Frontier Settlement
and Market Revolution

CHARLES E. BROOKS

Frontier Settlement and Market Revolution

The Holland Land Purchase

Cornell University Press   *Ithaca and London*

The illustrations on the title pages are (left) "The Pioneer
Settler upon the Holland Purchase, and His Progress" and
(right) "Third Sketch of the Pioneer." Both are reprinted
from Orsamus Turner, *Pioneer History of the Holland
Purchase of Western New York* (Buffalo, N.Y., 1850).

First published 1996 by Cornell University Press.

Printed in the United States of America

Library of Congress Cataloging-in-Publication Data
Brooks, Charles E.
    Frontier settlement and market revolution : the Holland Land
Purchase / Charles E. Brooks.
        p. cm.
    ISBN 0-8014-3120-4 (cloth : alk. paper)
    1. Holland Puchase.   2. Frontier and pioneer life—New York
(State)   3. Land use, Rural—New York (State)—History—19th
century.   I. Title.
F127.H7B76 1996
974.7'03'092—dc20   95-32732

♾ The paper in this book meets the minimum requirements
of the American National Standard for Information Sciences—
Permanence of Paper for Printed Library Materials, ANSI Z39.48-1984.

For my mother and father,
Dorothy and Donald Brooks,
and in memory of Elayne's mother and father,
Adeline and Leon Surowiec

CONTENTS

ACKNOWLEDGMENTS

I have incurred many debts, intellectual and otherwise, during the research and writing of this book. I acknowledge them with gratitude. First, thanks to the public libraries and historical societies of western New York: the Cattaraugus County Historical Museum (Little Valley), the James Prendergast Library Association (Jamestown), the Patterson Library (Westfield), the Chautauqua County Historical Society (Westfield), the Fenton Historical Society Museum and Research Center (Jamestown), the Holland Land Company Museum (Batavia), the Lockport Historical Center (Lockport), the Buffalo and Erie County Public Library, the Pendleton Town Hall archives (Pendleton), the Perrysburg Town Hall archives (Gowanda), and the Town of Porter Historical Society (Youngstown). Special thanks to the Buffalo and Erie County Historical Society which provided permission to quote from archival material in the Joseph Ellicott Collection and the Ira A. Blossom Papers and from Robert W. Bingham, ed., *Reports of Joseph Ellicott*, 2 vols. (Buffalo, N.Y., 1937–41). Former librarian Herman Sass and current librarian Mary Bell have always been generous with their time and expertise. Special thanks also go to the Holland Land Company Project at Reed Library, State University College at Fredonia, for permission to quote from the microfilm version of the Archives of the Holland Land Company. Project director Franciska Safran gave help and encouragement from the beginning. Financial support for research and travel came from the history department at Texas A&M University. Faculty Mini-Grant Awards in 1990, 1991, and 1994 also provided crucial support. Parts of Chapter 2 appear as an article in *Forest & Conservation History*, January 1995.

My greatest debts are owed to former teachers and current colleagues. When I was an undergraduate at the State University College at Buffalo, Eric Brunger, John Aiken, and Edward Smith encouraged and inspired me to become a historian. At the State University of New York at Buffalo, Richard Ellis introduced me to the study of the early American republic and the elusive problem of economic change in the countryside. I also thank my friends and colleagues at Texas A&M. James Bradford, John Canup, and John Lenihan have exhibited great patience and forbearance, reading more than one early draft of this book. Likewise, a former colleague at A&M, Donald Pisani, shared my enthusiasm for the history of frontier land development and has been a generous supporter of my work since we first met in 1989. Alan Taylor and Christopher Clark deserve special thanks for their critical and thoughtful reviews of the manuscript for Cornell University Press. I also thank my editor, Peter Agree. His steady hand has helped immeasurably.

Finally, it is with great joy that I say thank you to my wife, Elayne. She is the perfect life partner. Despite her own busy schedule running a small furniture refinishing business, she always had time to listen and encourage. Without her, my work and my life would be incomplete.

CHARLES E. BROOKS

College Station, Texas

Frontier Settlement
and Market Revolution

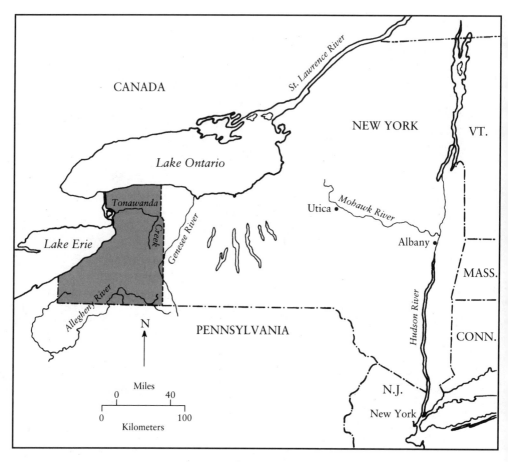

MAP 1. Holland Land Purchase

Introduction

In 1850 Orsamus Turner published the *Pioneer History of the Holland Purchase of Western New York,* an odd collection of facts, recollections, and biographical sketches that included four engraved views showing the progress of settlement during the early nineteenth century. The first view shows a pioneer farm in winter; a "rude log house" stands alone in the otherwise unbroken forest. In the foreground a settler has chopped down a large tree to provide browse for cattle and sheep. The second sketch portrays the same farm the following summer. The opening in the forest has expanded; underbrush has been burned to make room for a garden, and corn, potatoes, beans, and pumpkins grow among the stumps and logs. A "logging bee" is in progress behind the cabin; cattle and hogs graze in the surrounding forest. The third scene depicts summer ten years later. A frame house and barn have replaced the primitive cabin, crops are growing, livestock are visible in a distant woodland pasture, and "the whole premises begin to have the appearance of careful management, of thrift, comfort, and even plenty." In the fourth view it is winter, and forty-five years have passed. "The scene has progressed to a consummation," Turner rhapsodizes. "The pioneer is an independent Farmer of the Holland Purchase. . . . He has added to his primitive possessions; and ten to one that he has secured lands for his sons in some of the western states, to make pioneers and founders of settlements of them. He has flocks and herds; large surplus of produce in his granaries, which he may sell or keep as he chooses. He is the founder, and worker out, of his own fortunes."[1]

1. Orsamus Turner, *Pioneer History of the Holland Land Purchase of Western New York* (1850; rpr. Geneseo, N.Y., 1974), 565, 566.

This agrarian patriarch is truly free, Turner explains. He has created property and a modest level of physical comfort for his family in the wilderness. He both manages his household's labor and disposes of its output. By acquiring land to provide his sons with new farms, he is perpetuating the culture of independent producers that was at the center of an agrarian vision of American society.

Turner's settler and family strove to reproduce the independent patriarchal household that was central to rural New England society. Achieving independent status was largely dependent on access to land and control over the resources needed for making a "comfortable subsistence." A local newspaper in the Holland Purchase described the ideal: "How many clever people think that a new country affords no amusement. The idea is a log house, . . . hog and hominy, forests of trees, lean cattle and no reward for labor. They never think there is a bright side to the picture. The man who raises his necessary crops, stays at home from enticing allurements, keeps a little library of useful knowledge; who gathers his friends, his children, his neighbors around a fire of light wood, who owes nothing at the store in town and does not wish to borrow money, is indeed a nabob."[2]

The independence to which frontier farm households aspired could not be achieved by individual effort. Independent did not mean self-sufficient. Farm families needed and relied upon one another; local exchanges of goods and services were essential to the well-being of all. The logging bee shown in Turner's second sketch underscores this interdependence. Small farmers did not strive for the self-sufficiency historians once believed they did.[3]

The independent farm households that settled the Holland Purchase of western New York rested on patriarchal authority and family labor. Tasks were divided on the basis of sex and age. Men cleared land, cultivated crops, raised livestock, and made potash. The work was arduous, but it

2. *Cattaraugus Republican* (Ellicottville, N.Y.), June 11, 1835. For the nature of rural patriarchal society, see Christopher Clark, *Roots of Rural Capitalism: Western Massachusetts, 1780–1860* (Ithaca, N.Y., 1990), 21–58; James Henretta, "Families and Farms: Mentalité in Pre-Industrial America," *William and Mary Quarterly* 35 (1978), 3–32; Michael Merrill, "Cash Is Good to Eat: Self-Sufficiency and Exchange in the Rural Economy of the United States," *Radical History Review* 4 (1977), 42–71; Sarah F. McMahon, "A Comfortable Subsistence: The Changing Composition of Diet in Rural New England, 1620–1840," *William and Mary Quarterly* 42 (1985), 23–51; Daniel Vickers, "Competency and Competition: Economic Culture in Early America," *William and Mary Quarterly* 47 (1990), 3–29; Allan Kulikoff, "The Rise and Demise of the American Yeoman Classes," in his *The Agrarian Origins of American Capitalism* (Charlottesville, Va., 1992), 34–59.
3. Carol Shammas, "How Self-Sufficient Was Early America?" *Journal of Interdisciplinary History* 13 (Autumn 1982), 247–72.

was spread out over the entire year. The hard chores of planting and tilling took place in April and May. Extensive agriculture, adopted from Native Americans, minimized the labor, and planting was usually followed by periods of relative inactivity. Corn, a staple of pioneer agriculture, required little attention after planting. Meanwhile, cattle, sheep, and hogs were turned out into summer woodland pastures. Fall was harvest time and the beginning of market season. Some livestock were butchered or sold, the number usually depending on the supply of hay and forage for the coming winter. With the onset of cold weather and snow, settlers turned their attention to chopping clearings, cutting lumber, and piling and burning refuse timber for potash. Winter was also the season to market any cash product or subsistence surplus that was available. Transportation to market by sleigh or sled was easy and fast. Overall, winter constituted another period of relative leisure for men.[4]

Women's work, some of which is evident in Turner's second scene, was more regular and monotonous. Women bore and raised children, cooked and preserved food, spun and wove clothing from wool and flax, looked after the garden, made soap, and attended to many other routine chores. During peak seasons of labor it was not unusual for women to assist with field work. At the beginning of the nineteenth century most rural women gave birth to seven or eight children at roughly two-year intervals. The maternal rhythm of getting pregnant and giving birth, followed by extended nursing, lasted for fifteen or twenty years. Children were readily integrated into the system of family labor that was critical to sustaining the independent farm household.[5]

Preserving and protecting household independence also required pass-

4. Clark, *Roots of Rural Capitalism*, 25; Jared Van Wagenen, Jr., *The Golden Age of Homespun* (New York, 1953); Eric Sloane, *The Seasons of America Past* (New York, 1958). Robert Gallman has concluded that "the typical agricultural worker—slaves apart—was unable (and perhaps unwilling) to fill his year with work. The seasonal pattern of agricultural labor—certainly in the north, in places distant from urban centers—produced twelve- or fourteen-hour days and six- or seven-day weeks at active times of the year, but substantial leisure at other times" ("The Agricultural Sector and the Pace of Economic Growth: U.S. Experience in the Nineteenth Century," in David C. Klingaman and Richard K. Vedder, eds., *Essays in Nineteenth Century Economic History: The Old Northwest* [Athens, Ohio, 1975], 56).

5. Clark, *Roots of Rural Capitalism*, 26; Charles Sellers, *The Market Revolution: Jacksonian America, 1815–1846* (New York, 1991), 11. The patriarchy of traditional rural culture is examined in John Mack Faragher, *Women and Men on the Overland Trail* (New Haven, Conn., 1979). The political consequences of rural patriarchal independence are explored in Stephanie McCurry, "The Two Faces of Republicanism: Gender and Pro-Slavery Politics in Antebellum South Carolina," *Journal of American History* 78 (March 1992), 1245–64, and Rachel Klein, *Unification of a Slave State: The Rise of the Planter Class in the South Carolina Backcountry, 1760–1808* (Chapel Hill, N.C., 1990), 149–50 n. 1.

ing the resources that made it possible on to the next generation. Family patriarchs struggled to acquire enough land to settle their sons on nearby farms. The ability to provide land was the linchpin of the patriarch's authority and status. In the areas of New England longest settled, a Malthusian demographic and ecological crisis threatened rural culture by the mid-eighteenth century. The imaginary settler depicted by Orsamus Turner probably left New England in search of the fresh land needed to reproduce the independent rural household in which he and his wife had been raised.[6]

THIS book examines frontier settlement and land development in western New York. Specifically it tells the story of landlords and settlers, of capitalist and agrarian models of land use and commercial development, and of the negotiation, accommodation, and confrontation that alternately characterized relations between landlord and settler during the period 1800 to 1845. In 1792 a consortium of Dutch bankers and businessmen, later organized as the Holland Land Company, made a series of large land purchases that included 3.3 million acres in western New York. Stretching westward from the Genesee River to Lake Erie and northward from Pennsylvania to Lake Ontario, this vast area became known as the Holland Land Purchase. The Dutch landlords opened the region for sale in 1800, and during the next thirty-six years the company had a major influence on its settlement and development.[7]

Like other eighteenth-century landlords who purchased extensive tracts of land in the backcountry, the Dutch proprietors of the Holland Land Company counted on attracting good, hardworking, family-oriented farmers who would clear the forests, cultivate the land, enhance land values, and produce a marketable commodity. They also expressed a strong preference for settlers who would behave themselves and do what

6. Kenneth Lockridge, "Land, Population, and the Evolution of New England Society, 1630–1790," *Past and Present* 39 (April 1968), 62–80; Lockridge, "Social Change and the Meaning of the American Revolution," *Journal of Social History* 6 (1972–73), 403–39. For the effects of agrarian crisis elsewhere, see Duane E. Bell, "Dynamics of Population and Wealth in Eighteenth-Century Chester County, Pennsylvania," *Journal of Interdisciplinary History* 6 (Spring 1976), 621–44; Paul G. E. Clemens and Lucy Simler, "Rural Labor and the Farm Household in Chester County, Pennsylvania, 1750–1820," in Stephen Innes, ed., *Work and Labor in Early America* (Chapel Hill, N.C., 1988), 106–43.

7. For the history of the Holland Land Company, see Paul Evans, *The Holland Land Company* (Buffalo, N.Y., 1924); William Wyckoff, *The Developer's Frontier: The Making of the Western New York Landscape* (New Haven, Conn., 1988); William Chazanof, *Joseph Ellicott and the Holland Land Company: The Opening of Western New York* (Syracuse, N.Y., 1970).

the landlords wanted.[8] Overall the Dutch sought capitalist land development, and they expected to profit from sales of undeveloped land, from
rising land values, and from interest paid by settlers who bought land on
credit.

The settlers, however, had their own goals and objectives. Drawn to the
Holland Purchase by the hope of finding a better life, they used and
harvested this land in ways that were compatible with the outlook of a
small producer. They used resources and produced commodities for both
subsistence and sale that could be made and marketed within the con-
straints of a frontier exchange economy.[9]

The primary limitation, as it affected both landlords and settlers and
mediated their relations, resulted from the high ratio of land to labor.[10]
Even though the Holland Land Company controlled the local real estate
market several years before widespread settlement began, the urgent need
to attract labor and encourage improvement compelled the proprietors to
offer generous terms of sale and possession. The critical shortage of labor
underlay the landlords' strategy of counting on small seminomadic
farmers and herdsmen to begin the process of land development. The
company realized that most of its profits would have to wait until the first
pioneers sold their possession claims to more prosperous farmers from
back east who were looking for partially cleared land upon which to build
new farms. The landlords expected this second wave of more stable and
better established settlers to pay for the land in full and make the necessary improvements to allow continuous cropping on permanent fields so
that land values would rise throughout the Purchase and finally compensate the landlords for all of the earlier delinquencies.

8. See, for example, Alan Taylor, *Liberty Men and Great Proprietors: The Revolutionary Settlement on the Maine Frontier, 1760–1820* (Chapel Hill, N.C., 1990), 31–59; Thomas P. Slaughter, *The Whiskey Rebellion: Frontier Epilogue to the American Revolution* (New York, 1986), 78–89; Andrew R. L. Cayton, *The Frontier Republic: Ideology and Politics in the Ohio Country* (Kent, Ohio, 1986), 1–11; and Richard R. Beeman, *The Evolution of the Southern Backcountry: A Case Study of Lunenburg County, Virginia, 1746–1832* (Phila-delphia, 1984), 14–24.

9. See Taylor, *Liberty Men and Great Proprietors*, 61–87; Kulikoff, "Rise and Demise of Yeoman Classes," 37–43; Michael A. Bellesiles, *Revolutionary Outlaws: Ethan Allen and the Struggle for Independence on the Early American Frontier* (Charlottesville, Va., 1993), 32–41, 53–55; J. Ritchie Garrison, *Landscape and Material Life in Franklin County, Massa-chusetts, 1770–1860* (Knoxville, Tenn., 1991), 94–114, esp. 249–50.

10. Studies that highlight the significance of a high land-to-labor ratio include David Potter, *People of Plenty: Economic Abundance and the American Character* (Chicago, 1954); William Cronon, "Revisiting the Vanishing Frontier: The Legacy of Frederick Jack-son Turner," *Western Historical Quarterly* 18 (April 1987), 157–76; Sellers, *Market Revolution*, 17.

The high ratio of land to labor freed the settlers from potential domination and oppression by the landlords. It created the social and cultural space that allowed them to pursue, largely uninterrupted, their agrarian model of land development. Adapting to this labor-scarce environment, the settlers carefully husbanded their labor, investing it only in commodities that had both subsistence and market value. Labor input had to be minimal but the resulting exchange value high enough to cover the cost of shipment to market. Furthermore, the settlers desired to participate in a democratic market system in which small independent producers met and exchanged goods as equals. The ideal was for every rural household to enjoy complete managerial autonomy over what it produced as well as over what and how much it kept or exchanged.[11]

The spirit of negotiation and accommodation between landlords and settlers, which was primarily a result of demographic factors, eroded after 1819. Slumping land values and rising indebtedness generated a crisis for both landlords and settlers which deepened as the 1820s progressed, sparking a conflict over the use and control of land. The settlers, drawing on their cultural resources and experiences, resisted the landlords' encroachments and refused to surrender their improvements without compensation for their equity.[12] Their labor theory of property had plebeian cultural roots; neither John Locke nor anyone else had to tell them what their labor was worth. Moreover, their experience with developing land in the Holland Purchase during the early years of accommodation and coop-

11. My understanding of the link between small producers' values and individual managerial control over land and productive resources is based on Richard L. Bushman, "Massachusetts Farmers and the Revolution," in Richard M. Jellison, ed., *Society, Freedom, and Conscience: The American Revolution in Virginia, Massachusetts, and New York* (New York, 1976), 77–124; Richard Maxwell Brown, "Back Country Rebellions and the Homestead Ethic in America, 1740–1799," in Richard Maxwell Brown and Don E. Fehrenbacher, eds., *Tradition, Conflict, and Modernization: Perspectives on the American Revolution* (New York, 1977), 73–99; Ruth Bogin, "Petitioning and the New Moral Economy of Post-Revolutionary America," *William and Mary Quarterly* 45 (1988), 391–425; Taylor, *Liberty Men and Great Proprietors*, 6–8, 14, 16–18, 28, 94–96, 100–114, 150, 186–89, 216, 222, 229–30; William B. Scott, *In Pursuit of Happiness: American Conceptions of Property from the Seventeenth to the Twentieth Century* (Bloomington, Ind., 1977); Paul Conkin, *The Southern Agrarians* (Knoxville, Tenn., 1988); Allen Tate, "Notes on Liberty and Property," in Herbert Agar and Allen Tate, eds., *Who Owns America? A New Declaration of Independence* (Boston, 1936), 80–93; Samuel Eliot Morison, ed., "William Manning's 'The Key of Libberty,'" *William and Mary Quarterly* 13 (1956), 202–54; Stephen Hahn, "Hunting, Fishing, and Foraging: Common Rights and Class Relations in the Post-Bellum South," *Radical History Review* 26 (1982), 37–64.

12. Alfred F. Young, "How Radical Was the American Revolution?" in Young, ed., *Beyond the American Revolution: Explorations in the History of American Radicalism* (DeKalb, Ill., 1993), 319–22, 329–33.

eration affirmed and validated the moral power and dignity associated with a free man's labor. The opportunity to mix labor with land and productive resources in whatever combination individual initiative and personal judgment determined, coupled with the right to use, exchange, or trade away the property that resulted, was what made and kept a yeoman family free.[13]

THIS book is a regional study, but recent explorations into the history of the early American countryside have helped me keep sight of its wider implications. No historical work, of course, can stand alone. Any book's larger meaning and significance depend on its place within and connection to the current dialogue among historians as well as other scholars.

Recent studies of economic change in early America emphasize that there was no single road to capitalist development. Historians have just begun to appreciate the diversity of social, cultural, and material circumstances that structured economic change and market involvement. In studies of four major regions in eighteenth-century America, New England, the Mid-Atlantic area, the plantation South, and the backcountry, historians have found that four interrelated developments contributed to the emergence of a capitalist economic system after 1770. First, the opening of a booming transatlantic market for grain and other agricultural products enticed many Americans into expanding their market participation. At the same time, population growth through natural increase and in-migration created a surplus of laborers who were forced to work for wages. Third, a growing number of merchants, landowners, and artisans, animated by the new opportunities to increase their income and make a profit, became capitalist entrepreneurs seeking to control labor and production as well as market exchange. Last, the creation of the American republic produced new governments at both the national and state levels

13. Several historians have argued that by the time of the American Revolution the idea of productive labor had become imbued with the moral power to make men free and equal. No longer associated with slavery and servitude, labor achieved a new dignity that was primarily a consequence of the labor theory of value operating in an environment where the ratio of land to labor was high. In revolutionary America labor became the vital source of wealth and property as well as the foundation of liberty and equality. See Gordon S. Wood, *The Radicalism of the American Revolution* (New York, 1992), 136, 170–71, 413 n. 50; Taylor, *Liberty Men and Great Proprietors,* 25, 28. For the traditional view of labor as a painful necessity, see J. E. Crowley, *This Sheba, Self: The Conceptualization of Economic Life in Eighteenth-Century America* (Baltimore, 1974), 42; Richard Morris, *Government and Labor in Early America* (1946; rpr. Boston, 1981), 1–54. On the impact of industrialization, see Daniel T. Rodgers, *The Work Ethic in Industrial America, 1850–1920* (Chicago, 1974).

which actively encouraged economic growth and supported the needs and interests of entrepreneurial-minded Americans.[14]

The relative importance of these developments varied from region to region, yet each one hinged to some degree on the capacity of Americans to work harder and longer, whether by choice or coercion. Because early America was land-rich and labor-poor, the transition to capitalism depended on intensive organization and mobilization of labor. In New England rural folk pushed themselves to work harder as part of a strategy to preserve household autonomy in the face of a Malthusian ecological crisis and the need to shift from extensive agriculture to more intensive practices. In southeastern Pennsylvania labor was reorganized mainly by aggressive entrepreneurs taking advantage of landless German and Scots-Irish migrants who had to work for wages to survive. Meanwhile, in the plantation South, new management practices, principally the expansion of the task system, resulted in more efficient organization and use of slave labor.[15]

Throughout the frontier backcountry, entrepreneurs encountered serious obstacles that impeded their capacity to direct and control labor more efficiently. The abundance of land and the scarcity of labor were particularly pronounced on the frontier. Euro-American elites tried to impose their own social and economic interests, but whether renting or selling lands, they had to offer terms attractive to yeomen, who had their own ideas and plans. The folk memory of the enclosure movements and the expropriation of peasants' land during the sixteenth and seventeenth centuries, the desire to secure a modest independence of their own choosing, and their contact with the natural abundance that had shaped the Indian world encouraged frontier people to act on their own. Conse-

---

14. My discussion is based on James A. Henretta, "The Transition to Capitalism in America," in James A. Henretta, Michael Kammen, and Stanley N. Katz, eds., *The Transformation of Early American History* (New York, 1991), 218–38, esp. 220–21; Christopher Clark, "Economics and Culture: Opening Up the Rural History of the Early American Northeast," *American Quarterly* 43 (1991), 279–301; Kulikoff, "The Transition to Capitalism in Rural America," in his *Agrarian Origins*, 13–33; Richard L. Bushman, "Opening the American Countryside," in Henretta, Kammen, and Katz, eds., *Transformation of Early American History*, 239–56; Gregory H. Nobles, "Breaking into the Backcountry: New Approaches to the Early American Frontier," *William and Mary Quarterly* 46 (1989), 641–70. For a different view of economic change in rural America, see Winifred B. Rothenberg, *From Market-Places to a Market Economy: The Transformation of Rural Massachusetts, 1750–1850* (Chicago, 1992). See also Gordon S. Wood, "Inventing American Capitalism," *New York Review of Books*, June 9, 1994, 44–49.

15. Henretta, "Transition to Capitalism," 221–34.

quently, they refused to behave in the respectable way demanded by land-owning elites.[16]

This study of the Holland Land Purchase helps to further understanding of economic change on the early American frontier. It emphasizes that the struggle for dominion over labor and land underlay the economic change of the region as well as the conflict between landlords and settlers and their respective capitalist and agrarian systems of land and resource management. Moreover, it highlights the progress and the limitations of economic change in a region that was undergoing the rural capitalist development that historians of Jacksonian politics and society in particular now call the Market Revolution.[17]

Since this book is set in the context of that revolution, a definition is in order. The Market Revolution refers not to the birth of capitalism but rather to a particularly dynamic chapter in its early growth and expansion that was largely a consequence of active government promotion of a market economy. But the shift away from long fallow agriculture, the reorganization and mobilization of labor, and the spread of market-oriented production and exchange generated sharp conflict between capitalists and agrarians. In this book I use the term "capitalist" in neither its Marxist nor its modern liberal sense. The capitalists in this story of rural economic change in the Holland Purchase are neither the agents of proletarianization nor the unblushing champions of free enterprise. Rather they are the large landowners of the Holland Land Company and their American successors who sought to direct and manage new property and market development by trying to dictate the behavior of the majority of small farmers and herdsmen in the region. The agrarians are the small settlers and their entrepreneurial neighbors who fought to check the landlords' aspirations and keep dominion of land and productive resources in the hands of the producing classes. In its original meaning, capitalism was

16. Nobles, "Breaking into the Backcountry," 643–49.

17. For the Market Revolution in early nineteenth-century America, see Sellers, *Market Revolution;* Harry L. Watson, *Liberty and Power: The Politics of Jacksonian America* (New York, 1990); Sean Wilentz, "Society, Politics, and the Market Revolution, 1815–1848," in Eric Foner, ed., *The New American History* (Philadelphia, 1990), 51–72. The general literature about capitalist transformation is vast, but a good introduction to the far-reaching effects of this revolution can be gleaned from Karl Polanyi, *The Great Transformation: The Political and Economic Origins of Our Time* (Boston, 1944); Rodney Hilton, ed., *The Transition from Feudalism to Capitalism* (London, 1976); T. H. Aston and C. H. E. Philpin, eds., *The Brenner Debate: Agrarian Class Structure and Economic Development in Pre-Industrial Europe* (Cambridge, Eng., 1985).

as much a political as an economic system in which various commercial, financial, and landowning elites, the so-called moneyed men, ran government and everything else to benefit themselves. The confrontation between the moneyed few and the producing majority was at the heart of the Market Revolution both in the Holland Purchase and the rest of Jacksonian America.[18]

The Holland Purchase of western New York makes a good case study of frontier settlement and land development in the early American republic because it stood in the vanguard of the changes that were convulsing antebellum America. Powerful cultural and religious impulses turned western New York into the "burned-over district," producing a rich harvest of converts for ministers and exhorters preaching the doctrine of human perfectibility and self-improvement. Equally potent social and economic currents marked by internal improvements and intensification of market activity in the countryside put this area in the forefront of rural capitalist development.[19]

As a case study of private land development, this book goes well beyond studies of public land policy, which seldom follow landlords or settlers after the first distribution of land.[20] It also probes deeper than the many quantitative studies of land and property distribution in antebellum America which emphasize structural economic inequality. Such profiles are useful, but they tell us little about the experience of social and economic change as it was really lived.[21] This in-depth examination of one

18. For the crucial role of government promotion of economic growth in the Market Revolution, see Sellers, *Market Revolution*, 3–102; my conception and definition of capitalism are taken from Michael Merrill, "The Anticapitalist Origins of the United States," *Review: A Journal of the Fernand Braudel Center* 13 (Fall 1990), 465–97, esp. 470–73 and 483–94. See also Merrill, "Putting 'Capitalism' in Its Place: A Review of Recent Literature," *William and Mary Quarterly* 52 (1995), 315–26.

19. For the "burned-over district," see Whitney Cross, *The Burned-Over District: The Social and Intellectual History of Enthusiastic Religion in Western New York* (Ithaca, N.Y., 1950), and Paul E. Johnson, *A Shopkeeper's Millennium: Society and Revival in Rochester, New York, 1815–1837* (New York, 1978). For the significance of rural western New York as center stage for the Market Revolution, see Watson, *Liberty and Power*. "In all probability," Watson observes (177), "the economic effects of internal improvements and the Market Revolution were more dramatic in western New York than in any other region of rural America."

20. For the limitations of public land studies, see Thomas Le Duc, "History and Appraisal of U.S. Land Policy to 1862," in Howard W. Ottoson, ed., *Land Use Policy and Problems in the United States* (Lincoln, Neb., 1963), 3–27.

21. See, for example, Lee Soltow, *Distribution of Wealth and Income in the United States in 1798* (Pittsburgh, 1989); Soltow, "Inequality amidst Abundance: Land Ownership in Early Nineteenth Century Ohio," *Ohio History* 88 (Spring 1979), 133–51; Soltow, "Land Inequality on the Frontier: The Distribution of Land in East Tennessee at the Beginning of

case history of private land development illuminates the actual process of rural economic growth and change. It examines the dynamic interaction between culture and the social, ecological, and material circumstances in which both the landlords' and the settlers' consciousness and behavior were rooted.

Like many other studies of the early American countryside, this one emphasizes that ordinary rural and frontier folk participated openly and actively in economic change. Historians must avoid the trap of viewing the Market Revolution as an external behemoth that forced convulsive changes upon a reluctant but essentially passive countryside. As Christopher Clark has said, rural people "did not just respond to things, they made them happen."[22]

Likewise, historians must avoid the pitfall of conflating the sentiments and values of ordinary farmers and artisans with those of established or emerging entrepreneurial elites. In the long run, agrarian attitudes toward labor may have legitimized wage labor and industrial capitalism, but if agrarian producers' ideology was co-opted by various elites, historians should not allow this fact to obscure the consciousness and agency of ordinary rural folk. Rural people deserve to be understood on their own terms. The settlers of the Holland Purchase were neither communitarians bound by the tradition of the moral economy nor petty capitalists looking for the main chance. Their goals and plans cannot be explained in terms of the transition from classical republican values to bourgeois liberal ones. Hence they cannot easily be placed along a continuum that stretches from republican virtue at one end to liberal self-interest at the other. These settlers cleared land, produced commodities from the forest, and created new property; yet their objective was to live in an egalitarian society of small independent producers. Even though they participated in markets and subscribed to the doctrine of private property, they were a world apart from capitalist developers who preferred to avoid continuous physical labor. Their agrarian culture represented an important alternative system of political economy that was conceived by and for small producers, and it is a tradition of which historians have just become aware.[23]

---

the Nineteenth Century," *Social Science History* 5 (Summer 1981), 275–91. See also R. Eugene Harper, *The Transformation of Western Pennsylvania, 1770–1800* (Pittsburgh, 1991).

22. Clark, *Roots of Rural Capitalism*, 8.

23. Michael Merrill and Sean Wilentz, "'The Key of Libberty': William Manning and Plebeian Democracy 1747–1814," in Young, ed., *Beyond the American Revolution*, 246–82, esp. 248, 270–71, 273–74 n. 5; Michael Merrill and Sean Wilentz, eds., *The Key of*

Finally, this regional story of frontier settlement, land development, and agrarian conflict is part of the larger story of how the yeomanry helped to shape the course and direction of American life from the mid-eighteenth to the early twentieth centuries. The small producers of the Holland Purchase shared the sentiments of agrarians before and after them. They believed that a direct and tangible relationship between labor and the creation of property separated honest people who worked for a living from the moneyed few who lived on the labor of others. Consequently, the small frontier farmers and herdsmen of western New York used their dominion over the means of subsistence and production to resist centralized control or exploitation. Their struggle with the large landowners of the region underscored the fundamental importance they attached to economic independence and individual managerial control over the use and development of land and natural resources.[24]

Liberty: The Life and Democratic Writings of William Manning, "A Laborer," 1747–1814 (Cambridge, Mass., 1993), 3–86; Merrill, "Anticapitalist Origins," 465–97; Taylor, *Liberty Men and Great Proprietors,* 8, 246–49. The literature about republicanism and the transition to liberal capitalism is vast, but a good starting point is Daniel T. Rodgers, "Republicanism: The Career of a Concept," *Journal of American History* 79 (June 1992), 11–38.

24. Merrill and Wilentz, eds., *Key of Liberty,* 59–70, 135–38; Taylor, *Liberty Men and Great Proprietors,* 6, 85–87. For postbellum agrarianism, see Robert C. McMath, Jr., *American Populism: A Social History, 1877–1898* (New York, 1993); Bruce Palmer, *"Man over Money": The Southern Populist Critique of American Capitalism* (Chapel Hill, N.C., 1980); and Lawrence Goodwyn, *Democratic Promise: The Populist Moment in America* (New York, 1976).

I

The Holland Land Company

The Holland Land Company, formally organized in 1796, was the largest private land developer in antebellum America. The Dutch banking houses that purchased 3.3 million acres of wild land in western New York first became interested in America ten years earlier, when the prestigious financial houses of Pieter Stadnitski and Son, Nicholas and Jacob Van Staphorst, P. & C. Van Eeghen, and Ten Cate and Vollenhoven sent an agent to America in search of investment opportunities. Theophile Cazenove invested the Dutch capitalists' money in U.S. public securities and internal improvement projects, but in 1792 he was authorized to purchase large tracts of wild land. Among other projects, the Dutch hoped to develop a maple sugar industry.[1]

The Dutch bankers acquired the territory that became known as the Holland Land Purchase in two transactions. Theophile Cazenove purchased 1.5 million acres from Robert Morris, the financier of the American Revolution, in December 1792. Morris's son, who was in Amsterdam, sold another 1.8 million acres to the same Dutch bankers. This second transaction was completed before the elder Morris could tell his son not to sell any more land in western New York.

---

1. For the Holland Land Company's acquisition, see Paul Evans, *The Holland Land Company* (Buffalo, N.Y., 1924), 3–36; William Wyckoff, *The Developer's Frontier: The Making of the Western New York Landscape* (New Haven, Conn., 1988), 16–18; William Chazanof, *Joseph Ellicott and the Holland Land Company: The Opening of Western New York* (Syracuse, N.Y., 1970), 15–24; Eric Brunger, John Aiken, and Robert Silsby, "Historical Land Valuation of the Big Tree Cession" (1970), unpublished report on file at the Buffalo and Erie County Historical Society, Buffalo, N.Y.

As part of the deal struck between Robert Morris and the Dutch investors, Morris agreed to do a survey and purchase the lands that were under
contract from the Indians. The right to purchase Indian lands had been
transferred to Morris by the state of Massachusetts, which had acquired
preemption rights to the region at a convention held in Hartford, Connecticut, in 1786. That convention had resolved the conflicting claims of
Massachusetts and New York by giving Massachusetts the right to sell
more than six million acres and allowing New York to retain political
sovereignty over the area. Indian title was extinguished at the Treaty of
Big Tree in 1797.[2]

The Holland Purchase was not the only tract of wild land purchased by
the Dutch bankers. They also acquired sizable parcels in central New
York, including one hundred thousand acres around Cazenovia and two
other tracts near the Black River, north of Cazenovia. The Dutch capitalists also bought 1.4 million acres of wild land in north-central and northeastern Pennsylvania. These lands were divided into the East Allegheny
and West Allegheny land agencies. But their lands in western New York
proved to be the best suited for settlement and development, and the
Dutch landlords committed their principal managerial energy and resources to the Holland Purchase.[3]

Presettlement Landscape and Ecology

The terrain of the Holland Land Purchase was diverse, ranging from
lowland plains along Lake Ontario in the north to rounded hills and
steeper mountains in the south. The broad belt of lake plain that made up
the northern third of the Purchase extended to the southwest, where it
formed a narrow strip bordering Lake Erie. The entire lowland region
occupied an ancient glacial lake bottom. The Ontario Lake plain was flat
and featureless until it reached a limestone escarpment, where it ended
abruptly. South of this steep slope, low, mounded hills and ridges appeared; in other places the plain flattened out again to form vast areas of

2. For Robert Morris and the early land transactions that predated the Dutch purchase,
see Barbara A. Chernow, "Robert Morris: Genesee Land Speculator," *New York History* 58
(1977), 195–220; Paul Evans, "The Pulteney Purchase," *Proceedings of the New York State
Historical Society* 20 (1922), 83–103; William H. Siles, "Pioneering in the Genesee Country:
Entrepreneurial Strategy and the Concept of a Central Place," in Manfred Jonas and Robert
V. Wells, eds., *New Opportunities in a New Nation: The Development of New York after
the Revolution* (Schenectady, N.Y., 1982), 35–68.
   3. Wyckoff, *Developer's Frontier,* 17–18.

swamp and bottomlands that were drained by small, sluggish streams. The remaining two-thirds of the Purchase constituted a portion of the Appalachian uplands known as the Cattaraugus Hills. In the extreme southern part of this region the Allegheny hills, which today are state park lands, rose upward more steeply.[4]

The soil regions and types also varied throughout the Holland Purchase. In the northern lake plain glaciers had ground up limestone outcrops, building a deep layer of soil rich in agricultural potential. To the south the uplands were not so blessed. The acid soil was thinner, with more rocks and stones, and less suited for cultivation of crops. When the organic debris created by the forest ecosystem was used up, the potential for tillage and crop production would be small, and the land would require regular applications of fertilizer. The steeper grade of the uplands made them vulnerable to erosion. Only the alluvial bottomlands along the major rivers and streams promised more than marginal fertility. Of course, most of this was not known at the time widespread settlement began. In 1800 the rolling hills and protected valleys, the fast-running streams of crystal-clear water, and the thickness and height of the towering trees beckoned to the settlers. Even today this upland region of western New York, its pastoral charm still intact, is a pleasant place to visit but a hard place to make a living.[5]

The creeks and rivers of the Holland Purchase divided the region into different watersheds, which complicated the Holland Land Company's task of choosing a strategy for development. The streams of the northern lake plain, including the Genesee River just to the east of the Purchase, flowed into Lake Ontario, which together with the St. Lawrence River provided a navigable market outlet to Montreal. In the central region of the Purchase, the Buffalo and Tonawanda creeks, muddy, slow-moving streams, formed a system that drained into Lake Erie or the Niagara River. Cattaraugus Creek rose in the middle section of the Purchase and also flowed west into Lake Erie. The Allegheny River and its feeder streams linked the steeper hill country well to the south with Pittsburgh and the Ohio River Valley. Finally, a little bit to the east of the Holland Purchase yet another network of streams eventually made up the Susquehanna, flowing east and then south toward Baltimore into Chesapeake Bay.[6]

The extensive forests covering the Holland Purchase constituted the

4. John H. Thompson, ed., *Geography of New York State* (Syracuse, N.Y., 1966), 25–34; Wyckoff, *Developer's Frontier,* 20–21.

5. Thompson, *New York State,* 104–10, 32; Wyckoff, *Developer's Frontier,* 21.

6. Wyckoff, *Developer's Frontier,* 21.

most conspicuous feature of the landscape before white settlement. About 65 percent of the region, consisting of the central and southern uplands plateau, featured a forest of beech, sugar maple, basswood, elm, and hemlock. Within this climax forest association, distinctive stands of oak and oak-chestnut mixed with the dominants, particularly in the far southern region of the Purchase. On the moister upland sites butternut and cucumber trees were interspersed among the other more common hardwoods. In the drier upland regions oak, chestnut, red maple, yellow birch, white pine, black cherry, and other species controlled the higher slopes. The Ontario Lake plain, which occupied the northern third of the Purchase, was also clothed with beech-maple forest. But in the flat bottomland areas, wetland forests prevailed, mostly black ash–silver maple–elm communities, along with some northern white cedar–larch–alder–black spruce associations.[7]

The understory of these forests also displayed variety. There was comparatively little undergrowth in some areas of the dominant beech-maple forests. Hobblebush, a shrub of the honeysuckle family, was sometimes the only species found. In areas where moister conditions prevailed, the undergrowth was rich in both shrubs and ground cover. Honeysuckle, witch hazel, and dogwood shrubs flourished. The ground cover was especially rich in ferns and early spring flowers. Wild leeks abounded during the earliest weeks of spring. The settlers' cattle grazed on these plants, producing milk tinged with the strong odor of onions. In the drier areas of the upper slopes the undergrowth consisted of shrubs and half shrubs, including black huckleberry, arrowwood, and mountain laurel, along with a layer of herbaceous vegetation. The undergrowth found in the upland beech-maple forests of the Ontario Lake plain was similar to that which grew in the moist upland forests of the south. In the bottomland and swamp forests of the lake plain, the undergrowth was made up of elderberry, American yew, winterberry, spice-bush, and poison ivy. The mass of shrubs and woody vines found there often formed a junglelike tangle of brush and bramble.[8]

7. Franz K. Seischab, "Forests of the Holland Land Company in Western New York, circa 1798," in *Late Eighteenth Century Vegetation of Central and Western New York State on the Basis of Original Land Survey Records,* New York State Museum Bulletin 484 (Albany, N.Y., 1992), 36, 41, 43–49.

8. Robert B. Gordon, *The Primeval Forest Types of Southwestern New York,* New York State Museum Bulletin 321 (Albany, N.Y., 1940), 37, 38–39, 36, 42; L. A. Kenoyer, "A Botanical Survey of a Portion of Allegany State Park," *New York State Museum Handbook* 17 (1937), 151–97; Fred W. Emerson, "A Botanical Survey of Big Basin in the Allegany State Park," *New York State Museum Handbook* 17 (1937), 89–150; H. J. Lutz, "The Vegetation

The beech-maple-hemlock forest was primarily a climax ecosystem. There is little evidence of any catastrophic disturbances in the presettlement forests of the Holland Purchase. Analysis of land survey records from both the Holland Purchase and the Phelps and Gorham Purchase situated just to the east shows that less than 2 percent of the total area had been affected by disturbances resulting from windthrow, agricultural fields, dead trees, or burns. Yet company surveyors reported many instances of windthrow and downed timber. This was not an unchanging forest, but it appears that most disturbances occurred on a small scale. The loss of a single tree primarily from old age, disease, or drought was common. The small openings in the canopy these events created favored shade-tolerant species such as beech and hemlock. Hence the climax forest was able to reproduce itself, remaining stable and constant over a long period of time.[9]

Clearly, the Senecas' land use had modified the environment of western New York. Indian villages, cornfields, and orchards produced a mosaic of ecological zones, ranging from open meadow to partial clearing to denser forest. But the overall impact of these Native Americans appears to have been not as great as some recent studies of other areas have found. Quantitative distribution studies of land survey records show very little indication of Indian disturbance. The study of the Holland Purchase pinpointed only two areas of grassland that might be attributed to Indian activity. One was found in the northeast corner of the Tonawanda Reservation. The largest area of grassland or open prairie identified by surveyors was found along the old Indian trail running from Batavia to Buffalo Creek. There was no evidence of pitch pine communities created by Indian fire practices. Even in the Military Tract, in the heart of the traditional Iroquois homeland, less than 1 percent of the total area could be identified as an old Indian clearing. It seems probable that the ecological impact of the

---

of Heart's Content, a Virgin Forest in Northwestern Pennsylvania," *Ecology* 11 (1930), 1–29; Wyckoff, *Developer's Frontier,* 30–38; Wyckoff, "Assessing Land Quality in Western New York: The Township Surveys of 1797–1799," unpublished paper in the manuscripts division of the Buffalo and Erie County Historical Society, Buffalo, N.Y.

9. Franz K. Seischab and David Orwig, "Catastrophic Disturbances in the Presettlement Forests of Western New York," *Bulletin of the Torrey Botanical Club* 118 (1991), 117; P. L. Marks and Sana Gardescu, "Vegetation of the Central Finger Lakes Region of New York in the 1790's," in *Late Eighteenth Century Vegetation of Central and Western New York State on the Basis of Original Land Survey Records,* New York State Museum Bulletin 484 (Albany, N.Y., 1992), 23–28; Seischab, "Forests of the Holland Land Company," 49–51; Gordon, "Primeval Forest Types," 15; G. G. Whitney, "The History and Status of the Hemlock-Hardwood Forests of the Allegheny Plateau," *Journal of Ecology* 78 (1990), 454.

Seneca and other Iroquois people must have been greater in earlier times. During the almost twenty years that had passed since the Sullivan raid against the Iroquois, nature had reclaimed many of the village sites that had been destroyed or abandoned in 1779.[10]

Choosing a Strategy

Like other speculators, the Dutch proprietors of the Holland Land Purchase had to choose between reselling their lands to other speculators and developing their capital investment in wild lands slowly over time. It was a choice between quick profits and deferred income generated by rising land values and future interest or rent payments. The Dutch bankers gave considerable thought to the strategy they selected, seeking advice from several individuals who had direct experience with land development in western New York.

Theophile Cazenove received plans and suggestions from Charles Williamson, James Wadsworth, and Joseph Ellicott. Charles Williamson, the Scottish-born land agent for the English-owned Pulteney Estate situated just to the east of the Holland Purchase, came to America in 1791. He served as principal agent for the Pulteney Association until 1800, spending over one million dollars building roads and frontier service centers and establishing a land office headquarters at Bath which featured a theater, a racetrack, and a grand hotel. James Wadsworth emigrated, with his brother William, from Connecticut to the Genesee Country in 1790. Buying land from their cousin, Colonel Jeremiah Wadsworth, the two brothers built a large estate in the fertile Genesee River Valley at Geneseo. Aside from managing his own estate, James Wadsworth also served as an agent for other large buyers in the area.[11]

10. For Indian land use, see Michael Williams, *Americans and Their Forests: A Historical Geography* (Cambridge, Eng., 1989), 32–40; Gordon M. Day, "The Indian as an Ecological Factor in the Northeastern Forest," *Ecology* 34 (1953), 329–46; Carolyn Merchant, *Ecological Revolutions: Nature, Gender, and Science in New England* (Chapel Hill, N.C., 1989), 69–85; William Cronon, *Changes in the Land: Indians, Colonists, and the Ecology of New England* (New York, 1983), 51; Timothy Silver, *A New Face on the Countryside: Indians, Colonists, and Slaves in South Atlantic Forests, 1500–1800* (Cambridge, Eng., 1990), 35–66; Seischab and Orwig, "Catastrophic Disturbances," 118, 120; Marks and Gardescu, "Vegetation of the Central Finger Lakes," 28, 32, 27.

11. In 1791 a group of English capitalists purchased about one million acres between Seneca Lake and the Genesee River from Robert Morris. This area became known as the Pulteney Estate or Purchase. Chazanof, *Joseph Ellicott*, 83, 29; Evans, "The Pulteney Purchase," 83–92; Helen I. Cowan, *Charles Williamson: Genesee Promoter, Friend of Anglo-*

Joseph Ellicott deserves special mention because he served as the company's resident agent from 1800 to 1821. Both family background and early professional experience prepared him for the task he undertook in November 1800. The fifth child of a Quaker family, he was born in Bucks County, Pennsylvania, in 1760. At the age of fourteen he moved with his family to a new home in Maryland, ten miles west of Baltimore. Homesteading on seven hundred acres of wild, undeveloped land, the Ellicotts learned firsthand about the rigors and opportunities of new settlements. They built a series of mills and a store that grew into Ellicott City. As a young man Joseph Ellicott became a surveyor, following in the footsteps of his older brother Andrew. Field experience in Pennsylvania, Georgia, and Washington, D.C., taught him how to survey and assess the potential value of unsettled lands. In 1797 Ellicott was asked to conduct a survey of the Holland Purchase that laid out and divided the entire tract into a grid of individual townships; each one covered six square miles. By the time the Holland Land Company hired him to serve as its resident agent, Joseph Ellicott had spent almost all of his thirty-seven years learning the skills he would put to use in the Holland Purchase.[12]

Williamson's and Wadsworth's proposals outlining a strategy of settlement and development were in sharp conflict; Ellicott's ideas fell somewhere in between. Williamson recommended that the Dutch bankers "hurry civilization" along by building roads and market facilities. "Want of communications is the great draw back on back settlements distant from the rivers which run into the Atlantic," he explained. "Remove this difficulty and there can be no doubt that the gentlemen . . . will reap an advantage fifty times their outlay; and come to their purpose many years sooner." Williamson pointed to the importance of establishing towns, with stores, inns, and gristmills, to serve as market centers. Landlord-subsidized improvements justified selling wild land at the comparatively high price of three to five dollars an acre. Selling land at these prices in lots of no less than 320 acres ensured that only the best class of settlers could afford to buy them.[13]

James Wadsworth advised Cazenove and his Dutch principals to "avoid

American Rapprochement (1941; rpr. Clifton, N.J., 1973). For James Wadsworth, see Orsamus Turner, *History of the Pioneer Settlement of Phelps and Gorham's Purchase and Morris' Reserve* (1851; rpr. Geneseo, N.Y., 1976), 324–48, and Neil McNall, *An Agricultural History of the Genesee Valley, 1790–1860* (Philadelphia, 1952).

12. My sketch of Joseph Ellicott is drawn from Chazanof, *Joseph Ellicott*, 9–15; Charles W. Evans, *Biographical and Historical Accounts of the Fox, Ellicott, and Evans Families* (Buffalo, N.Y., 1882), 166–77; Wyckoff, *Developer's Frontier*, 18–20.

13. Evans, "The Pulteney Purchase," 86–87; Wyckoff, *Developer's Frontier*, 46.

all considerable expenses, . . . to sell rather at low prices than to give long credits, and to make the purchase of these Lands an object to rich individuals and Societies." The latter injunction notwithstanding, Wadsworth believed the quickest route to rapid settlement was to encourage the "birds of passage" who constituted the first pioneers of new lands. These early settlers were essential to development of wild lands, contributing cheap labor to the work of clearing the forest. Accordingly, Wadsworth advised offering these "first adventurers" discount prices of $1.00 to $1.50 per acre with no down payments.[14]

Ellicott favored keeping company expenditures for improvements to a minimum. He proposed that it build a few main roads, a business office for the land agent, and a nearby tavern for prospective buyers. All subsequent development should be left to the settlers. Ellicott agreed with Williamson that substantial farmers should be lured from Pennsylvania, Maryland, and New Jersey to the Genesee Country. Ellicott was particularly interested in attracting ethnic German farmers from Lancaster County, Pennsylvania, but he also anticipated the migration of many poor settlers from the hill country of New England. Consequently, he suggested a system of credit purchases with five years or more to complete payment. Ellicott originally proposed a substantial down payment of 25 percent, but when settlement began only 15 percent was required.[15]

Ellicott recommended opening as much of the Purchase for sale as possible, particularly the elevated table lands of the middle third of the region. Neither the swamps and lowland plains of the northern townships nor the mountains of the extreme southern townships were likely to attract many settlers. Within the favored middle region, Ellicott urged selling good and bad lands in equal proportion. If the landlords reserved all the best lands for future sale at high prices, many potential settlers would be lost to other regions of the West. And unless some poor quality lands also were sold, the company faced the double burden of paying taxes on these lands while maintaining an agent to sell them.[16]

Cazenove and the Dutch landlords selected Ellicott to be their resident land agent for western New York. Ellicott's ideas skillfully blended the conflicting strategies proposed by Williamson and Wadsworth. The Dutch especially appreciated Ellicott's commitment to hold company expenditures to a minimum. Cazenove also admired the judicious balance of Ellicott's plan, which combined sales to other speculators with retail sales

14. Chazanof, *Joseph Ellicott,* 29; Wyckoff, *Developer's Frontier,* 45.
15. Evans, *Holland Land Company,* 219; Wyckoff, *Developer's Frontier,* 69–70.
16. "Remarks on Ellicott's Plan," Letter Books, 1795–1800, Joseph Ellicott Collection, Buffalo and Erie County Historical Society, Buffalo, N.Y.; cited hereafter as JEC.

on credit to actual settlers. Neither Ellicott nor the company ever lost their appetite for speculative sales that generated quick profits without the expense of subsidized development. Hence Cazenove and the Dutch responded enthusiastically to Ellicott's proposal to reserve some land for future speculation by keeping it off the market until prices rose.[17]

When Ellicott took up his position in November 1800, the Dutch proprietors granted him an agency of 500,000 acres. They authorized him to offer 300,000 acres for immediate sale, reserving the balance for future sale at higher prices. Of the 300,000 acres offered for immediate sale, one-third was earmarked for retail sale to actual settlers in lots of 120 and 240 acres. The other 200,000 acres were to be sold in units of at least 3,000 acres.[18]

The Dutch proprietors approved credit sales with terms of payment spread out over either four or six years. This policy was compatible with the system of credit purchases instituted by the national government in the Land Act of 1800. Credit purchases required a substantial down payment, ranging from one-third of the purchase price when buyers chose four-year terms to one-quarter in cash when they chose six-year plans. The Dutch proprietors also granted two- or three-year exemptions from interest charges. This was an important provision of Ellicott's plan. Cazenove agreed that the company should not make persistent demands for interest charges. Dunning deprived the frontier farmer, he pointed out, "of making his ground bear a crop, for if he is compelled to sacrifice from the beginning in payments of interest the small surplus he has earned by his industry he cannot again throw it in the ground [and] recover it thence tenfold by the sweat of his brow."[19]

No one expected settling this region was going to be easy. The Genesee Country was so vast, Cazenove noted, that "several generations would pass away before it could be called a populous country." Likewise, Paul Busti, Cazenove's replacement, pointed to the disparity between land and labor that made settlement of any new lands slow and difficult. "It is more easy to determine the passage of emigrating birds than that of adventurers looking out for land," he said. Settlement of the Holland Purchase lands might take fifty years to complete. Ellicott agreed that the frontier ratio of land to labor could not "be altered by human power."[20]

17. Wyckoff, *Developer's Frontier,* 52.
18. Evans, *Holland Land Company,* 221.
19. Ibid., 222–23; "Remarks on Ellicott's Plan."
20. "Remarks on Ellicott's Plan"; Paul Busti to Joseph Ellicott, March 9, 1802, June 5, 1804, JEC; Robert W. Bingham, ed., *Reports of Joseph Ellicott,* 2 vols. (Buffalo, N.Y., 1937–41), 1:1804, 261; cited hereafter as *RJE*.

"To get these lands settled"

To understand Ellicott's sales and settlement strategy one must examine
the larger conceptual framework guiding his thinking about the American
frontier. Settlement and development of new lands was a daunting task
because it involved compressing the social evolution of human society
into three or four decades. "The great objective in my opinion," Joseph
Ellicott said in 1809, "is for the Company to get these lands settled and
under improvement. Whilever they remain in a state of nature they have
no real value; because they are not productive to any individual, and their
value will be enhanced in proportion to the extent and populousness of
the settlement." Ellicott realized that "to get these lands settled and under
improvement" encompassed much more than a business or investment
strategy. Like most men of his time, he viewed social and economic
development as an evolutionary process with several distinctive stages and
particular types of settlers and economic activity. This thinking pointed to
a four-stage progression of hunting, pasturage, agriculture, and commerce. Each phase of development featured a distinct form of livelihood
and particular "habits and propensities" of behavior that changed greatly
as one stage succeeded to the next.[21]

The western New York frontier was part of a great laboratory of social
evolution. In America, Scottish historian William Robertson once explained, man could at last be studied "in his progress through the different
stages of society as he gradually advances from the infant state of civil life
towards its maturity and decline." This idea persisted well into the nineteenth century, becoming the basis of Frederick Jackson Turner's frontier
thesis. Like Robertson, Turner traced social development from "the disin-
tegration of savagery" through "the pastoral stage in ranch life" to "the
intensive culture of the denser farm settlement; and finally the manufacturing organization with city and factory system."[22]

On the western New York frontier Ellicott anticipated a progressive
transition from a society of seminomadic improvers and herdsmen to one
of permanent settlers and farmers. The Indian had already passed from the
scene, but the commercial stage could not be reached until men became

21. *RJE*, 2:1809, 27; Ronald L. Meek, *Social Science and the Ignoble Savage* (Cambridge,
Mass., 1976), 230; Michael Lienesch, *New Order of the Ages: Time, the Constitution, and
the Making of Modern American Political Thought* (Princeton, N.J., 1988), 82–115.
22. Robertson is quoted in Lienesch, *New Order of the Ages*, 84; Frederick Jackson
Turner, "The Significance of the Frontier in American History," in Ray Allen Billington, ed.,
Frontier and Section (Englewood Cliffs, N.J., 1961), 43.

sufficiently preoccupied with the middling opportunities trade and markets provided. In 1808 he generalized about the social process then under way.

> It is an old saying and a very correct one (with exceptions) that a considerable number of those who first emigrate to new lands may be called Pioneers. They go forward to clear and prepare the way for another description of people, who are generally in better circumstances. Those pioneer settlers erect a kind of a house, clear a few acres of land and remain there until the wild herbage that grows spontaneously in the forest is pretty much destroyed by their cattle. They then dispose of their improvements to the next description of emigrants and move further into the forest where the herbage is not destroyed by domestic animals and make other improvements but in reality for the purpose of sale when the wild food is exhausted.[23]

The transition from pioneer to farmer that structured Ellicott's thinking about settlement and development is represented in the four sketches adorning Turner's *Pioneer History*, which depict the transition from a pioneer backcountry clearing to a rural landscape of farms, fields, and country villages. In the third sketch the buildings, fences, and growing crops give the "whole premises . . . the appearance of careful management, of thrift, comfort, and even plenty." The outward appearance of this farm underscored the commitment of its proprietor to the middle-class values of refinement and respectability. "A neat framed barn, a well dug, a curb and sweep; a garden surrounded with a picket fence" testified to its owner's active industry and "finished husbandry."[24]

During the first ten years of Ellicott's tenure as resident agent, he adopted a sales and settlement policy to encourage the transition from pioneer to farmer. Inviting pioneers to improve the Holland Purchase was the first step in an overall strategy to create populous rural settlements and raise the market value of the company's property. Because Ellicott realized that "the extent of uninhabited Counties wanting settlers" was

23. *RJE*, 1:1808, 400.
24. Orsamus Turner, *Pioneer History of the Holland Purchase of Western New York* (1850; rpr. Geneseo, N.Y., 1974), 563–66; Paul Busti to Joseph Ellicott, June 5, 1804, JEC. For an examination of the idea of improvement, see Jack P. Greene, "Independence, Improvement, and Authority: Toward a Framework for Understanding the Histories of the Southern Backcountry during the Era of the American Revolution," in Ronald Hoffman, Thad W. Tate, and Peter J. Albert, eds., *An Uncivil War: The Southern Backcountry during the American Revolution* (Charlottesville, Va., 1985), 3–36; Joan Thirsk, *Economic Policy and Projects: The Development of a Consumer Society in Early Modern England* (Oxford, 1978); Joyce Appleby, *Economic Thought and Ideology in Seventeenth-Century England* (Princeton, N.J., 1978).

vast and the number of actual settlers comparatively small, he advocated generous terms of sale and "lenient conduct" when settlers fell into arrears.[25]

During his first year sales were disappointing. He reported in 1802, "When it is considered that emigrants from the old settlements are generally that class of people who are compelled by indigence and the pressure of misfortunes at home to remove to new countries in hopes of bettering their situation, . . . we may reasonably infer that from the pecuniary abilities of such emigrants we are to form but very slender expectations." Land seekers objected strongly to the down payment required by the Dutch because it left them without the means of making "their intended Improvements." During his first year Ellicott dropped the requirement of a 15 percent down payment and refunded even the small amounts some settlers offered. "Had I implicitly adhered to the strict principles of my instructions in exacting the advance required," he explained, "we would not now have had more than fifteen settlers on our lands."[26]

Ellicott argued that requiring a down payment was counterproductive; the ultimate objective was settlement and development of wild lands, so the labor of the pioneer settler was far more valuable than his cash down payment. Ellicott explained:

> These advances, as Experience will ever prove will be very inconsiderable when contrasted with the Improvements they prevent. For every acre of the Company's land that is cleared and fenced at the labour and expence of others to whose support we contribute nothing will enhance the value of the District at least 20 dollars. Thus supposing we refuse admission to a family on our lands unless 33 dollars, the advance on a lot, is paid, who would clear and fence ten acres, which improvement would be worth 200 dollars, we totally postpone that increase of property, which is received by lands in other quarters, for the sake of 33 dollars.[27]

To encourage labor and industry, Ellicott believed the landlords should give these first settlers the right of "peaceable possession" and then leave them alone. Little or no payment should be expected over the five- to ten-year period required to build a farm and produce the surplus needed for making regular payments. "It is an object in my opinion," Ellicott declared, "that the most lenient conduct should be pursued towards them,

25. *RJE*, 1:1804, 261.
26. *RJE*, 1:1801, 161.
27. Ibid., 162.

because those who come into the country in quest of land never fail to inquire minutely into the manner the landholder deals with them; and if they find they are treated with a lenient hand, and not crowded for their payments it is an inducement for other persons to become purchasers and settlers." Settlement and improvement of the Holland Purchase required that "lenient measures should be continued until the territory is pretty well settled."[28]

During his first year as resident agent, Ellicott decided to let "actual settlers . . . take up lands without requiring any advance money." Under the terms of what he called a provisional or unarticled sale, he required that each settler build a cabin, clear and improve four acres of land, and pay five or ten dollars during the next year.[29] Paul Busti, the company's agent in Philadelphia, approved Ellicott's decision, believing the original sales policy adopted by the Dutch was unrealistic. Busti encouraged Ellicott to go even further, advising him to accept a settler's personal note in lieu of the small cash payment required of provisional buyers and to exempt provisional buyers who made improvements from paying interest for the first two years after beginning an improvement.[30]

Ellicott and his Dutch principals preferred that their land buyers take articles of agreement. The landlords refused to convey title to any buyer until all the purchase money was paid. New York State law had given alien proprietors the right to purchase and hold property but prohibited them from recovering property after the title was transferred. When a default occurred on property deeded by aliens, it reverted to the use of the people of New York. Consequently, Ellicott and the Holland Land Company required that land buyers who paid an advance or made an improvement also enter into articles of agreement. These articles of agreement, preparatory to the execution of a formal deed, declared the landlords' promise to transfer title when all the conditions of the sale were met.[31]

During his first year Ellicott executed thirty-two articles of agreement selling 4,558 acres of land in five townships. The total purchase money amounted to $12,073.99, and the advance paid in cash, labor, or promissory notes came to $1,135.82. He also sold 5,164 acres on provisional

28. *RJE*, 2:1809, 28.
29. *RJE*, 1:1801, 171–72.
30. Paul Busti to Joseph Ellicott, March 9, 1802, JEC.
31. An act of March 26, 1802, made it possible for aliens to transfer title through a mortgage and then recover the property if a default occurred. But the property could be recovered only by a case brought before the chancellor of New York. Such litigation was tedious and expensive (Evans, *Holland Land Company*, 245).

terms. The purchase price of these lands was $14,269.55 and was secured, Ellicott believed, by the improvements he required of such buyers. On the lots sold provisionally he recorded a total of 20 houses built, 74 acres cleared, 15 acres plowed, and 46 acres sowed in grain.[32]

Both articled and provisional sales continued in 1802. Ellicott tightened the conditions of provisional sales to ensure that buyers entered into articles of agreement. Within the first two months a provisional settler had to "chop over" at least two acres. By the end of eight months he had to build a house and move his family into residence. Two to six months later Ellicott expected at least six acres to be "well cleared and fenced." If all these improvements were made on time, an advance payment of 10 percent of the total purchase price entitled a provisional settler to enter into an article of agreement. If a provisional settler failed to comply with these stipulations, Ellicott disposed of the lot to another "applicant."[33]

Ellicott also proposed to extend the length of contracts from six to ten years. "This would give the settler," Ellicott believed, "full time to clear up his land and pay for it by the produce of the farm if he possessed industry and only a tolerable share of good fortune. . . . And if at expiration of 10 years such purchasers should not be able to make the stipulated payments the Company might with every propriety re-enter, and take the Lands and improvements thereon." By extending the period of credit Ellicott hoped to encourage sales, stimulate the work of improvement, and protect his principals' investment. Ellicott knew many provisional buyers intended to sell their improvements before taking articles of agreement. Yet as long as they made improvements and helped "to make way for the accommodation of more permanent and wealthy settlers," they were "beneficial."[34]

The quantity of land sold by provisional agreements continued to increase. More than 45,000 acres were sold in 1804. During the period 1807–9 provisional sales accounted for more than 462,000 acres, roughly two-thirds of the total acreage sold. In 1809 alone Ellicott sold 228,468 acres with a purchase price of $551,216 under provisional terms. Precisely how many sales of this type were made cannot be determined because Ellicott did not register the names of individual buyers. Since "it is always uncertain which of the persons, or how many of them will comply with such contracts," Ellicott explained, "detailing the names of the purchasers or quantity of land that each . . . provisionally contracted to

32. *RJE,* 1:1801, 157–58, 179, 181.
33. *RJE,* 1:1802, 199.
34. Ibid., 202, 200.

purchase" was unnecessary. He recorded only the total number of acres sold by provisional terms in any given year.[35]

In late 1809 Ellicott abandoned the practice of provisional sales. "I found by experience," he said, "there is a period that a system of that kind must for the benefit and advantage of the land holders be discontinued, because the plan is too susceptible of abuse that eventually more injury arises from it than all the benefits derived." The large number of provisional sales encouraged an active market for improved lands. This buying and selling of wild or partially improved land occurred outside of the company's control and led to many abuses. New settlers ended up buying land from provisional settlers. They "paid over all" their money to provisional settlers, Ellicott complained, "what we obtained was the settler without any money."[36]

Ellicott also believed that many of the provisional buyers were dishonest. They did not make any of the stipulated improvements yet found ways to prolong their possession until they could sell out. "These people would by means of a second person, who would lend his name, obtain another provisional term, and so on until an opportunity offered to make 50, 100, 150 or $200 [from] some coming in settler." The sheer volume of land sold on provisional terms became a problem. "We had in many townships," Ellicott noted, "scarcely a feaseable lot of land for sale and the coming on settler was compelled, if he . . . got land, to buy second handed of provisional purchasers." For all of these reasons he decided that unarticled sales should be discontinued. "In short the business in this large extent of country became so complex and confused," he declared, "I was compelled to abandon provisional sales altogether, and resort to real ones where the 5 to 10 percent of the money was paid in hand, and an article of agreement issued at once."[37]

After ten years it was also time, Ellicott believed, for the second stage of settlement to begin. In this stage permanent farmers would make valuable improvements and pay for their land. Ellicott worried about the great number of provisional buyers already in the Purchase because they were particularly susceptible to environmental influences. The negative effect of the frontier on these settlers was explained by Congressman Peter B. Porter in 1810:

35. "Report of Land Tables," 1804–6, 1807, 1808, 1809, Reel 109, Inventory no. 485, Holland Land Company Project, State University of New York College at Fredonia; *RJE*, 2:1809, 24.

36. *RJE*, 2:1809, 75.

37. Ibid., 75–76.

The great evil, and it is a serious one indeed, sir, under which the inhabitants of the Western country labor, arises from the want of a market. . . . The single circumstance, of the want of a market, is already beginning to produce the most disastrous effects not only on the industry but upon the morals of the inhabitants. Such is the fertility of their lands, that one half of their time spent in labor is sufficient to produce every article, which their farms are capable of yielding in sufficient quantities, for their own consumption, and there is nothing to incite them to produce more. They are, therefore, naturally led to spend the other part of their time in idleness and dissipation.[38]

This was the nightmare of underdevelopment—poverty and idleness in the midst of natural abundance. Without markets to encourage industry and improvement, settlers succumbed to the lure of easy living.[39]

As Ellicott and other company agents grew impatient with the slow pace of social evolution in western New York, they distinguished between two types of settlers. From the company's perspective, good settlers resisted and overcame the pernicious effects of the frontier environment, whereas bad settlers became lazy and dissolute. Good settlers made valuable improvements; they cleared, fenced, and cultivated their land. Bad settlers made improvements of negligible value, preferring to strip the land rather than cultivate it.

Good, "profitable settlers" helped to convert the Holland Purchase from a wilderness to a rural landscape of fields and fences. The model for such a settler, Joseph Ellicott believed, was the Pennsylvania German farmer. In 1808 he told Paul Busti: "Should the Lancaster County Germans turn their attention to settling on the Holland Purchase they will doubtless be the means of introducing many others from other parts of Pennsylvania." Ellicott liked the German farmers because they had money to buy land as well as "industry and economy" to cultivate it. The agents of the Holland Land Company often used the word "industry" to characterize a good settler. "Industry," for them, meant "habitual diligence in any employment" or "steady attention to business." A "sober industrious" settler applied his labor with energy, direction, discipline, and perseverance. He also strove for more than mere subsistence. The spirit of

38. *Annals of the Congress of the United States, Eleventh Congress, First and Second Sessions,* 1810 (Washington, D.C., 1853), 1388. For a discussion of early American environmental theory, see Bernard W. Sheehan, *Seeds of Extinction: Jeffersonian Philanthropy and the American Indian* (1973; New York, 1974), 32–35; Leo Marx, *The Machine in the Garden: Technology and the Pastoral Ideal in America* (New York, 1964), 75–81.

39. Peter S. Onuf, *Statehood and Union: A History of the Northwest Ordinance* (Bloomington, Ind., 1977), 1–20; Drew R. McCoy, *The Elusive Republic: Political Economy in Jeffersonian America* (New York, 1980), 236–59.

improvement guiding his personal conduct and work habits encouraged respect for private property rights established by title and deed. The solicitude for property rights, in turn, encouraged respect for land contracts and the obligation to pay the agreed-upon price for the land.[40]

Finally, good settlers made "good improvements." The willingness to clear and fence land was viewed by the company as confirmation that a settler was a "real farmer," who used the land to raise crops, including wheat and corn. "Before wheat can be raised," a company agent explained in 1824, "the soil must be well cleared, which is, at present, attended with much labour; the putting in the crop, is also expensive; and afterwards, it must be well fenced, for security. If a few fields on a farm are in this state of improvement, we are certain of final payment." Growing wheat, then, represented the investment of "industry" and the intensive use of land and productive resources that the landlords desired and sought to promote.[41]

If industry and "good improvements" distinguished desirable settlers, laziness and negligible improvements marred the character and signified the casual work habits of bad settlers. "Their improvements are inconsiderable," a company agent reported in 1821, "and in many instances scarcely deserve the name. Large families, exhibiting all the appearances of poverty and misery," he added, "drag out a wretched existence without a chance of bettering their condition." Far too many of the first settlers, the company believed, "built a kind of a house," cleared "a few acres of land," and stayed only long enough for their cattle to consume "the wild herbage that grows spontaneously in the forest." Eventually these nomads would sell their primitive improvements to more permanent settlers who could be counted on to cultivate and pay for the soil.[42]

"The interest compounded and added to the principal due"

From 1801 to 1809 Ellicott encouraged any improvement of company lands. "Every person who emigrates hither," he reported in 1809, "and clears up an acre of land, adds $16 more value to the Holland Company's territory. Hence I consider every person who does even this and makes not

---

40. *RJE*, 1:1805, 303; *RJE*, 2:1809, 28; Reports of Jacob Otto in *RJE*, 2:1821–22, 295–96; Joseph Ellicott to Paul Busti, Dec. 24, 1808, JEC.

41. Reports of Jacob Otto, 1824, 374.

42. Reports of Jacob Otto, 1821–22, 298.

any payment an acquisition." Good improvements protected the company against loss because the value of the property created grew more rapidly than the unpaid land debt. Even the "lazy" pioneer who extracted what he could from the partially cleared forest before selling out and moving on made a contribution. As land changed hands, "property was improved," and the company received "a more wealthy and better settler."[43]

At the conclusion of his annual report for 1810, Ellicott confidently predicted that the "most sanguine expectations" concerning the settlement and development of the Holland Purchase were coming true. New settlers appeared to be wealthier and better off than those of just a few years before. New emigrants were able to pay "at least 5 percent of the purchase money." Their arrival signified the beginning of the second stage of social evolution and affirmed Ellicott's decision to end provisional sales.[44]

Meanwhile, the administrative business of issuing articles to past provisional buyers and renewing old articles that had expired presented Ellicott with an opportunity to encourage the industry and economy of those pioneers who had apparently succumbed to the lure of indolence and easy subsistence. Provisional buyers who had not yet taken articles of agreement were required to enter into a contract at current land prices and terms of credit. This meant they now had to pay more for their land than the original provisional agreement stipulated. By 1812 many original articles issued during the first years of settlement had expired. The business of renewing these articles grew increasingly complicated because the current settler was seldom "the person who made the first purchase or was the first settler." Some articles changed hands, according to Ellicott, on average once every twelve months over the entire ten years the original contracts were in effect.[45]

When Ellicott renewed an expired contract, he computed a new purchase price by assessing compound interest over the life of the old contract, subtracting any previous payments. For instance, if a settler purchased land on credit at $2.50 per acre, eight years of simple interest added to the principal raised the cost to $3.90 per acre. If the agreed-upon terms were not met after ten years, Ellicott renewed the contract but computed a new price based on compound interest that raised the cost to $4.39 per acre. The new purchase price was $.49 more per acre than the

43. *RJE,* 2:1809, 29; *RJE,* 1:1808, 401.
44. *RJE,* 2:1810, 91; *RJE,* 2:1811, 95.
45. *RJE,* 2:1811, 95; *RJE,* 2:1812, 122.

original agreement, and the increased value of the property was largely owing to the settler's own improvements. Ellicott reported to his boss in 1813 that in some instances "it may be only equitable to charge a still greater sum than the interest compounded and added to the principal due." Sometimes it was necessary to increase the price of land even more because the objective was to keep the price of the company's land commensurate with rising property values throughout western New York.[46]

Ellicott assessed compound interest for the first time in 1812, but the practice quickly became central to his system of management. Assessing compound interest improved the personal discipline of settlers and encouraged them to make the transition from pioneer to farmer. "I have generally made it a practice in renewing the article," he observed, "to make the new principal greater than the sum due, interest compounded. Experience proves that this mode of dealing with the article holders is productive of advantages to the proprietors as well as to the people. It is a powerful stimulus to industry and economy." It encouraged settlers to save money, to make punctual payments, and "to keep the interest paid off." Ellicott justified the practice of compounding interest because of the large number of pioneer settlers who migrated to western New York. "I well recollect," he declared, "that until the arrangement was adopted of requiring interest on unpaid interest, . . . we seldom received little more money during the year than sufficient to defray administration expenses."[47]

The practice of assessing compound interest was also compatible with the landlords' concept of property. Ellicott and the Dutch owners viewed property as a legal right established by title and deed. Title to the Holland Land Purchase had descended to the Dutch proprietors in 1792, when they purchased over 3 million acres of land in western New York from Robert Morris. The new landlords viewed their property in wild lands as equivalent to money. Hence they expected an annual return in the form of interest. The assessment of interest was critical to their overall strategy. It protected the company's investment by keeping the price of land on a par with the rising value of property throughout western New York resulting from the settlers' improvements. It also covered the cost of extending credit for land purchases and represented that portion of the settlers' labor due the landlords as a return on their capital.[48]

46. *RJE*, 2:1812, 122–23.
47. *RJE*, 2:1813, 127–28; *RJE*, 2:1817, 229.
48. *RJE*, 2:1814, 145.

Ellicott's annual reports carefully documented how the system of compound interest raised "the price of the land so high as to keep pace with the increasing value of the territory." Compounding interest maximized the landlords' profits. In 1813, for instance, he showed that compounding interest added $13,309.98 to the landlords' property. The Dutch were fully entitled to this increment even though it was largely a product of the settlers' labor. Ellicott and later agents argued that the landowners' contribution to settlement fully justified the return they received. Once the settlers had time, through "sufficient indulgence" granted by the company, to create a farm and produce a surplus, the landlords had a "right" to some portion of the settlers' labor. The amount of that portion was the difference between the price of wild land and the added value resulting from compounding interest over eight years on the original ten-year contracts.[49]

The practice of assessing compound interest became a cornerstone of Ellicott's policy for settling and developing new lands, and it took full advantage of the company's decision to enter into articles of agreement with most settlers. In 1807 Ellicott estimated that "nineteen twentieths of the settlers" held their land under articles of agreement. Entering into articles of agreement permitted the landlords to assess compound interest, whereas if land was sold "on bond and mortgage simple interest only [was] legally obtainable." Ellicott concluded: "Experience tests that if the objects of Land Companies are to make the greatest profits in the sale of their lands that the most beneficial plan is at retail, and by article of agreement."[50]

"Affording them a regular and certain market"

Up to this point I have focused on the system of provisional sales, articles of agreement, and renewed land contracts based on compound interest that underlay the Dutch landlords' strategy for settling and developing wild lands. Now we must turn to what Ellicott described as "a powerful auxiliary" of social evolution on the American frontier. Access to markets and other manufacturing services encouraged settlers to work beyond what mere subsistence required. Only when settlers practiced the sober industry and prudent economy necessary to produce an agricultural surplus for market could they pay for their land. Congressman Peter B.

49. Ibid.; Reports of Jacob Otto, 1821–22, 296.
50. Joseph Ellicott to Paul Busti, Jan. 9, 1807, JEC; *RJE,* 2:1813, 128.

Porter declared "the want of a market" the principal source of "the most disastrous effects . . . on the industry [and] morals" of western settlers. Without markets, there was no incentive to labor, and settlers spent a large portion of their time "in idleness and dissipation."[51]

The Holland Land Purchase was strategically located adjoining Lakes Erie and Ontario. Settlers in the northern half of the Purchase thus had access to a good market at Montreal for agricultural products, potash, and lumber because transportation over the lakes and down the St. Lawrence was comparatively cheap. The high cost of transportation to market severely limited market activity in the backcountry. Ellicott appreciated the geographic advantage enjoyed by the Holland Purchase. "Boats and vessels of proper construction for navigating the lakes and the river St. Lawrence were built and it was soon found that a barrel of flour could be carried from any part of Lake Ontario to Montreal for a less premium than a barrel of flour could be carried from any place 80 and 100 miles west from Philadelphia by land to Philadelphia even along their best turnpike roads. Hence . . . as to expence of carrying articles to market," he added, "the lands of the Holland Company adjoining and contiguous to Lake Ontario became better situated than lands 100 miles west of Philadelphia." Since lands within a hundred-mile radius of Philadelphia were selling at from $60 to $100 per acre, Ellicott concluded that "the period is fast arriving when these very lands of the Holland Company will be in a degree as valuable as the lands . . . in Pennsylvania."[52]

Access to market increased the value of the company's property and encouraged settlers to improve their land. If settlers had to travel more than twenty-five to thirty miles to a local market center such as a grist or sawmill, this "great inconvenience" sometimes compelled them "to abandon their improvements." Ellicott reported such a case in 1813. Settlers had abandoned their improvements in township 14, range 4, "in consequence of the great distance to a grist mill."[53]

Lake Ontario provided a natural market outlet to Montreal, yet Ellicott knew roads and other frontier services were needed to open up the interior of the Purchase. Although he had pledged to keep down company expenses, he spent some of his principals' money to open roads throughout western New York. Roads, "more than any other objects," he said in 1803, encouraged settlement and promoted commercial development of company lands. All of his early annual reports included a statement about

51. *RJE*, 2:1810, 78; *Annals of the Congress*, 1810, 1387.
52. *RJE*, 2:1810, 78–79.
53. *RJE*, 2:1812, 105.

the need for roads. In 1805 he observed: "In order to introduce and extend the Settlements of new Countries it is always necessary to open roads of Communication in various Directions for the Accommodation of the Settlers, which are at present and perhaps will continue for some time to be requisite for the Sale of our Land." In 1810 he noted that "unless Roads are opened at our Expence in interior Parts to enable Settlers to carry their Property thither, Settlements would progress very slowly indeed." Without roads, settlers could not reach the lands they desired to purchase, nor could they transport to market any surplus they produced or extracted from the land.[54]

Roads also increased the value of the company's property. Lands located in the interior, where access was difficult, sold for less than lands of equal or lesser quality in more desirable locations. Ellicott believed isolated lands could be sold at $1.75 to $2.50 per acre. Lands adjacent to roads brought much higher prices. Ellicott set out to build a network of roads radiating outward from Batavia like the spokes of a wheel. During his first year, he "partially opened a road from Batavia towards Queenstown in Upper Canada as far as the Indian Village of Tonnawonta." He also instructed teams of surveyors to "mark out" a road from Batavia to the mouth of Oak Orchard Creek for "the immigration of settlers, and for the transportation of salt and other articles deposited on the Lake." Opening roads cost the Holland Land Company $942.23 during the first year of settlement.[55]

The next year Ellicott directed construction of a road from Batavia to the mouth of Oak Orchard Creek on Lake Ontario. He opened another road that extended from Batavia southward into townships 10 and 11 in the second range. Work proceeded on another road running from Batavia to the southeast in the direction of Big Tree. The road from Batavia to Buffalo Creek was "causewayed and bridged." Considerable progress was also made laying out a road from Batavia to Queenstown despite the wet and swampy ground through which it passed. By the end of 1802, Ellicott had opened 170 miles of roads running from Batavia to points north, west, and south in the Purchase.[56]

At the end of Ellicott's first ten years as resident agent, many major routes were in some degree of service. The Buffalo Road was the most important one. It extended west from Batavia, passed just south of the Tonawanda Indian Reservation, and continued to Vandeventer's settle-

54. *RJE*, 1:1803, 214; *RJE*, 1:1805, 271; *RJE*, 2:1809, 10.
55. *RJE*, 1:1801, 172, 144–45, 175.
56. *RJE*, 1:1802, 187–88.

ment and Asa Ransom's tavern, where it turned south toward Buffalo Creek. This road became the focus of early settlement and economic development. The Niagara Road linked Batavia to the busy trading corridor along the Niagara River. It ran in a northwesterly direction, turning almost due west when it reached the Niagara limestone escarpment and ended at the new village of Lewiston. Several other roads also tied the Holland Purchase to the historic portage route linking Lakes Erie and Ontario. The Military Road followed the course of the river and connected Buffalo Creek, Lewiston, and Fort Niagara. The Ellicott Creek Road linked the Niagara River, across from Grand Island, with the Buffalo Road as it turned south toward Buffalo.[57]

Ellicott built roads by exchanging cash and land for the settlers' labor. He entered into such an arrangement with a settler named Samuel Berry on June 29, 1808. Berry agreed to open a road from Canadaway Creek "to the line of the town of Pomfret" in Chautauqua County. He was "to cut all the timbers level with the surface of ground for the full breadth of 14 . . . feet and to remove all the old logs and underbrush." Ellicott promised to credit Berry's land account ten dollars for every mile of road he opened. Crediting land accounts for labor expended on road building was successful, but it required great patience and steadfastness on the part of Ellicott. Many settlers, especially during the first years of development, could not honor their agreements. Some of them shirked their responsibility, others fell sick with fevers, while still others spent "the principal part of their time . . . clearing their Lands in order to procure Subsistence for their Families and Cattle during the Winter."[58]

The Holland Land Company assisted road building in other ways too. In 1807, Busti proposed that the company "make a Donation of $100 in Cash and $100 in Land for every Mile of Road any Turnpike Company would effect between the Eastern Transit Line and New Amsterdam." And in 1810 Ellicott urged the company to encourage construction of a road linking Mayville on Chautauqua Lake with Lake Erie. The Portage Turnpike Company, recently chartered by the state legislature, had undertaken this project. Ellicott recommended that the landlords accept shares of stock issued by the turnpike company at face value in payment for land.[59]

---

57. Brunger, "Historical Land Valuation," 18–20; Wyckoff, *Developer's Frontier,* 76, 81–82; Chazanof, *Joseph Ellicott,* 81–93.

58. Joseph Ellicott to Samuel Berry, June 29, 1808, JEC; *RJE,* 1:1801, 143; *RJE,* 1:1807, 331.

59. *RJE,* 1:1807, 336; *RJE,* 2:1810, 52–53.

Busti and the Dutch landlords supported Ellicott's efforts to open roads. "If the people show an eagerness to settle in the townships through which the new road is to pass," he instructed Ellicott, "you may cut it out." At the same time, he expressed the company's hope that once a few main roads were opened, future road building would be left to the settlers. Meanwhile, new land seekers should be encouraged to take up land along roads already built.[60]

Ellicott built roads following "the most economical plan." His roads measured seventeen feet across and cost ten dollars per mile. Ellicott insisted that all trees under one foot in diameter be cut "close to the ground." In the northern part of the Purchase, where numerous swamps dotted the low-lying plains, the ground was soaked or covered by standing water at least one or two seasons of the year. Here causeways were built, rows of timber placed "parallel to each other" that raised the level of the road, making it more passable. But the bottom layer of logs pressed against wet earth, and the wood rotted quickly. Ellicott tried to lengthen the short life of causewayed roads by making them wider. More sunlight and greater air circulation helped to keep the roads drier. He also tried covering the logs with a layer of "earth from 4 to 8 inches in depth" to slow the rate of decay.[61]

Roads required continuous maintenance and repair. Busti instructed Ellicott to make sure local pathmasters kept them in good repair. He also cautioned against building roads and turnpikes prematurely. "Large buildings, turnpike roads etc. in an unsettled country decay and perish," he warned. For that reason he opposed John Church's plan to extend a turnpike west from Bath to Lake Erie in 1805. Church had purchased a large amount of company land at wholesale the previous year, but because his lands were unsettled, Busti predicted that the proposed road would get little use. In a season or two it would become indistinguishable from the surrounding forest.[62]

Ellicott and the Erie Canal

The Holland Land Company's attitude toward the greatest internal improvement of the age, the Erie Canal, deserves special attention. When the idea of building a canal from Lake Erie to the Hudson River came

60. Paul Busti to Joseph Ellicott, April 25, 1806, June 5, 1804, JEC.
61. *RJE*, 1:1805, 271; *RJE*, 1:1802, 187; *RJE*, 1:1807, 337–38.
62. Paul Busti to Joseph Ellicott, April 20, 1803, May 11, 1805, JEC.

under serious consideration in 1808, Ellicott immediately endorsed it. He recognized the contribution such an outlet "to our Atlantic Markets" would make to the rapid settlement and development of company lands in western New York. He estimated that the proposed canal would increase the value of company lands by at least $1 million. From the beginning, he supported an internal canal route that traversed the Tonawanda wetlands in the thirteenth and fourteenth tiers of townships. He preferred this route over an external canal passing through Lake Ontario from Oswego to Lewiston because it would be cheaper to build and once in operation would require fewer points of transshipment. Less loading and unloading reduced freight costs and promised to keep the cost of transportation to a minimum. The external canal route through Lake Ontario, on the other hand, risked diverting western trade and commerce to Montreal and Canada and raised serious questions for the future of American economic development and political union.[63]

To support construction of the canal, Ellicott offered the state alternate lots of land along the entire distance it cut through the Purchase. The company hoped this generous offer might encourage other land companies in the state to do likewise. If they did, the canal could be built without running up a large public debt.[64]

By 1811, however, Ellicott had undergone a change of heart about the proposed canal. He now referred to it as "a wild visionary moonshine Piece of Business." "Such a Work might possibly be effected," he said, "by a despot who had the Power of a whole Nation at his Command," but the prospect of its success in America was slim. Ellicott's loss of interest in the canal was attributable to the opening of the Montreal trade. "At the Period I wrote my Report of 1808, 1809," he conceded, "the Market of Montreal was hardly thought of and it was not at that Time known with what Facility Articles of Produce could be transported through the Lakes and down the River St. Lawrence to that Place, or what would be the Expence of Transportation."[65]

Jefferson's Embargo of 1807 made Montreal "a better Market than

63. *RJE,* 1:1808, 423; Joseph Ellicott to Paul Busti, July 16, 1808, and Joseph Ellicott to Simeon DeWitt, July 30, 1808, JEC. See also Chazanof, *Joseph Ellicott,* 157–80; Ronald E. Shaw, *Erie Water West: A History of the Erie Canal, 1792–1854* (Lexington, Ky., 1966), 31–33, 42–44, 59, 64; Frank H. Severance, ed., *The Holland Land Co. and Canal Construction in Western New York; Buffalo–Black Rock Harbor Papers; Journals and Documents,* vol. 14 of the *Buffalo Historical Society Publications* (Buffalo, N.Y., 1910).

64. Paul Busti to Joseph Ellicott, Oct. 14, 1808, and Joseph Ellicott to Simeon DeWitt, Nov. 19, 1808, JEC.

65. *RJE,* 2:1810, 84–85.

New York on Account of the Trade of the United States being so much shackled by the European Powers." Ellicott reported the export of 500 barrels of cider and 100 barrels of apples from Charlotte at the mouth of the Genesee River in 1810. The following spring 445 barrels of pork, 5,557 barrels of flour, 611 barrels of wheat, and 10,000 pounds of cheese were shipped from Charlotte. Lake schooners carried these products from the Genesee River to Ogdensburg; scows and boats took the cargo from there to Montreal. The early success of this trade convinced Ellicott that even if the "great Canal should never be compleated," the Holland Purchase enjoyed a major market outlet.[66]

When the state went forward with plans for the canal, Ellicott worked to ensure that the proposed route passed through as much of the Holland Purchase as possible. In 1816 Ellicott was appointed to a group of five canal commissioners, and he convinced this group to let him lay out the route from the Genesee River to Buffalo. Ellicott got his nephew and Holland Company subagent, William Peacock, appointed as engineer and his brother Andrew to conduct the survey. He pushed for a canal that passed south of the Niagara escarpment, a limestone ridge dividing the Ontario Lake Plain into two areas. Ellicott preferred this route to one that passed north of the escarpment because it traversed more of the company's lands. Ultimately, however, the canal commissioners chose the route that ran north of the escarpment. Though disappointed, Ellicott did not lose interest in the canal, and he played an important part in the decision to make Buffalo its western terminus.[67]

About the time Ellicott was appointed a canal commissioner, he became involved in another project intended to promote trade and commerce. Ellicott understood, like William Cooper, a fellow land developer in central New York, who wrote a manual for those engaged in the management of settling wild lands, that "where there is trade there will be money; and where there is money the landlord will succeed."[68] To promote more trade and to facilitate larger land payments from the settlers, Ellicott helped to establish and run the Bank of Niagara, the first bank chartered in the Holland Purchase. In May 1816, as the bank was being organized, its board of directors asked Ellicott to supervise the subscription of stock because the new directors were "unacquainted with monied institutions or the mode of organizing them." In July 1818, he became the bank's

66. Ibid., 84–85, 80–82.
67. Chazanof, *Joseph Ellicott,* 168–70, 175–76.
68. Quoted in Wyckoff, *Developer's Frontier,* 11. The original source is William Cooper, *A Guide in the Wilderness* (Dublin, 1810), 7.

president. Throughout the first years of the Bank of Niagara's operation, Ellicott, along with his family and friends, subscribed to its stock, discounted loans to one another, and used the institution to convert their personal property into capital simply by giving personal notes. When the bank was threatened by insolvency in 1818, Ellicott even committed the resources of the Holland Land Company to bolster its flagging credit. To the extent that the bank's paper became "the circulating medium in this quarter," Ellicott supported the institution as a vital source of credit and money needed for frontier settlement and land development.[69]

Encouraging Local Manufacturing

The company tried to create markets and stimulate improvement by subsidizing the establishment of local manufacturing facilities. "The Erection of Grist and Saw Mills," Ellicott said in 1804, "contributes as much and probably more than any other object to the sale and settlement of a tract of country, and it has generally been the practice of large landholders to turn their attention to their erection." Sawmills provided essential building materials, and gristmills encouraged pioneers to cultivate wheat and corn for home consumption and local exchange as well as for sale and profit in the marketplace. The company preferred that its settlers raise more crops and herd fewer cattle.[70]

Although Ellicott believed settlement and development should be left to private enterprise, he favored building a sawmill and a gristmill at company expense. He also initiated an aggressive policy to encourage development of mills throughout the Purchase. First, he offered assistance to prospective mill operators by helping them find good sites. When Ellicott supervised the survey of company lands, he had instructed his men to note the location of potential mill sites. He shared this information with prospective millers who stopped at his Batavia office. Second, Ellicott often provided loans to get mills built and into operation, even supplying critical parts. Asa Ransom received a small loan to help build a sawmill in 1801. The following year, he received further assistance to build a

69. Isaac Leake to Joseph Ellicott, July 17, 1818, Charles W. Evans Papers, Buffalo and Erie County Historical Society, Buffalo, N.Y.; Joseph Ellicott to Myron Holley, Aug. 21, 1818, and Joseph Ellicott to Paul Busti, Aug. 24, 1818, JEC; Jonas Harrison to Joseph Ellicott, May 28, 1816, Evans Papers; Joseph Ellicott to Paul Busti, May 19, 1819, JEC; Joseph Ellicott to Paul Busti, Jan. 31, 1817, JEC. For a discussion of Ellicott and the Bank of Niagara, albeit a sympathetic one, see Chazanof, *Joseph Ellicott*, 134–56.

70. *RJE*, 1:1804, 255; *RJE*, 1:1801, 148.

gristmill. In 1808 Ellicott loaned D. Bowers fifty dollars as startup money to erect a series of mills in township 3, range 7. He also "loaned a Mr. Wilder" fifty dollars to help rebuild a mill destroyed by fire. Of a total of twenty-seven early mills encouraged by Ellicott and built between 1801 and 1812, eleven of the operators received loans from him.[71]

Ellicott also helped new mill operators purchase equipment. In 1805 he furnished J. Cummings with mill irons and stones. He helped Asa Ransom purchase "Irons Mill Stones, bolting Cloths, and . . . the running Gears." And he advanced $100 to M. Dunham for millstones to open a gristmill in township 16, range 2. During his first year as resident agent he spent a total of $1,869.20 to encourage the construction of saw and gristmills.[72]

Ellicott also assisted the establishment of mills by offering special terms to operators. James Dewey wrote to Ellicott in March 1801 to inquire whether the Holland Company would furnish the money to construct a sawmill on Allen's Creek near Buttermilk Falls and then turn over "the direction" of it "for a certain share of the profits." In 1805 Ellicott entered into such an arrangement with Zerah Phelps, who opened a gristmill with the help of a company loan. Phelps ran the mill and turned over a share of the profits, $373.10, the first season it was in operation. In 1807 Ellicott proposed building grist and sawmills at Eighteen Mile and Johnson's creeks respectively. He offered any prospective operator free rent for five years. In return, he asked only that the mills be kept running and in good repair. Sometimes the terms offered by Ellicott and the company required a settler to open a mill in exchange for a reduction in the purchase price of land. In 1808, for instance, Ellicott entered into a contract with a settler who agreed to build both a saw and a gristmill on Quottehonyaiga Creek in township 15, range 7. The settler agreed to pay $2.25 per acre with the required down payment of 5 percent deferred for two years.[73]

In the early years of Ellicott's tenure, the company itself built three mills. A company sawmill opened at Batavia in 1802; another one, on Oak Orchard Creek in township 15, range 3, opened in 1804. A company gristmill, also at Batavia, went into operation in late 1804. All three mills taxed Ellicott's patience and the company's finances. The gristmill opened for business after many delays. Ellicott noted that "agues and fevers in the early Part of the Season" kept the millwrights from completing its con-

---

71. Evans, *Holland Land Company,* 223; *RJE,* 1:1801, 148; *RJE,* 1:1808, 386–87; Wyckoff, *Developer's Frontier,* 44, 47–49, 57, 84–85, 90–94.
72. *RJE,* 1:1804, 250; *RJE,* 1:1801, 201; *RJE,* 1:1807, 339; *RJE,* 1:1801, 175.
73. James Dewey to Joseph Ellicott, March 28, 1801, JEC; *RJE,* 1:1805, 275; *RJE,* 1:1807, 339; Joseph Ellicott to Paul Busti, June 30, 1808, JEC.

struction. He hesitated to open the mill because he judged that the newness of the settlement lessened the need for it. Busti concurred with
Ellicott's decision but added: "It would . . . be painful to me if three years
after the settlement began the cultivators around Batavia should not be in
want of such a Building, for it would be evidence that their agricultural
pursuits are not carried on with great spirit." Busti was worried about the
slow progress of improvements.[74]

The company's strong commitment to stimulate commerce and production for market also prompted it to invest in the local manufacture of salt.
Salt was a critical commodity, necessary for the preservation of food and
to keep the settlers' cattle healthy. In 1801 Ellicott reported the discovery
of a salt spring in township 15, range 4, that supplied enough water "to
make 50 bushels of salt" per day. Busti recommended some experimenta-
tion, but Ellicott reported poor results in 1803. Four barrels of salt were
made, but it took five hundred gallons of water to produce one barrel.
Nonetheless, Ellicott remained optimistic about the prospect of manufacturing salt in the region. He believed the company's investment in this
undertaking would generate a profit for the landlords as well as provide a
critical resource for the settlers of the Holland Purchase.[75]

Ellicott also tried to divert the western salt trade through the southern
part of the Purchase. Salt produced at the Onondaga works in central
New York was shipped to Pittsburgh and the West via Lake Ontario, the
Niagara portage, Lake Erie, the portage at Erie, Pennsylvania, and from
there to Pittsburgh. As the population west of the Appalachian Mountains
grew, the demand for salt increased. Only 714 barrels of salt were trans-
shipped from Erie in 1800, but 6,659 barrels changed conveyance there
just five years later.[76]

In 1805 a settler named Thomas Kennedy wrote to Ellicott pointing out
how the salt trade could be diverted through company lands. If navigation
of Connewongo Creek could be opened for boats of twenty-five or thirty
tons, the salt trade could be diverted through Portland, Mayville, and the
southern part of the Purchase. In 1806 Ellicott announced the impending
sale of two thousand acres near Mayville to several merchants "who have
it in contemplation to erect wharfs and stone houses at the landing in
Mayville and carry on the salt trade from Onondaga to Pittsburgh thro the
Chautauqua Lake, and in Return bring back from Pittsburgh glass, iron

74. *RJE*, 1:1804, 249; Paul Busti to Joseph Ellicott, June 5, 1804, JEC.
75. *RJE*, 1:1801, 166; *RJE*, 1:1803, 222–23. I am indebted to Alan Taylor for the
observation concerning the need for salt to keep the settlers' cattle healthy.
76. Wyckoff, *Developer's Frontier*, 77–78, 96–99; *RJE*, 1:1805, 282.

and hollow ware." Ellicott offered the company's assistance in opening a road from Mayville to Lake Erie and in clearing navigation through Chautauqua Lake to the Allegheny River. "Should that portage from Lake Erie to Lake Chautauqua become generally in use," he told Busti, "and the navigation from Chautauqua to the Allegheny River with some Improvement be made passible for Boats there is not the smallest doubt but that the Lands in that Quarter will meet with a more rapid sale than any other Lands on the Purchase."[77]

When the Portage Road opened with company help in 1809, it became an important route for the western salt trade, and the lands adjacent to it were settled quickly. The opening of the salt trade through the southern region of the Purchase created other opportunities for trade too. Ellicott believed Pittsburgh could supply badly needed manufactures to the isolated hinterlands of western New York. "There are many articles necessary for the use of the people in this quarter," he noted, "that come more reasonable from Pittsburgh than from Albany."[78]

Finally, Ellicott and the Holland Land Company encouraged settlement and improvement in the early years by helping to attract the services of tavern keepers, merchants, artisans, and doctors. Taverns would provide shelter and food to curious travelers and prospective land buyers and serve as meeting places for social, political, and religious activities. In his original proposal submitted to Theophile Cazenove outlining a policy of development for the Purchase, Ellicott recommended building a hotel near the land office to serve the needs of land seekers. When it opened in 1804, the hotel occupied half of a large building that included the courthouse and the jail.[79]

Ellicott offered special terms to settlers who promised to build and operate a tavern or hotel. In 1799 he received company authorization to offer 150-acre parcels of land to any settler who expressed an interest in opening a tavern. Three settlers soon took advantage of this offer and built taverns along the Buffalo and Niagara Road. Between 1800 and 1811, sixty-five taverns were established in the Holland Purchase; another eighty-three were built during the next ten years.[80]

Ellicott encouraged the opening of stores in the Purchase by making loans to aspiring merchants. During the first year of settlement, he extended loans to James Brisbane, who proposed to build a store in Batavia,

77. Joseph Ellicott to Paul Busti, March 16, 1806, JEC.
78. *RJE*, 2:1809, 18–19.
79. Evans, *Holland Land Company*, 296–97.
80. Brunger, "Historical Land Valuation," 25–26.

and John Thompson, who planned to build one near Ellicott's Creek. Ellicott also offered special terms to blacksmiths who would settle in the Purchase. "The establishment of blacksmiths in our district," he explained, "is a subject that intimately regards the interests of the settlers; the various concerns of husbandry cannot be directed without their services." Ellicott wooed two of them to the Purchase in 1801. William Wood opened a shop in Batavia on land he received from Ellicott. In return, Wood agreed to provide blacksmith services for five years. When Wood fell into debt to James Brisbane, the local storekeeper, Ellicott assumed the debt of $381.72 on behalf of the company. Finally, Ellicott secured the services of a doctor in 1806. He loaned Dr. David McCraken $600 "to enable him to set up an Apothecaries Shop, so that the Country should always be supplied with Drugs and Medicine."[81]

THE Holland Land Company and Joseph Ellicott devised a settlement plan based on the concepts of social evolution and improvement. As a consequence of the high ratio of land to labor, settlement and development of the Holland Land Purchase required an overall strategy that encouraged pioneers to take up and improve wild land. This strategy counted on these pioneers to begin the arduous task of converting wilderness into settled rural communities. With this objective in mind, Ellicott tailored a system of provisional and articled sales of land that attracted settlers and then left them alone to make their improvements. This strategy was based on the Enlightenment belief that social evolution took place in stages. Applied to the American frontier, this theory predicted an early social stage dominated by seminomadic pioneers and herdsmen followed by a more settled agricultural stage featuring more permanent farmers and artisans. While this crucial transition was under way, the landlords' capital investment was protected by the pioneers' improvements, which rose in value faster than their cumulative land debt.

The Holland Land Company's plan for settling western New York also rested on the concept of improvement. For the company, an improvement was an investment of labor contributing to creation of a farm. Clearing forest, planting crops, fencing arable fields, and draining low-lying land all constituted good improvements that secured the landlords' capital investment. But the landlords' strategy encouraged more than just the physical transformation of the land. The outward appearance of the land mirrored the inner character of the inhabitants. Good fences, well-

81. *RJE,* 1:1801, 153; *RJE,* 1:1807, 358–59, 342.

cultivated fields, and strongly built barns were signs of a settler who was becoming a farmer. These improvements testified to his adoption of intensive work habits and his commitment to abandon easy living on the frontier for the material comfort and social status afforded by the market economy. As wild lands were cleared, cultivated, and made into farms, the company expected the lazy pioneer who had been drawn west by the lure of easy subsistence to make a fundamental choice. He could sell or abandon his negligible improvement and move to another frontier, or he could become a new man full of respect for private property and animated by the sober industry and prudent economy necessary to turn his bush pasture into a real farm.

Ellicott and the landlords encouraged improvement in two ways. After the first decade of settlement, Ellicott ended provisional sales and adopted a new policy of renewing expired land contracts that was designed to help discipline the pioneers. When settlers needed more time to pay, he renewed their contracts, computing a new purchase price by compounding interest over the life of the old contract. This practice kept the price of company land proportionate with the rising value of the Holland Land Purchase. It also stimulated the settlers' industry. To avoid paying interest on unpaid interest, Ellicott argued, settlers intensified their efforts to build a farm and pay for their land before another contract expired. Renewing land contracts on the basis of compound interest, therefore, facilitated the progress of social evolution, promoting physical improvement of the land while transforming the personal character of the first pioneer inhabitants.

Ellicott and the company also encouraged improvement through positive incentives. If the settlers were to labor beyond what subsistence required, Ellicott believed the universal wellspring of self-interest had to be engaged. Without regional markets, without cheap transportation to those markets, without money, and without local manufacturing centers to process the raw materials of field and forest, settlers quickly succumbed to the debilitating effects of the frontier environment. Ellicott and the company leaned heavily on the region's natural market outlet to Montreal. But Ellicott also built an internal infrastructure of roads, radiating outward from Batavia into the interior of the Purchase. These roads opened up the Purchase to settlement while providing potential commercial links with the outside world. Ellicott also encouraged local market centers, helping to establish grist and sawmills throughout the region. His efforts to promote local manufacturing even extended to a company saltworks. When this failed, he tried to divert the western salt trade through Mayville in the southern part of the Purchase. All of these efforts grew from his conviction that commerce was a powerful stimulus to improvement.

The transition from pioneer to farmer, upon which the Holland Land Company's policy rested, is the frontier equivalent of the transformation of work, culture, and society that E. P. Thompson, Herbert Gutman, and others have associated with the rise of industrial capitalism. E. P. Thompson argued that the transition to industrial society "entailed a severe restructuring of work habits—new disciplines, new incentives, and a new human nature upon which these incentives could bite effectively."[82] From the landlords' perspective, in western New York the transition from pioneer to farmer required a similar restructuring that encouraged steady industry, personal discipline, and new habits of land use. As we shall see, the transition from pioneer to farmer and the hierarchical control that was necessary to establish it created a pervasive and sometimes open conflict between the settlers' agrarian culture and the Holland Land Company's capitalist objectives.

82. E. P. Thompson, "Time, Work-Discipline, and Industrial Capitalism," *Past and Present* 38 (1967), 56–97, quote on 57; Herbert G. Gutman, "Work, Culture, and Society in Industrializing America, 1815–1919," *American Historical Review* 78 (June 1973), 531–88; and Jonathan Prude, *The Coming of Industrial Order: Town and Factory Life in Rural Massachusetts, 1810–1860* (Cambridge, Eng., 1983), 36–37, 45–46, 135–44.

2

The Settlers

The settlers who came to the Holland Purchase of western New York migrated from three principal areas: from New England, from central New York south of Lake Ontario eastward along the Mohawk River, and from Pennsylvania. Western New York congressman Albert Tracy described the settlers as a "hardy yeomanry" from New England. Joseph Ellicott noted that many of them came from Vermont. Travelers through the region, including Joseph Avery, J. U. Niemciwicz, and John Melish, also described the predominance of New England Yankees in western New York.[1]

Settlers from New England clustered throughout the hill country in the central and southern region of the Purchase. By 1811 notable concentrations of New Englanders, many from Vermont, had settled in southern Erie and Genesee counties, as well as in some portions of Cattaraugus and Chautauqua counties. David Eddy, for example, came to southern Erie

1. My analysis of the geographical sources of immigration to western New York is taken from William Wyckoff, *The Developer's Frontier: The Making of the Western New York Landscape* (New Haven, Conn., 1988), 104–15. Tracy's analysis of the settlers' origins appeared in his second "Agricola" letter, *Niagara Journal* (Buffalo, N.Y.), Oct. 12, 1819. Joseph Ellicott to Paul Busti, May 22, 1807, Joseph Ellicott Collection, Buffalo and Erie County Historical Society, Buffalo, N.Y.; cited hereafter as JEC. See also James W. Darlington, "Peopling the Post-Revolutionary New York Frontier," paper given at the Conference on New York State History, June 4–5, 1993, Seneca Falls, N.Y.; Lewis D. Stilwell, *Migration from Vermont* (Montpelier, Vt., 1948); Harold F. Wilson, *The Hill Country of Northern New England: Its Social and Economic History, 1790–1930* (New York, 1936); Lois K. Mathews Rosenberry, *The Expansion of New England: The Spread of New England Settlement and Institutions to the Mississippi River, 1620–1865* (1909; rpr. New York, 1962).

County from Vermont in 1804 with his brother Aaron, his brother-in-law Nathan Peters, and his sister Mary. Similarly, Solomon Jones, born in Milford, Massachusetts, moved to Vermont in 1785. Eventually he left there, stacking his belongings into two wagons, and settling at last in Chautauqua County.[2]

Although the early census data do not record places of birth, the 1845 state census provides this information at the end of the settlement period in western New York. By 1845 settlement had been under way for more than two generations. Yet the state census of that year still found that significant proportions of the population had been born in New England. The numbers ranged from 16 percent of the population in Cattaraugus County to 10 percent in Niagara County.[3]

Many of the settlers who came from central New York were the children of migrants from New England, as documented in William Wyckoff's study. By analyzing the postmarked letters of inquiries about land received by Joseph Ellicott, he concluded that settlers living just to the east of the Holland Purchase showed great interest in moving westward.[4]

Reuben Wilson was such a settler. He left Massachusetts in 1805, lived briefly in Otsego County, not far from Cooperstown, and then moved to Upper Canada near Toronto. Wilson stayed there three years. In April 1810, he moved his wife and children, crossing the western end of Lake Ontario, and settled in Niagara County at the mouth of Twelve Mile Creek. Andrew Putnam, a native of Greenfield, Massachusetts, moved with his wife and two children to Madison County in 1795. After the births of an additional eight sons, Putnam took his family to Chautauqua County in February 1817, arriving "with 4 yoke of oxen and 2 sleds, 1 span of horses and a sleigh, 13 cows and young cattle." James Bates left Massachusetts and moved to Onondaga County in 1803. Twelve years later he resettled in the township of Cherry Creek in Chautauqua County.[5]

The third source of migration to the Purchase was Pennsylvania. The Holland Land Company had important Pennsylvania connections. Its general agent Paul Busti kept his office in Philadelphia, and the company

2. Orsamus Turner, *Pioneer History of the Holland Purchase of Western New York* (1850; rpr. Geneseo, N.Y., 1974), 475. Andrew W. Young, *History of Chautauqua County, New York* (1875; rpr. Bowie, Md., 1990), 365.

3. These figures are derived from the *Census of the State of New York, for 1845* (Albany, N.Y., 1846).

4. Wyckoff, *Developer's Frontier,* 110.

5. Turner, *Pioneer History of the Holland Purchase,* 548; Young, *History of Chautauqua County,* 566, 287.

owned an extensive tract of land in the northwest part of the state. Joseph Ellicott admired the German farmers of Pennsylvania and urged the company to advertise the Purchase among them. Chautauqua and Cattaraugus counties did attract a sizable number of settlers from Pennsylvania, but not all were Germans. Some of the Pennsylvanians were Scotch-Irish, and they struck Ellicott as troublemakers. When a group of them stopped at the land office in 1808, Ellicott complained that "it is characteristic of those people to possess the largest share of downright effrontery and blunt impudence of any other, at least ever since I have had any acquaintance with the manners and customs of mankind."[6]

Not all of the ethnic German farmers turned out to be as desirable as Ellicott and others hoped. After the War of 1812 eastern Cattaraugus County attracted Pennsylvania settlers from the Wyoming Valley region. Two brothers, George and Jacob Learn, arrived in 1823 with little more than the oxen and wagons that brought them. For the next twenty-one years they harvested the resources of forest and farm but remained cash poor, unable to complete their land purchases. In 1844–45 Jacob and George Learn, along with their Dutch Hill neighbors, became prominent figures in a rebellion that brought out the local militia.[7]

Rural folk left the longest settled regions of the country for the Holland Land Purchase for two reasons. First, they were drawn by the appeal of the celebrated Genesee Country. The second reason concerned the demographic and ecological crisis that gripped mid- and late eighteenth-century America. The latter had a pronounced effect on the lower and middle classes living in urban areas as well as the countryside. Before examining the specific appeal of the Genesee Country, consideration must be given to what historians have discovered about the Malthusian crisis of early America. By the mid-eighteenth century the oldest settled regions of America were becoming crowded places with too many people and too many animals. Throughout the colonial era the land base remained fairly constant, but the population doubled every twenty-five years. As the growing population pushed against a finite supply of land and productive resources, opportunity diminished and social polarization resulted. The widely shared experience of declining per capita wealth in eastern urban areas helped to mobilize popular support there for the American Revolution.[8]

6. Quoted in Wyckoff, *Developer's Frontier,* 115
7. Franklin Ellis, *History of Cattaraugus County, New York* (Philadelphia, 1879), 44–51.
8. Kenneth Lockridge has explored the Malthusian crisis of eighteenth-century America in "Land, Population, and the Evolution of New England Society, 1630–1790," *Past and*

In the countryside the land-population-wealth crisis was a result of agricultural practices that required abundant supplies of fresh or regenerated land. As long as the supply was abundant, farmers could bring new fields into cultivation whenever old ones were depleted. Old fields became brush pasture for livestock; twenty years might pass before they were hoed or tilled again. By the time of the Revolution, population pressure in the longest settled areas of New England had reduced the period of fallow to a year or two. The great reduction in the length of time allowed for fallow clearly signified the mounting pressure on the land. Meanwhile, the effects of animal crowding also became apparent in New England. As early as 1750 it started to become evident "that the necessary stock of the country hath outgrown the meadows, so that there is not hay for such stock as the present increased number of people really need." The importance of livestock in the rural economy made the need for meadow and pasture a crucial force encouraging westward expansion.[9]

As a growing population pressed against limited supplies of fresh or fully regenerated land, the young, the unlucky, the dissatisfied, and the adventurous were pushed westward in search of new land.[10] "Emigrants from the old settlements," Joseph Ellicott reported in 1802, "are generally that class of people who are compelled by indigence and the pressure of

Present 39 (1968), 62–80, and in "Social Change and the Meaning of the American Revolution," *Journal of Social History* 6 (1972–73), 403–39. The economic decline of the lower and middle classes in urban areas that coincided with the American Revolution has been documented by James Henretta, "Economic Development and Social Structure in Colonial Boston," *William and Mary Quarterly* 22 (1965), 75–92; Allan Kulikoff, "The Progress of Inequality in Revolutionary Boston," *William and Mary Quarterly* 28 (1971), 375–412; Gary B. Nash, "Social Change and the Growth of Prerevolutionary Urban Radicalism," in Alfred Young, ed., *The American Revolution: Explorations in the History of American Radicalism* (DeKalb, Ill., 1976), 5–36, and Nash, "Urban Wealth and Poverty in Pre-Revolutionary America," *Journal of Interdisciplinary History* 6 (1975–76), 545–84.

9. Harry J. Carman, ed., *American Husbandry* (1776; rpr. New York, 1939), 93–94. See also Richard Maxwell Brown, "Back Country Rebellions and the Homestead Ethic in America, 1740–1799," in Richard Maxwell Brown and Don E. Fehrenbacher, eds., *Tradition, Conflict, and Modernization: Perspectives on the American Revolution* (New York, 1977), 74–76. For the importance of livestock in early America see Edmund S. Morgan, *American Slavery, American Freedom: The Ordeal of Colonial Virginia* (New York, 1975), 87, 136–42, and William Cronon, *Changes in the Land: Indians, Colonists, and the Ecology of New England* (New York, 1983), 139. The quote is from Jared Eliot, *Essays upon Field Husbandry in New England and Other Papers, 1748–1762,* ed. Harry Carman, Rexford G. Tugwell, and Rodney H. True (New York, 1967), 27. William Cronon's *Changes in the Land* (141) concluded that "pastoralism became a significant force for expansion."

10. This conclusion is based on the studies by Lockridge, Brown, and Cronon cited above. See also Robert A. Gross, *The Minutemen and Their World* (New York, 1976), 68–108, 177–86, and James A. Henretta, *The Evolution of American Society, 1700–1815* (Lexington, Mass., 1973), 15–21.

misfortunes at home to remove to new countries."[11] For James Cochrane, a journalist living in New Haven, Connecticut, the connection between overcrowding and out-migration was unmistakable. In June 1804 he told Ellicott: "In this thickly settled Country they are highly in the spirit of moving to the westward."[12]

Newcomers to the Holland Land Purchase had felt the pinch of growing scarcity, and they had experienced firsthand its disruption of agrarian culture and rural household independence. Agents for the Holland Land Company often explained that one of the main reasons why settlers moved west was to acquire enough land to raise a large family and provide farms for their children when they grew up. When Jan Lincklaen was sent to investigate the wild lands of America on behalf of the Dutch bankers who eventually negotiated the Holland Land Purchase, he traveled extensively. One day in Vermont, he came upon the house of a man he had previously met in the Genesee Country. Thomas Rice was about to give up "a good farm" in exchange for four hundred acres of wild land recently purchased in western New York. "It is astonishing," Lincklaen observed, "to see a man 50 years old who has spent the best part of his life in clearing his land and enhancing its value, leaving it all just as he begins to enjoy the fruits of his labor, in order to bury himself anew in the forest, and expose himself to all the difficulties of forming a new settlement!"[13]

This Vermont farmer, like many other Americans, according to Lincklaen, was ready to give up his established farm because at age fifty he had a "numerous family" that his old lands could no longer support. So he had decided to sell his farm for "a sufficient sum to buy in the Genesee, where the lands are cheaper, three times the quantity, enough to maintain and establish around [him] a dozen children." A sufficient quantity of land to raise such a large family included not only the material resources to feed and nurture the family but also the ample reserves of land needed to settle "a dozen children" on surrounding farms when they grew up. The capacity of a father to provide land for his children remained an important instrument of patriarchal authority in the early American countryside of western New York.[14]

Almost forty years later, another agent of the Holland Land Company,

---

11. Robert W. Bingham, ed., *Reports of Joseph Ellicott*, 2 vols. (Buffalo, N.Y., 1937–41), 1:1801, 161; cited hereafter as *RJE*.

12. Wyckoff, *Developer's Frontier*, 104.

13. Helen Fairchild, ed., *Journals of John Lincklaen: Travels in the Years 1791 and 1792 in Pennsylvania, New York and Vermont* (New York, 1897), 83–84.

14. Ibid.

David Evans, found the same concerns among the settlers. In a report to the general agent, J. J. Vanderkemp, Evans analyzed the settlers' long-standing proclivity to buy more land than they could clear or cultivate. "The temptation," he explained in 1831, "to purchase more than three times the quantity of land, of as good quality, for the same money, is difficult for a man to resist, whose principal motive in disposing of a farm, on which he has long resided, is to make provision for his children." Evans believed this was the reason for "the immense migration from the eastern states."[15]

"There is little or no underwood, and excellent pasture in the forests between the trees"

If overcrowding, human and animal, encouraged rural folk to leave New England, the reputation of the Genesee Country acted as a magnet drawing settlers to western New York (for population growth see Table 1). The Holland Purchase was situated immediately to the west of the Genesee Country, but in the minds of travelers and settlers alike it was linked to this celebrated region. The topography of the Holland Land Purchase signified the region's ideal suitability for new settlements. Early accounts of the Genesee Country proclaimed its potential for raising live-stock. "In many parts of the tract," Gilbert Imlay reported in 1797, "there is little or no underwood, and excellent pasture in the forests between the trees." Cattle and hogs could be "reared in the woods at little or no expence to the farmer." Robert Munro described the area in 1804 and likewise promoted the opportunity to raise livestock. Cattle, he said, could be easily "kept in the woods. There are many instances," he added, "of cattle being kept throughout the winter only by browsing, or eating the tops of basswood and some other sorts of trees cut down for them."[16]

The beech-maple forests spread over the uplands contained many valu-able resources. Sugar maple trees were found throughout the tract. Conse-quently, maple sugar and syrup could be manufactured in large quantities as every tree could furnish enough sap to produce several pounds of sugar. Most of the equipment required could be made from other resources

15. Reports of David Evans in *RJE*, 2:1830, 474.

16. Wyckoff, *Developer's Frontier*, 106; Gilbert Imlay, *A Topographical Description of the Western Territory of North America* (1797; rpr. New York, 1969), 465; Robert Munro, *A Description of the Genesee Country in the State of New York* (1804) in E. B. O'Callaghan, *The Documentary History of the State of New York*, 4 vols. (Albany, N.Y., 1850), 2:687.

Table 1. Population growth in the Holland Land Purchase of Western New York

County	1820–21	1825	1835
Allegany	4,010	7,871	15,649
Cattaraugus	4,090	8,643	24,986
Chautauauqa	12,568	20,639	44,869
Erie	15,668	24,316	57,614
Niagara	7,322	14,069	26,490
Orleans		10,346	17,459
Genesee	25,314	26,022	39,280

Sources: H. G. Spafford, *Gazetteer of the State of New York* (1824; repr. Interlaken, N.Y., 1981); New York State Census for 1825, in David Burr, *Atlas of the State of New York* (New York, 1829); *Census of the State of New York for 1835* (Albany, N.Y., 1835); Thomas F. Gordon, *Gazetteer of the State of New York* (Albany, N.Y., 1836).

found in the region. The sugaring season came at the end of winter, and this was important, the promoters emphasized, for two reasons. First, it was a time of the year when there was little other work to do. Second, maple sugar was a highly nutritious and good-tasting food that became available at a critical season of the year when other food supplies were running low. William Cooper's *Guide in the Wilderness* also noted that the sugar maple tree provided the "best fuel the forest yields."[17]

Jan Lincklaen explained that raising livestock and manufacturing maple sugar were compatible activities. Limited markets in the western country meant that "people could never raise more grain than they need[ed] for their own use." Lincklaen proposed, therefore, that settlers of the uplands, where the sugar maple abounded, enhance the outlook for raising cattle by "cutting all trees except the maple." The selective clearing would make maple sugar production easy and at the same time create excellent pasture for livestock.[18]

The superior timber in western New York indicated several other advantages of particular interest to new settlers. Careful accounting of the size and types of trees showed that ample supplies of timber were available for building and farm making as well as for producing potash. All the early accounts of the Genesee Country emphasized that pot and pearl ashes were an important resource of the American forest. A by-product of

17. Imlay, *Topographical Description*, 459, 471; Munro, *Description of the Genesee Country*, 683; Terry G. Jordan and Matti Kaups, *The American Backwoods Frontier: An Ethnic and Ecological Interpretation* (Baltimore, 1989), 231; William Cooper, *A Guide in the Wilderness* (Dublin, 1810), 26.

18. Fairchild, ed., *Journals of John Lincklaen*, 88–89.

the slash-and-burn technique used to clear wooded lands, "ashes" offered cash-poor settlers a good source of money for purchasing land. Jacob Otto, who replaced Joseph Ellicott as resident agent of the Holland Land Company in 1822, noted shortly afterward that "the wood when cut down and converted into ashes will pay for the soil." The extensive stands of beech and northern hardwoods covering most of the Holland Purchase were a potential market resource of great value.[19]

The Holland Land Company's own assessment of the environment and its potential for nurturing new settlements affirmed the advantages attributed to the larger Genesee Country. The township surveys of the Holland Purchase, conducted under the supervision of Joseph Ellicott, assessed the agricultural potential of the company's wild lands. During the two years (1797–99) it took to complete the survey, Ellicott gave precise instructions to the surveyors to make careful observations about the terrain, whether it was bottomland, intervale, upland, swamp, or barren. He also insisted that each type of terrain be designated as first-, second-, or third-quality land.[20]

Bottomland of the first quality, the best in the region, was "generally that description of Land which lies adjoining Rivers, Creeks, and other water Courses, and appears to be formed of an accumulation of the soil brought there by the overflowing of . . . water over the banks, and depositing the sediment thereon." Intervale was defined as "those rich swales of land . . . frequently found where there are no streams." Upland of the first quality referred to elevated table lands, "calculated for the production of grain and grass, as well as roots, vines, and other garden productions." Swamps and other areas unfit for cultivation denoted third-quality lands of little value. Nevertheless, Ellicott required his surveyors to note the particular features of swamps—"to mention whether they are open swamps, cat-tail, and flag, drowned, black ash, tamarack or whatever description they may be."[21]

19. Imlay, *Topographical Description*, 466; Reports of Jacob Otto in *RJE*, 2:1822, 315–16; Cooper, *Guide in the Wilderness*, 26–27; F. W. Beers and Co., *History of Allegany County, N.Y.* (New York, 1879), 67.

20. William Wyckoff, "Assessing Land Quality in Western New York: The Township Surveys of 1797–1799," unpublished paper in the manuscripts division of the Buffalo and Erie County Historical Society, Buffalo, N.Y.; Wyckoff, "Joseph Ellicott and the Western New York Frontier: Environmental Assessments, Geographical Strategies, and Authored Landscapes 1797–1811" (Ph.D. diss., Syracuse University, 1982); Wyckoff, *Developer's Frontier*, 24–41.

21. Joseph Ellicott's Letter Books in vol. 26 of *Buffalo Historical Society Publications* (Buffalo, N.Y., 1922), 109–10.

Ellicott also instructed his surveyors to observe and document the soil, the types and frequency of trees, and the undercover of plants. The surveyors were to note color, texture, and depth of the soil. Soil that was black or dark was considered the most fertile. Sometimes referred to as "black muck," the dark color signified a rich organic composition that was a product of natural decay and regeneration. Deep soil, of course, was better than thin soil.[22]

The type of tree and the thickness of growth were taken as a measure of soil and land quality. Particular types and stands of trees were associated with the three respective qualities of land. Bottomland and upland of the first quality were covered by stands of mixed hardwoods, including beech, sugar maple, elm, butternut, birch, and basswood. The frequency of the ubiquitous sugar maple may have been exaggerated by the surveyors and Joseph Ellicott because of its potential market value. Hemlock trees often signified second- or third-quality lands. Hemlocks growing on steep hillsides and in low-lying areas of standing water marked terrain less suited for agriculture.[23]

The undercover of plants growing on the land also distinguished its fertility and quality. "Thick herbage" was a sign of good land. Descriptions of the ground cover were usually detailed. In township 11, range 1, for instance, surveyors reported that the herbage consisted of nettles, brakes, ox balm, richweed, ginseng, and black snakeroot. But the amount of undergrowth seemed a more important measure of the land's agricultural potential than any precise accounting of the species present.[24]

Ellicott used the surveyors' field notes to create Range Books that defined the boundaries of each township and described the terrain, soil, trees, and vegetation found along its perimeter. The Range Books gave Ellicott a detailed picture of the topography of the Holland Land Purchase and were often consulted by settlers when they visited the Batavia office to purchase land. The books provide an interesting overview of the resources settlers could expect to find. A broad swath of good land, running southwest from Batavia and extending to the shore of Lake Erie and the Pennsylvania boundary, covered a large portion of the southern two-thirds of the Purchase. It was an area of uplands; the terrain was described in the books as "gently uneven" or as "land beautifully diversified with small eminences." Beech and maple old-growth forests covered much of the

22. Wyckoff, *Developer's Frontier*, 36.
23. Ibid., 37–38.
24. Range Books, microfilm ed., New York State Library, Township 11, Range 1; Wyckoff, *Developer's Frontier*, 38.

region. Large trees, spaced far apart with little underbrush in between except ferns and a species of honeysuckle bush, formed a landscape of great appeal for new settlers. Less arduous to clear than the regenerating woodlands so common back east, these forests also featured a rich organic topsoil that promised easy cultivation and abundant yields of corn and grain. The region was full of resources for raising livestock, manufacturing maple sugar, making potash, and milling lumber.

Four specific areas of the Holland Purchase appealed to the early settlers.[25] The area around Batavia attracted early settlements when more than a half dozen townships were opened for sale in 1802. This belt of settlement extended to the south, running through the first and second range of townships. Early settlements also reached north of Batavia; by 1811 they stretched westward through the lowland plains of townships 14 and 15 all the way to the Niagara River. Growing trade with Canada encouraged a spurt of settlement there just before the War of 1812 began.

A second area of early settlement developed along the Buffalo and Genesee Road. "The prairies, or unwooded plains," referred to by all the early visitors, were the most prominent feature of this region. Describing the township of Clarence in 1813, Horatio G. Spafford's *Gazetteer of the State of New York* affirmed that "there are extensive prairies of rich and valuable lands." The townships in this corridor were settled as soon as Ellicott opened them for sale. Ellicott anticipated the value of these lands, and he set the prices accordingly. In 1804 the median price of land in the townships through which the Buffalo and Genesee Road passed was $2.50 to $2.75 per acre. By 1811 the median price in these same townships had increased to $3.50 to $3.75 per acre.[26]

A third area of early settlement occurred in the townships that lay east and south of the Buffalo Creek Reservation and north of Cattaraugus Creek. Vermont settlers, in particular, including some who migrated directly to the Purchase, along with others who had settled down for a while in central New York before moving farther west, found the rolling hills and old-growth forests of this region very much to their liking. At least thirteen of the townships in this area were first settled by emigrants from Vermont. These hill country people were especially drawn to townships where the mixed hardwood forests featured high concentrations of sugar maple trees. The highest concentrations of sugar maple found anywhere in the Holland Purchase occurred northeast of the Allegheny Reser-

25. Wyckoff, *Developer's Frontier*, 119–25.

26. Horatio G. Spafford, *Gazetteer of the State of New York* (Albany, N.Y., 1813), 87, 162; Wyckoff, *Developer's Frontier*, 72–73.

vation and east and southeast of the Buffalo Creek Reservation, precisely the areas where Vermont folk chose to settle. These settlers selected their woodland farms with great care. Their decisions shaped the evolving landscape as much as the company's development strategy.[27]

The fourth area of early settlement clustered around the elevated table lands bordering the lowland plain of Lake Erie and reaching into the hill country around Chautauqua Lake. The old-growth forests found there contained large quantities of stately white pine that became the basis of an early lumber trade. This region was rated as a good grazing country yet capable of producing grain enough for home consumption. By 1810 the area had two thousand settlers and two growing frontier centers at Mayville and Fredonia.[28]

Early settlers avoided the low-lying tracts situated throughout the northern Ontario Lake plain. One settler named Armstrong explained that bottomlands were "not so good . . . being swampy with a great deal of hemlock." Swamps and poorly drained bottomlands were considered unhealthy as well as unsuited for cultivation. Widely believed to be a source of fevers and agues, such lands could not be made "productive until ditched and drained." Most of the early settlers proved unwilling to invest the labor necessary to make such improvements.[29]

The Right of "Peaceable Possession"

Settlers arriving in western New York in search of land took an article of agreement issued directly by the company or one transferred sometimes third- or fourthhand from another settler. An article of agreement

27. My conclusions concerning the proclivity of Vermont settlers for the hilly uplands of the central Purchase, especially for the townships that featured high concentrations of sugar maple forest, are based on capsule histories of early settlement documented township by township in J. H. French, *Gazetteer of the State of New York* (1860; rpr. Interlaken, N.Y., 1980), 710–16, 284–93, 186–95, 208–16, 168–76, and also on Franz K. Seischab, "Forests of the Holland Land Company, circa 1798," in *Late Eighteenth Century Vegetation of Central and Western New York State on the Basis of Original Land Survey Records,* New York State Museum Bulletin 484 (Albany, N.Y., 1992), 44–45. My understanding of cultural preadaptation is drawn from Milton Newton, "Cultural Preadaptation and the Upland South," *Geoscience and Man* 5 (1974), 143–54, and Frank L. Owsley, *Plain Folk of the Old South* (1949; rpr. Baton Rouge, 1982), 52–55.

28. Horatio G. Spafford, *Gazetteer of the State of New York* (1824; rpr. Interlaken, N.Y., 1981), 104; Elisha Smith to Jacob Otto, March 8, 1823, Reel 151, Holland Land Company Project, State University of New York College at Fredonia; cited hereafter as HLCP.

29. *RJE,* 2:1817, 230; Reports of Jacob Otto, 1822, 326; B. Armstrong to Jacob Otto, Dec. 29, 1821, Reel 151, HLCP.

described the conditions of sale, including the price per acre, the terms of credit, and the schedule of payments. Settlers considered an article a sort of license to occupy and improve the company's land. It gave them what the law called a color of title. Settlers acknowledged the authority of the company to sell wild land on terms set by the proprietors. But permission to occupy wild land, once granted, conferred the right to create property and wealth by mixing labor with "vacant lands." Because wilderness had no value until human labor improved it, any use that transformed wild land into property gave the improver a strong claim to ownership.[30]

The company conceded that the settlers' improvements gave them a claim to ownership. Both Ellicott and Busti believed the company should scrupulously refrain from taking any action that denied a settler just compensation for his improvement. "The Dutch Gentlemen," Busti told Ellicott in April 1803, "are far from wishing to take any advantage for their own benefit from the labour and improvements that sober and industrious squatters may bestow upon a particular spot of their possession." Consequently, no "improving squatter" was "to be driven away." Rather, he should be granted an article, Busti instructed, and treated "on the same footing" as a settler who was making payments. Because "squattering, intrusion and occupation . . . in America" conferred "a kind of title" to land, Busti concluded that it was too "troublesome" to enforce "the legal rights of the proprietor against the claims of an occupant." Ellicott, thinking of the social stages of development, agreed. The first "pioneers" of the Purchase would never pay for their lands or become permanent farmers. The only benefit most of them could hope to claim was the equity created by their labor and improvements.[31]

The opportunity to trade or sell an improvement protected every settler against the loss of his equity without compensation. The articles of agreement the company used to convey land to settlers permitted the holder of an article to sell his improvement "to the Party of the Second Part, and to his Heirs and Assigns forever, or to whom he or they shall appoint or direct." This concession encouraged an active and flourishing trade in improved land. "Every Settler and every Labourer," Ellicott reported in 1810, "as well as every Man who came into the Country were taking up

30. Bates Cooke to Jacob Otto, Jan. 27, 1827, Reel 153, HLCP. See also Alan Taylor, *Liberty Men and Great Proprietors: The Revolutionary Settlement on the Maine Frontier, 1760–1820* (Chapel Hill, N.C., 1990), 25, 28; and Taylor, "'A Kind of Warr': The Contest for Land on the Northeastern Frontier, 1750–1820," *William and Mary Quarterly* 46 (1989), 7.

31. Paul Busti to Joseph Ellicott, April 21, 1803, JEC.

lots on provisional Agreements without any Intention of making Settlements, or even making any Payment for the Land; having no other object in View than to dispose of that provisional agreement to a second Person, a coming-in Settler to an Advance as high as he could obtain."[32]

"The traffic in articles," Ellicott's successor agreed in 1821, "constitutes a large portion of the trade of this country. . . . Since the first settlement of this country," Jacob Otto noted, "it is probable that more money has passed between individuals in this transfer of contracts than has been received by the Company in payment of lands." Company officials thought articles were transferred too frequently, often ending up in "hands unknown." As a result, a settler who renewed an expired article was seldom the same person to whom the land was originally conveyed. Payment seldom reached the company until an article had been exchanged three or four times.[33]

The opportunity to trade or sell an improvement, from a settler's point of view, was principally a matter of exercising dominion over the product of his labor. Once a settler "had liberty to go on" a piece of land, he appealed to the right of "peaceable possession" to support his individual managerial freedom to barter, sell, or keep his improvement as he saw fit. For instance, Gilbert Smith took an article on lot 7, township 11, range 6, in July 1815. He assigned the lot as "collateral security for the payment of certain notes" to a mercantile firm in Canandaigua, New York. According to Smith, the article was to be reassigned to him when the notes were paid. Early in 1823 the company issued a new article to Davis, one of Smith's creditors. Alarmed about the loss of his equity, Smith argued that if the lot was "to be sold" he was "equitably entitled to the refusal of it in preference to one who never bestowed any labor on the lot." The matter ended when another settler, William Grinall, purchased the lot and paid Smith's wife (he was in jail in Buffalo) fifty dollars for the improvements. Resolution of the conflicting property claims in this case affirmed the company's authority to sell land and collect payments, yet it also upheld the settler's claim to any improvements resulting from his labor.[34]

Similarly, Cornelius Ashton took an article for the northern part of lot 17 in township 14, range 4, on November 11, 1811. Seven years later he assigned the ninety-two acres to Horace Church "for a debt owed him." Then on July 14, 1819, "Church for a good consideration" sold the article to George Harris. The new holder tried to convey the article to a creditor,

32. *RJE*, 1:1807, 370; ibid., 1808, 400; *RJE*, 2:1810, 74.
33. Reports of Jacob Otto, 1821–22, 304; *RJE*, 1:1807, 370, *RJE*, 2:1812, 122.
34. J. Clary (for Gilbert Smith) to Jacob Otto, April 22, 1823, Reel 151, HLCP.

who refused to accept it. Harris then offered it to another settler named Wheaton. Meanwhile, Cornelius Ashton, the settler to whom the lot was originally conveyed, persuaded the company to issue him a new article. In turn, George Harris asked the company for a new article, appealing to the general agent to "say whether the wrong shall be righted or not." Harris believed the improvement had been "fairly transferred" and the property rightfully belonged to him.[35]

This settler's petition to the company for help underscores just how certain they felt both individually and as a group about the landlords' commitment not to deny them the fruits of their labor. It became fairly routine for a settler to appeal to the resident agent in Batavia to help mediate conflicting claims whenever disputes arose. In fact, the settlers counted on company agents to act as referees who could arbitrate the sale and exchange of articles. Jonathan Coomis appealed to David Evans for such help in February 1828. Coomis had taken an article in 1816 on 123½ acres located in township 15, range 7. In the spring of 1827 he sold the article to Israel Boardman, whom he later characterized as "a rogue," for eighty dollars. Coomis accepted Boardman's personal note as payment. The assignment carried the stipulation that Coomis could use "the improvements for a year." Coomis then leased the farm to another settler for a share of the twenty-eight acres of wheat which the lessee sowed. When Boardman claimed he was "entitled to all that is on the premises," Coomis asked Evans not to issue a new article to Boardman. Coomis argued that the fruits of what his tenant "sowed in peaceable possession" both he and the tenant "had an undoubted right to take off." Coomis asked Evans and the company to uphold what was right and just.[36]

Likewise, Bartholomew Armstrong appealed to Evans in November 1827 to save his farm from a debt judgment and sale. Armstrong came to western New York in 1805. "I came here when young," he explained, but "am now old." He was poor when he arrived, and despite the exertions of twenty years of labor, he was still poor. Armstrong assured Evans that he had never speculated in company lands. Instead his labor had created a "handsome" property that included an orchard with "fruit trees of all description." Armstrong estimated the property was worth at least $1,200, and as it was the first property he had ever owned he could not "think of losing it for the paltry sum of 50 or 100 dollars." Armstrong pleaded for consideration based on extenuating circumstances. He had a

35. Amos Bates to unknown, July 4, 1825, Reel 152, HLCP; George Harris to Paul Busti, Dec. 13, 1823, April 10, 1824, Reel 151, HLCP.
36. Jonathan Coomis to David Evans, Feb. 7, 1828, Reel 153, HLCP.

large family, several of whom were sick, and he had lost his job. The company still held the deed to the property, and he implored Evans not to give a deed to anyone but him.[37]

The settlers of the Holland Land Purchase believed that their contractual obligations to the landlords rested squarely on principles of equity and justice. The company had the legal right to sell land and collect payments, but the settlers could not be denied the improvements their labor had created. A committee of three appointed to speak for the settlers of Chautauqua County stated:

> No matter whether that policy originated in selfishness or not, it was one under which this vast wilderness had been populated and converted into blooming fields with a rapidity before unknown in the settlement of new countries. It was a policy well adapted to the times and circumstances attending the settlement of this country and the character of the settlers, and which has enabled thousands of men who had no means but their axes and no property but in hope, to become useful, respectable and comparatively wealthy citizens—Under this system of indulgence and lenity, and an implied promise of its continuance, the present settlers took their contracts. No matter what the conditions of these contracts were not one in a hundred ever read them—the policy of the land holders was Known, established and relied on; and implicitly, and in many instances, expressly, became a part of the contract.[38]

From the settlers' perspective, then, the landlords were bound to respect "the strictest principles of moral philosophy" which accorded every free man dominion over the products of his labor.

Frontier Land Use

The early settlers of the Holland Land Purchase cleared the forest with axes and by fire. The process of clearing woodland usually began with a "chopping." A clearing could be cut at any time of the year, but when it was done affected how arduous a job it was and how long it took. If the chopping took place in the spring when the wood was green, the cutting

37. Bartholomew Armstrong to David Evans, Nov. 13, 1827, Reel 153, HLCP. I could not find any record of what happened to Bartholomew Armstrong.
38. James Mullett, Leverett Barker, and Chauncy Tucker to Trumbull Cary, Feb. 18, 1836, Reel 91, HLCP.

was comparatively easy; yet green timber was difficult to burn. A summer chopping offered the advantage of cutting trees when they were in leaf. The leaves continued to function even after the tree was down, drying out the branches and preparing the timber for a good burn in the early fall. But a winter chopping was preferred by most of the settlers in the Holland Land Purchase. Orsamus Turner's illustration of the first stage of settlement showed a clearing being cut during winter. Timber and brush could be skidded and piled or simply left where it was cut. Burning generally followed a season or two later. A winter chopping also had the advantage of taking place during a traditional season of rural unemployment. In addition, many incoming settlers preferred to start a farm when snow- and ice-covered ground made travel in sleighs easy and fast.[39]

Trees were cut at a height of three or four feet from the ground, and stumps were left to rot. Large trees were girdled, which caused them to wither and die in a season or two. Meanwhile, some of the timber was cut into logs, trimmed of branches, and fitted together to make one-room cabins. "The dwellings of new settlers," according to Duke De La Rochefoucault Liancourt, were built "in a very slight manner." With roofs and walls of bark, these "huts" offered little comfort. The settlers of western New York spent the winter season, Liancourt believed, "wrapped up in blankets." Thirty years later, another European visitor, Patrick Shirreff, found little improvement in the houses. Traveling through the northern third of the Purchase on the road between Rochester and Lewiston, he noted: "The houses were mere log-huts, and wanting in external comforts."[40]

Set in the middle of an irregular, half-cut clearing, the settler's log house was hardly distinguishable from the jumble of timber and debris that surrounded it. The "rugged and ill-dressed" scene included a straggling snake rail fence, put up to protect a hastily planted vegetable garden. A new homestead, according to Basil Hall, was covered "with an inextricable and confused mass of prostrate trunks, branches and trees, piles of split logs, and of squared timbers, planks, shingles, great stacks of fuel,

39. Michael Williams, *Americans and Their Forests: A Historical Geography* (Cambridge, Eng., 1989), 115; Wyckoff, *Developer's Frontier*, 108; Jared Van Wagenen, Jr., *The Golden Age of Homespun* (1953; rpr. New York, 1963), 30–31; B. Armstrong to Jacob Otto, Dec. 29, 1821, and Samuel Bradley to Jacob Otto, Feb. 10, 1823, Reel 151, HLCP.

40. Duke De La Rochefoucault Liancourt, *Travels through the United States of North America, the Country of the Iroquois and Upper Canada in the Years 1795, 1796, and 1797*, 2 vols. (London, 1799), 1:164; Patrick Shirreff, *A Tour through North America Together with a Comprehensive View of the Canadas and United States as Adapted for Agricultural Emigration* (Edinburgh, 1835), 87.

and often in the midst of all this could be detected a half smothered log hut."[41]

A season or two after the cabin was put up, the next phase of clearing began. The chopping that had been cut was burned. The objective was to build a hot, roaring fire that would consume as much as possible of the tangled mass of fallen trees and underbrush. If the wind was right and the timber was ready to burn, the fire spread quickly, engulfing the area in a rolling wave of flame and smoke. Whatever survived the burn, usually blackened stumps, trunks, or other large limbs, was cut, piled, and left to be burned again.[42]

Fire remained an important agent of frontier settlement throughout the period from 1800 through 1845. David Eddy, among the first settlers to migrate to the hill country south of Buffalo Creek, began clearing his farm lot in 1804. He set fire to the dry leaves, and the resulting burn consumed most of the recently cut logs and branches. In 1822 William Blane, an English traveler on his way to Niagara Falls, reported that "log-cabins were rising in all directions, and the work of clearing was going on rapidly. Each little spot was covered with masses of burning timber; and the large trees that had been girdled the year before, were in many places in flames even to the tops, producing at night a very extraordinary and splendid effect." Patrick Shirreff saw similar scenes on his trip to Niagara Falls more than a decade later. The "felling and burning of trees was going on in all directions."[43]

The early settlers tilled the soil using techniques borrowed from the Indians. The best system for growing food in a northern hardwood forest to maximize yield and minimize labor had been developed by eastern wood-land Indians such as the Seneca. Girdling trees opened up the forest to full sunlight, and burning over a new clearing eliminated the undermat of dead branches, fallen leaves, and woodland vegetation. The resulting topsoil was black and rich in humus and potash; it produced good crops of wheat and corn. By the time wind, weather, and decay brought down the last of the girdled hardwood trunks, depletion of the rich organic topsoil often forced abandonment of the old site and cultivation of a new one.[44]

41. Williams, *Americans and Their Forests,* 121. The original source is Basil Hall, *Travels in North America in the Years 1827 and 1828,* 3 vols. (Philadelphia, 1829), 2:135.

42. Van Wagenen, *Golden Age of Homespun,* 31.

43. Turner, *Pioneer History of the Holland Purchase,* 477; William Blane, *An Excursion through the United States and Canada during the Years 1822–1823* (1824; rpr. New York, 1969), 393–94; Shirreff, *Tour through North America,* 87.

44. My understanding of early American agriculture is based on Carl Sauer, "The Settlement of the Humid East," in *Selected Essays, 1963–1975* (Berkeley, 1981), 6–7; Morgan, *American Slavery, American Freedom,* 52–56, 141–42; Edward C. Papenfuse, Jr., "Planter

Most of the food grown by the early settlers was for home consumption. Wheat, corn, buckwheat, oats, peas, and potatoes were important food crops for both humans and livestock. Wheat was the earliest crop produced in quantity with some left over for local exchange or sale. It could be sown as soon as the forest was partially cleared, and as Thomas Jefferson said, it required little attention until harvest time. Reaping called for intense and heavy labor within a fixed period, but once it was accomplished, threshing could be done whenever time allowed. Little capital investment was needed because wheat could be sown and harvested with a few simple tools, including a hoe, a sickle, and a flail.[45]

During the first years of settlement, wheat was planted broadcast by hand. Joseph Ellicott reported that "grain was . . . strewed on the surface of the ground" and then covered over using "the top of a small tree." Harrows and small plows were also used to smooth the topsoil over the seed. Wheat and other food crops sprouted and grew in woodland clearings that bore all the marks of recent cutting and burning.[46] Basil Hall wrote: "Some of the fields were sown with wheat above which could be seen numerous ugly stumps of old trees; others allowed to lie in the grass guarded, as it were, by a set of gigantic black monsters, the girdled, scorched and withered remnants of the ancient woods."[47]

Early on the agents of the Holland Land Company encouraged the production of wheat because of its market value and the investment of labor it signified. From the company's perspective, the willingness to invest such labor denoted an industrious and valuable settler. Wheat met all the requirements of a market commodity in a frontier region. It had high

Behavior and Economic Opportunity in a Staple Economy," *Agricultural History* 46 (1972), 297–311; Paul W. Gates, *The Farmer's Age: Agriculture, 1815–1860* (New York, 1960); Lewis C. Gray, *History of Agriculture in the Southern United States to 1860*, 2 vols. (1932; rpr. New York, 1941); John T. Schlebecker, *Whereby We Thrive: A History of American Farming, 1607–1972* (Ames, Iowa, 1975); Ulysses P. Hedrick, *A History of Agriculture in the State of New York* (1933; rpr. New York, 1966); Van Wagenen, *Golden Age of Homespun*; Percy W. Bidwell, "Rural Economy in New England at the Beginning of the Nineteenth Century," Connecticut Academy of Arts and Sciences, *Transactions* 20 (April 1916), 241–399; Cronon, *Changes in the Land*; Timothy Silver, *New Face on the Countryside: Indians, Colonists, and Slaves in South Atlantic Forests, 1500–1800* (Cambridge, Eng., 1990). For the theoretical underpinnings of my discussion of extensive agriculture, see Ester Boserup, *The Conditions of Agricultural Growth: The Economics of Agricultural Change under Population Pressure* (Chicago, 1965).

45. Thomas Jefferson, *Notes on the State of Virginia*, ed. Thomas Perkins Abernethy (New York, 1964), 159; Gates, *Farmer's Age*, 35.

46. *RJE*, 1:1797–1800, 104; Clarence Danof, *Change in Agriculture: The Northern United States, 1820–1860* (Cambridge, Mass., 1969), 206.

47. Williams, *Americans and Their Forests*, 121. The original source is Hall, *Travels in North America*, 2:135.

value in relation to its bulk, which meant it could stand the high cost of overland transportation, and it was always in demand.

The labor required to grow wheat or any food crop was physically arduous and extended beyond the tasks of clearing, cultivating, and harvesting. Because livestock were afforded an open range in the Holland Purchase, crops had to be protected by a fence. Timber for fencing was abundant, but cutting logs and splitting rails was labor-intensive and physically demanding. Fences also had to meet the construction specifications concerning height and spacing between rails prescribed by the free electors of each town. Fences of inferior construction left the owner without any legal recourse if roving livestock broke into his field. Maintenance and repair of wooden fences was also laborious and time-consuming. Finally, since old fields readily were abandoned when the humus layer of soil wore out, new fields had to be fenced. The zigzag or Virginia rail fence became popular in western New York because its construction did not require digging post holes. Such fences could be moved from field to field and thus were perfectly suited to a system of agriculture that was based on rotation of land.[48]

Cutting and burning over areas of forest also produced one of the most valuable resources harvested from the woodlands of western New York—potash. Many settlers cut down trees, rolled them into piles, and burned the heaps of timber without any intention of preparing the ground for agriculture. When the fire went out, the ashes were collected and washed with water to extract the lye, which then was boiled down into a solid mass known as black salts. According to company agent, William Peacock, one acre "of hard timbered land" dominated by maple trees could yield up to five hundred pounds of black salts. Beech trees gave smaller yields, averaging about three hundred pounds. The weather could also affect the yield; a very wet season might result in loss of "much of the alkali."[49]

Black salts were particularly valuable because they could be sold for cash. In the words of an early settler of Orleans County, the market for potash "afforded the new settlers the first facilities they had to command

48. Danof, *Change in Agriculture*, 118; Danof, "The Fencing Problem in the Eighteen-Fifties," *Agricultural History* 19 (1944), 168–69. See also Richard Bushman, "Opening the American Countryside," in James A. Henretta, Michael Kammen, and Stanley N. Katz, eds., *The Transformation of Early American History: Society, Authority, and Ideology* (New York, 1991), 244.

49. Van Wagenen, *Golden Age of Homespun*, 165–67; William Peacock to Joseph Ellicott, April 10, 1819, JEC; Paul W. Gates, "Problems of Agricultural History, 1790–1840," *Agricultural History* 46 (1972), 39–41; Beers, *History of Allegany County*, 67.

a little money." The cash was used to pay taxes and purchase "goods and groceries." Local merchants bought ashes from the settlers, paying half in cash and the balance in goods. And the promoters of the Genesee Country, including the Holland Company's agents, told new settlers they could pay for land by converting timber into potash.[50]

Except for the cost of a large kettle, making potash required little capital investment. Labor was the principal factor of production. Nevertheless, the cost of potash kettles limited the quantity made during the first years of settlement. Kettles sold for $50 each in the Holland Purchase, nearly twice the price in Utica. Some pioneers, like Ephraim Hart, who settled south of Albion in the northeast region of the Holland Purchase in 1811, pooled resources with neighbors to buy a caldron for manufacturing potash. Utica became the first regional market for potash made in the Purchase. Yet the fourteen to twenty days it took to haul ashes from western New York to Utica left a very small margin of profit. The cost of overland transportation for western New York producers was seven to ten times higher than it was for farmers living in the longer settled regions of central New York.[51]

By 1810, Montreal had become the major regional market for potash manufactured in western New York. As a consequence of Jefferson's Embargo, the potash trade with Montreal was illegal for several years, but that never stopped it. Efforts to enforce the trade ban spawned a "potash rebellion" in upstate New York which Jefferson tried to suppress with the army. Meanwhile, merchants and storekeepers in western New York continued to pay cash for ashes at a rate of $2.50 to $3.00 per hundred pounds. Some merchants opened asheries for converting black salts into a more refined product. Brick kilns heated the black salts to a high temperature, burning off the carbon and leaving a bluish-white substance called pearl ash.[52]

Merchants bought ashes from local settlers or acted as middlemen, shipping the ashes in bulk to Montreal. In the northern part of the Purchase the village of Charlotte, at the mouth of the Genesee River where it flowed into Lake Ontario, was the primary shipping center. Records for a

50. Turner, *Pioneer History of the Holland Purchase*, 555; *Centennial History of Chautauqua County*, 2 vols. (Jamestown, N.Y., 1904), 1:123; Beers, *History of Allegany County*, 67; Reports of Jacob Otto, 1822, 315–16.

51. Turner, *Pioneer History of the Holland Purchase*, 555; Joseph Ellicott to Paul Busti, Aug. 21, 1807, JEC.

52. Richard P. Casey, "North Country Nemesis: The Potash Rebellion and the Embargo Act of 1807–1809," *New York Historical Quarterly* 64 (1980), 130–49; Van Wagenen, *Golden Age of Homespun*, 166–67.

three-month period during the spring of 1811 indicated that 668 barrels of potash were shipped to Montreal. In the southern region of the Purchase, Jamestown, Mayville, Westfield, and Fredonia served as collection and marketing depots. From these towns ashes were transported by boat to Black Rock and Fort Schlosser, by ox team to Lewiston, by lake vessel to Cape Vincent, and finally by bateau down the St. Lawrence to Montreal.[53]

Another important resource of the Holland Purchase was pasture for the settlers' cattle. Raising livestock required comparatively little labor and produced a commodity of high value that could be driven to market. In 1809 Joseph Ellicott said that "cattle in consequence of our distance from market must in a great measure be the staple commodity of this country." In fact, livestock were the "principal property," according to Jacob Otto, that the settlers possessed.[54]

Raising livestock was compatible with the tasks of chopping and burning over a clearing. Settlers often chopped clearings in winter and drove their hungry cattle into the opening to feed on the tops of the recently cut trees. Roswell Turner migrated to the rolling hill country southwest of Batavia in March 1804. That first winter "was one of severe trials and hardships." He fed sixteen head of cattle, "principally upon browse" cut from the surrounding forest. At times, Turner remembered, deep snow prevented the cattle from "getting into the woods," so he had to cut down trees, collect the browse, and haul it in bags to the animals. Similarly, Andrew Putnam, an early settler of the town of Stockton in Chautauqua County, recalled how his cattle subsisted mainly on browse during the remainder of the winter following his arrival in February 1817.[55]

When spring came, however, both Roswell Turner and Andrew Putnam, along with hundreds of other settlers, turned their cattle loose to feed in the woodland pastures, "which abounded with leeks and other green herbage."[56] Access to this resource constituted a vital part of every settler's relationship with the land and productive resources of the Holland Purchase. To ensure that vacant woodlands remained an open range for pasturing cattle and other livestock, settlers throughout the Purchase required that the small portion of land under cultivation be protected from roving livestock by lawful fences.

53. *RJE*, 2:1810, 82; Young, *History of Chautauqua County*, 96–97.
54. Quoted in Wyckoff, *Developer's Frontier*, 161; Reports of Jacob Otto, 1823, 336.
55. Turner, *Pioneer History of the Holland Purchase*, 481; Young, *History of Chautauqua County*, 566.
56. Young, *History of Chautauqua County*, 566.

By the early nineteenth century every state in the Union had enacted fencing laws adapted to the land requirements of extensive agriculture. Unlike many states, New York left fencing regulations to local authority. Regulating when various animals could run at large on the highways received attention at almost every town meeting. Pound keepers were appointed and fines were levied to enforce local laws. But the settlers' right to leave land unfenced or to turn cattle loose in the forest was not limited. When a town declared what constituted a "sufficient fence," crops had to be fenced in and livestock fenced out. In the town of Cambria a fence had to measure "five feet six inches high." In Perrysburg the electors "voted that the fences which are considered lawful shall be 4½ feet high and of sufficient tightness to stop a hog that will weigh 75 pounds."[57]

Once a town declared the dimensions of a "sufficient fence," a fence viewer had to oversee claims for damages against roving livestock. An elected town official who usually served in a dual capacity as pathmaster or overseer of the highway, the fence viewer determined whether damage to crops resulted from livestock breaking through a legal fence. If the enclosure met the specifications set by the town, the aggrieved party could receive damages as determined by the fence viewer. If the damaged crops were not enclosed by a legal fence, the owner of the roving livestock was not liable for any injury to property.

Sometimes town meetings featured hot debates over the issue of whether hogs or any livestock "should be free commoners or not." In spite of the disputes that arose over roving livestock doing damage to crops or other property, the fencing laws enacted by the settlers of the Holland Purchase extended an absolute right of property only to land enclosed and protected by a legal fence. The importance of raising livestock made access to woodland pasture a critical resource of subsistence and production.[58]

57. Ransom H. Tyler, *A Treatise on the Law of Boundaries and Fences* (Albany, N.Y., 1874), 371–72; Porter Town Meeting, Minutes, April 11, 1815, Lockport Historical Center; Pendleton Town Meeting, Minutes, April 7, 1829, Book 1, Pendleton Town Hall; Perrysburg Town Meeting, Minutes, March 5, 1824, March 6, 1827, Perrysburg Town Hall; Porter Town Meeting, Minutes, April 11, 1815; Pendleton Town Meeting, Minutes, March 6, 1830, Book 1; *History of Niagara County, New York* (New York, 1878), 227; Young, *History of Chautauqua County,* 328; Perrysburg Town Meeting, Minutes, March 3, 1829.
58. See Record of Strays, 1819–1865, Perrysburg Town Hall; Pendleton Town Records, Book 2, Pendleton Town Hall; Record of Strays, Porter Town Records, 1817–23, Lockport Historical Center. For an analysis of fencing and open range conflicts in nineteenth-century America, see Danof, "The Fencing Problem in the Eighteen-Fifties"; J. Crawford King, Jr.,

Table 2. Livestock in the Holland Land Purchase

County	1820–21		1825		1835	
	Cattle	Sheep	Cattle	Sheep	Cattle	Sheep
Allegany	4,931	7,192	9,472	16,219	18,365	31,325
Cattaraugus	3,683	2,922	10,499	10,275	28,644	39,509
Chautauqua	18,765	17,948	25,516	46,264	55,490	95,903
Erie	17,729	26,240	27,137	50,592	44,407	69,256
Niagara	7,846	11,265	11,210	19,823	21,833	29,197
Genesee	28,896	51,270	33,125	68,476	44,483	96,163
Orleans*	—	—	9,301	16,710	15,003	28,893

Sources: H. G. Spafford, *Gazetteer of the State of New York (1824; repr. Interlaken, N.Y., 1981);
New York State Census for 1825, in David Burr, Atlas of the State of New York* (New York, 1829);
Census of the State of New York for 1835 (Albany, N.Y., 1835); Thomas F. Gordon *Gazetteer of
the State of New York* (Philadelphia, 1836).
*Orleans was set off from Genesee County in 1824.

The settlers of the Holland Purchase raised cattle, sheep, and hogs
(Table 2). Their cattle were often referred to as "neat cattle" or "woods
cattle." The former designation signified that little distinction was made
between draft animals and those used for beef or dairy products. The
latter designation referred to the practice of grazing livestock in unfenced
forested pastures. Raising cattle on "the wood's feed" made them semi-
wild. It also gave their milk a peculiar odor. During the spring milk and
butter carried the strong scent of wild onions. Samuel Salisbury, a settler
from Genesee County, explained: "Our milk was strongly flavoured with
leeks occasionally, with which our native 'pastures' abounded, but we
used to correct this by eating a fresh leek before eating the milk."[59]

In addition to the work they performed and the food they provided,
cattle could be sold to local storekeepers for cash or trade. Settlers often
sold or "turned out" some of their animals during the fall. The peak
season of work was past, and the coming winter was always hard on man
and beast alike. Storekeepers in the Purchase collected cattle and regularly
drove herds to the markets at Philadelphia. James Brisbane set up a store
at Batavia in 1801 and was involved in the cattle business for many years.
Paul Busti, the company's general agent, considered raising cattle on two

"The Closing of the Southern Range: An Exploratory Study," *Journal of Southern History*
48 (Feb. 1982), 53–70; Steven Hahn, *The Roots of Southern Populism: Yeoman Farmers
and the Transformation of the Georgia Upcountry, 1850–1890* (New York, 1983), 239–68.
    59. B. Churchman to Jacob Otto, Sept. 28, 1824, Reel 152, HLCP; Turner, *Pioneer
History of the Holland Purchase*, 475; Samuel Salisbury is quoted in Arad Thomas, *Pioneer
History of Orleans County, New York* (Albion, N.Y., 1871), 224.

lots he purchased in 1804. He told Joseph Ellicott that "no part of agriculture required less trouble and expense . . . than the raising of these animals" and "none afford[ed] more certain profits if attended to with a middling care." The company itself got into the cattle business in 1807, when it agreed to accept livestock as payment in kind for land.[60]

Settlers in the Purchase also raised sheep, primarily to produce wool for home manufacturing (Table 3). Almost every family in the Purchase made and wore "their own clothing." Spinning wheels constituted "an article of furniture in every house" and looms were "almost as common." In 1820-21 the amount of cloth made at home ranged from 4.29 yards per capita in Cattaraugus County to 8.05 yards per capita in more populous Genesee County. This level of production compared favorably with that in older and more established counties to the east. Oneida County, considered a leader "in manufactures of various kinds, particularly in wool and cotton," produced 7.77 yards of cloth per capita in the same period. The raising of sheep for wool was an important activity in the local economy. It furnished a basic resource, required little capital investment, demanded minimal attention and work, and produced an "always saleable article."[61]

Hogs were particularly adapted to the woodland pastures of the Holland Land Purchase. But these animals' destructive habit of rooting up vegetation with their snouts required special attention from settlers who met annually in town meetings to regulate whether animals "might run at large." In the town of Ellicott, for instance, it was voted "that cattle and hogs might run at large." A year later, in 1814, it was decided that swine should not run at large. Then in 1817 hogs were voted free commoners on the condition that they wear yokes and rings. Throughout the Purchase hogs were often let loose to fatten on beechnuts before they were slaughtered in November or December. Pork was a valuable product in the local frontier economy. For many settlers it was their principal food, and storekeepers treated it as a cash item. In 1821 the Holland Land Company decided to accept pork as payment in kind for overdue interest, yet it received very little. Storekeepers dominated the local trade in pork throughout the settlement period.[62]

60. Wyckoff, *Developer's Frontier,* 85, 127–28; Paul Busti to Joseph Ellicott, Oct. 24, 1804, JEC.

61. Reports of Jacob Otto, 1822, 321–22; These statistics are derived from Spafford, *Gazetteer* (1824); ibid., 370; Reports of Jacob Otto, 1822, 322.

62. Young, *History of Chautauqua County,* 328–29; *Centennial History of Chautauqua County,* 154; Liancourt, *Travels,* 165; Reports of Jacob Otto, 1824, 368.

Table 3. Local manufactures in the Holland Purchase

County	1820–21				
	Yards of cloth made in families	Yards of cloth per capita	Gristmills	Sawmills	Asheries
Allegany	31,047	7.74	9	22	5
Cattaraugus	17,548	4.29	6	38	10
Chautauqua	83,550	6.65	30	74	9
Erie	118,931	7.59	25	62	25
Genesee	203,720	8.05	42	72	66
Niagara	36,950	5.05	9	23	22
County	1825				
	Yards of cloth made in families	Yards of cloth per capita	Gristmills	Sawmills	Asheries
Allegany	78,556	9.98	14	37	61
Cattaraugus	74,028	8.57	12	45	20
Chautauqua	212,104	10.28	36	83	27
Erie	198,673	8.17	34	85	33
Genesee	245,692	9.44	37	65	60
Niagara	60,171	4.28	12	35	17
Orleans	60,269	5.83	8	30	23
County	1835				
	Yards of cloth made in families	Yards of cloth per capita	Gristmills	Sawmills	Asheries
Allegany	97,788	6.25	22	85	16
Cattaraugus	140,341	5.62	28	108	19
Chautauqua	286,561	6.39	52	206	15
Erie	177,211	3.08	46	168	20
Genesee	227,528	5.79	31	92	32
Niagara	70,499	2.66	13	51	7
Orleans	68,086	3.90	12	44	7

Sources: H. G. Spafford, *Gazetteer of the State of New York* (1824; repr. Interlaken, N.Y., 1981); *New York State Census for 1825, in David Burr, Atlas of the State of New York* (New York, 1829); *Census of the State of New York for 1835* (Albany, N.Y., 1835); Thomas F. Gordon *Gazetteer of the State of New York* (Philadelphia, 1836).

Making maple sugar was compatible with using the woodlands as pasture for hogs, cattle, and other livestock. Settlers created sugar groves by thinning out a tract of woodlands, cutting down or girdling all timber except the sugar maple. The result was a fairly open area that encouraged growth of the preferred maples and offered excellent woodland pasture for livestock. Even well-fed cattle and sheep will browse on the leaves and tender new growth of deciduous trees, and when the settlers' chronically underfed livestock were turned out to pasture in a sugar grove, they consumed the wild grass and woody growth, getting free nourishment while keeping the grove clear of underbrush.[63]

Maple sugar was a vital resource of the settlers' farm and woodland economy. Its seasonal rhythm of production fit well into the work schedule, and it provided a useful food product that had subsistence as well as market value. Moreover, its manufacture in March and April became the center of an annual springtime festival. When the sap began to run, rural folk listened for a loud cracking noise that occurred when the nights were still cold enough to freeze the sap but the afternoons warm enough to get it moving freely. Cooking and boiling often went on far into the night. During the few weeks when conditions were just right, men, women, and children gathered in the forest, where they visited, enjoyed one another's company, and took turns stirring the kettle. Adolescents and young adults found the late nights to be ideal occasions for pursuing romantic relationships.[64]

The wealth of timber found throughout the Holland Purchase made lumber another important product of the forest. Timber was cut and milled for local building and fencing, but in some areas near lakes and rivers, lumber became a marketable export. Early lumber operations used only a few species of trees. Oak was the primary species cut for lumber in the northern region of the Purchase. The great stands of white pine found along the Allegheny River and its tributary streams attracted the most attention in the south of the Purchase. Harvesting trees for lumber did not result in clear-cutting of entire tracts of forest. Instead, the settler turned seasonal lumberman cut down the choice oak or white pines and then moved on in search of other premium specimens. Generally the difficulty of getting logs to a mill limited the cutting to areas of forest adjacent to

---

63. Van Wagenen, *Golden Age of Homespun,* 170–74, 83; Hedrick, *History of Agriculture,* 147–48.
64. Hedrick, *History of Agriculture,* 147; Van Wagenen, *Golden Age of Homespun,* 174.

Lake Ontario in the north and to the rushing rivers and streams of the hilly uplands in the south.[65]

Most of the early mills sawed logs for the owners on shares, usually half of the lumber produced. Settlers marked their logs with notches or letters that were cut or struck into the end of the log. This system of marking was similar to the earmarks used to identify the owners of livestock. Before the logs were sawed, the owners' marks were recorded on a slate. As the sawyers milled the timber, they listed the amount of lumber cut from each log. These slate accounts were transferred into the mill owner's book and became the basis for settling accounts with the owners of the logs. For instance, on January 26, 1828, Ephram Wilcox, a settler of the town of Ellicott in Chautauqua County, received credit for 713 feet of boards from mill operator William Forbes. This figure represented his share of the lumber cut from his logs.[66]

The Allegheny River became the major market outlet for lumber in the south. Olean was the center of the trade. Major Adam Hoops purchased a large tract of land, which included Olean, from the Holland Land Company in 1804. Within six years Olean had become one of the major points of departure for settlers bound for the Ohio and Mississippi valleys. Every spring throngs of eager emigrants gathered there to await the thawing of the river, creating a tremendous demand for wooden rafts and arks to float down the Allegheny River. To meet the demand, Hoops built a sawmill on Olean Creek. In 1807 Willis Thrall and William Shepard erected another sawmill about three miles above the mouth of Olean Creek. Other mills followed. James Green built a sawmill along Great Valley Creek in 1812. By 1820 the township of Olean had twenty operating sawmills. In nearby Ellicott, a township located in southeast Chautauqua County, twenty-eight sawmills sent over 3 million feet of pine boards and shingles to market every year.[67]

While part of the lumber milled along the Allegheny was used to build rafts for western emigrants, the rest of it found a market in Pittsburgh. In 1807 the Allegheny River was declared a public highway, and the "running of lumber" became the principal business done on the river. Mer-

65. James Elliott Defebaugh, *History of the Lumber Industry of America,* 2 vols. (Chicago, 1907), 1:436–44; George Perkins Marsh, *Man and Nature,* ed. David Lowenthal (Cambridge, Mass., 1965), 233; Young, *History of Chautauqua County,* 376–79.

66. Young, *History of Chautauqua County,* 377; William Forbes Lumber Book, Dec. 31, 1827 to Dec. 13, 1828, Fenton Historical Center, Jamestown, N.Y.

67. William Adams, *Historical Gazetteer and Biographical Memorial of Cattaraugus County, N.Y.* (Syracuse, N.Y., 1893), 72–73; Spafford, *Gazetteer* (1824), 157, 368.

chants and storekeepers received lumber from farmers in exchange for various goods. When the ice melted and the river rose in April, they rafted the lumber down the river to Pittsburgh, where the cargo was exchanged, according to Judge Foote, for "flour, bacon, dried apples and peaches, tobacco, and whiskey; also nails, glass, and castings."[68]

The seasonal rhythm of the lumber trade enabled many settlers to cut logs and shave shingles during the winter. The snow and ice made it easier to get logs into a stream where they could be floated to a sawmill. Throughout the southern part of the Purchase "cutting logs for lumber took place mainly during the winter." But if winter was the season for cutting logs, spring was the best season for sawing the logs into lumber. Many mills operated with a single saw powered by an undershot wheel that depended on a good volume of moving water to turn it. Spring was the only time such a volume of water could be counted on. After the lumber was sawed and ready for market, spring freshets carried it into the Allegheny River, where it was organized into rafts.[69]

The rafts were put together from thousands of board feet cut by scores of sawmills along the Connewongo, Cassadaga, Great Valley Creek, and the Allegheny itself. When the rafts reached Warren, Pennsylvania, they were often linked together to form one large raft known as an "Allegany Fleet." Depending on the size of the raft, crews, ranging in size from two to ten men, guided them down the river. A strong crew ready to pull at the heavy oars could make the difference between a successful trip and one ending in a pileup. When the rafts reached Pittsburgh, the crews might break them up and sell the lumber or continue down the Ohio bound for more distant markets. When the journey ended, the raftsmen walked back to western New York. One raftsman made the trip down the Allegheny 247 times.[70]

The settlers of the Holland Purchase also depended on timber for fuel-wood. Cutting and gathering firewood probably took up more of a farm family's time and energy than any other single activity. Every settler kept at least a third of his land as a cultivated woodlot, but throughout much of the settlement period the settlers cut firewood on any land that was vacant. A typical settler likely burned fifteen cords of wood per year for heating and cooking. To keep warm over the long, cold winters required

68. Ellis, *History of Cattaraugus County,* 51; Judge Foote is quoted in Young, *History of Chautauqua County,* 376.

69. Adams, *Historical Gazetteer,* 73–76; Defebaugh, *History of the Lumber Industry,* 438.

70. *Centennial History of Chautauqua County,* 124–25.

large amounts of firewood. Year-round cooking also accounted for the heavy consumption of fuelwood. Settlers also paid their school taxes in firewood, supplying half a cord of wood during the winter months for every child they sent to school.[71]

Cutting and selling fuelwood was an important winter activity, providing some cash income during a period when underemployment in rural communities was always a problem. When seasoned properly, hickory, sugar maple, beech, birch, and oak made the best fuelwood. It was sold by the cord. The timber was cut into four-foot lengths and then piled four feet high and eight feet long. A cord contained 128 cubic feet and sold for between one and two dollars.[72]

The settlers of the Holland Purchase were more than cultivators of the soil; they exploited the woodlands for a variety of products that could be used, exchanged, or sold. Trying to determine the volume and value of these forest products is difficult because available statistics before 1840 are limited. But the United States Census of 1840 provided some important data about the production and sale of potash, lumber, maple sugar, and fuelwood. Data for the nation indicate that at the end of the settlement period the counties and townships of the Holland Purchase ranked in the top two quintiles for the manufacture and sale of forest products. The settlers of western New York, even more than their rural counterparts elsewhere, had turned the forest and its resources into a host of marketable commodities.[73]

Ecological Transformation and a New Landscape

The settlers of the Holland Land Purchase used forested land for a variety of purposes. They built cabins, grew food, made potash, raised livestock, and cut timber for lumber and fuel. Slashing and burning the forest disrupted and altered the ecosystem existing at the time white settlement began. The Seneca had modified the environment too, but the sheer magnitude of white settlement hastened the pace of ecological change and

---

71. Gates, "Problems of Agricultural History," 36–39.

72. Van Wagenen, *Golden Age of Homespun,* 159; Michael Williams, "Clearing the United States Forests: Pivotal Years, 1810–1860," *Journal of Historical Geography* 8 (1982), 16–18; Williams, "Products of the Forest: Mapping the Census of 1840," *Journal of Forest History* 24 (1980), 6–9.

73. Williams, "Products of the Forest," 4–23. Williams did not look at maple sugar production, but the census data show high production in the Purchase equal to 30 percent of New York State's output. See *Compendium of the Enumeration of the Inhabitants and Statistics of the United States Sixth Census* (1841; rpr. New York, 1976), 122.

initiated other disruptions peculiar to the settlers' use of land and resources. The settlers harvested those resources that had a high market or cash value in the frontier economy of western New York. They were primarily interested in expending labor on products offering a quick and ready return. Careful consideration of the ratio between labor input and product yield was the critical variable governing their land use choices.

Production of wheat and other food crops depended heavily on the rich humus making up the top layer of soil. Settlers readily abandoned their fields at the first sign of declining yields. New fields replaced old ones; the abandoned sites usually were "turned out" to brush pasture. Other clearings cut for lumber, potash, or firewood were also used for brush pasture. The first stage of plant succession in an old field or abandoned clearing began immediately. Woodland ferns and grasses appeared first, followed by weeds, shrubs, and underbrush. Plants that grazing livestock avoided, including thistles and other thorn-bearing species, could become dominant because of their competitive advantage. In the Holland Land Purchase, Canada thistles, a European weed widely naturalized throughout North America, became a prominent and unwelcome feature of regenerating lands. The settlers tried to control the thistles by enacting regulations at their annual town meetings. In the town of Porter the settlers voted that "any person having Canada thistles growing on the farm that he owns or possesses, and does not cut them off near the middle of June and the middle of August, shall forfeit the sum of five dollars, one half to the complainant and the other half to the poor."[74]

The next stage of plant succession was marked by the appearance of small trees and second-growth forest. Pin cherry, sugar maple, black cherry, white ash, and red maple were the first trees to invade an old clearing in the upland forest regions. Elm and red maple trees quickly became established when openings occurred in the bottomlands.[75]

Cutting, burning over, and abandoning old clearings and fields enhanced woodland pasture for livestock, but open-range grazing changed the frontier ecosystem dramatically. Domestic livestock browsed the tops of tender new growth; other, less desirable vegetation was broken down,

74. Robert B. Gordon, *The Primeval Forest Types of Southwestern New York,* New York State Museum Bulletin 321 (Albany, N.Y., 1940), 58–61; P. L. Buttrick, "Forest Growth on Abandoned Agricultural Land," *Scientific Monthly* 5 (1917), 80–91; The town of Porter's Ordinance is cited in *History of Niagara County,* 334–35, 276; *Buffalo Emporium* (Buffalo, N.Y.), Sept. 25, 1824.

75. Gordon, *Primeval Forest Types,* 58–61; G. G. Whitney, "The History and Status of the Hemlock-Hardwood Forests of the Allegheny Plateau," *Journal of Ecology* 78 (1990), 443–58; John H. Thompson, ed., *Geography of New York State* (Syracuse, N.Y., 1966), 95.

trampled underfoot, or, as was the case with thorn-bearing plants, simply left alone. Saplings up to one foot in height were especially vulnerable. The heavy body weight of cattle often damaged shallow-rooted hemlock and beech trees; both were dominants in the forest that existed at the time white settlement began. Stamping hoofs also compacted the forest soil, reducing the amount of organic debris that gave new lands their celebrated fertility. Light grazing slowed or destroyed young tree growth but encouraged other woodland vegetation. Ferns, flowers, and grasses flourished in great abundance. Heavier grazing left an area covered by weeds and pasture trees, which were protected from hungry livestock by an array of burrs, prickles, and spines.[76]

Cutting timber for domestic fuel may have created the most serious ecological disruption stemming from the settlers' land use. Whether a woodlot was regularly thinned out or periodically clear-cut determined the magnitude of the disturbance. Light thinning over an extensive area probably reenacted the effects of small-scale natural disturbances caused by wind damage or old age. As long as the overhead canopy remained intact, shade-tolerant species like beech and hemlock continued to thrive. Heavier thinning or periodic clear-cutting had a more radical effect on the species composition of the forests. When larger openings occurred, sun-loving white ash, black cherry, and red maple trees became the pioneers of the cutover areas, and they dominated the second-growth forests that sprang up on these woodlots. Turning out cattle to pasture in a woodlot, a common practice, intensified the level of disturbance.[77]

Overall the slash-and-burn technique used by the settlers to produce both subsistence and market commodities transformed the old-growth forest ecosystem that existed throughout the region at the time white settlement began. Mapping the precise progress and extent of this transformation is difficult, but early statistics concerning the number of improved acres in the Holland Purchase provide a general picture. When the

76. H. J. Lutz, "Effect of Cattle Grazing on Vegetation of a Virgin Forest in Northwestern Pennsylvania," *Journal of Forest Research* 41 (1930), 561–70; E. L. Jones, "Creative Disruptions in American Agriculture, 1620–1820," *Agricultural History* 48 (Oct. 1974), 510–28; F. Fraser Darling, "Man's Ecological Dominion through Domesticated Animals on Wild Lands," in William L. Thomas, Jr., ed., *Man's Role in Changing the Face of the Earth* (Chicago, 1956), 778–87; W. G. Wahlenberg, "Pasturing Woodland in Relation to Southern Forestry," *Journal of Forestry* 35 (June 1937), 550–56; F. A. Welton and V. H. Morris, "Woodland Pasture," *Journal of Forestry* 26 (Oct. 1928), 794–96.

77. Whitney, "Hemlock-Hardwood Forests," 443–58; Philip Tome, *Pioneer Life; or Thirty Years a Hunter* (1854; rpr. New York, 1971), 149; Alexander van Peter Mills to Jacob Otto, Nov. 28, 1822, Reel 151, HLCP.

Table 4. Status of land in the Holland Purchase, 1825 and 1835

| County | Improved land in the Holland Purchase 1825 | | |
	Improved acres	Percent of total	Per capita
Allegany	24,309	7.5	3.09
Cattaraugus	26,513	3.3	3.07
Chautauqua	67,784	10.0	3.28
Erie	79,338	12.2	3.26
Genesee	116,510a	24.9	4.48
Niagara	44,197	14.3	3.14
Orleans	38,175	21.2	3.69

| County | Improved land in the Holland Purchase 1835 | | |
	Improved acres	Percent of total	Per capita
Allegany	59,649	17.9	3.81
Cattaraugus	87,576	11.1	3.51
Chautauqua	167,134	25.7	3.73
Erie	150,110	28.0	2.61
Genesee	215,418a	43.8	5.48
Niagara	98,330	31.9	3.71
Orleans	90,982	50.9	5.21

Sources: New York State Census for 1825, in David Burr, *Atlas of the State of New York* (1829); *Census of the State of New York for 1835* (Albany, N.Y., 1835); Thomas F. Gordon, *Gazetteer of the State of New York* (Philadelphia, 1836).

aIncludes town of Stafford, which is partially included in the Holland Purchase.

census takers and compilers of gazetteers referred to improved land, they meant land cleared of forest. Indeed, clearing the forest was the first step in creating a farm; hence the number of improved acres recorded in the state census for 1825, 1835, and 1845 measured the progress of clearing the forest (Tables 4 and 5).[78]

More specifically, improved land designated areas "in use, under cultivation, fenced and provided with farm buildings." The marshals and assistants of the United States Census of 1850, for instance, defined "improved land" as that cleared and used for grazing livestock, mowing hay, and growing crops. Cropland usually accounted for only a small proportion of the land that was designated as improved. For example, in Chautauqua County 38 percent of the total acreage was improved in 1845, but only 10 percent was actually under cultivation. In Niagara

78. Williams, *Americans and Their Forests,* 118.

Table 5. Status of land in the Holland Purchase and Western New York, 1845 and 1850

| County | Improved land in the Holland Purchase 1845 | | |
	Improved acres	Percent of total	Per capita
Allegany	75,457	27.3	5.03
Cattaraugus	157,443	18.5	5.22
Chautauqua	252,784	37.8	5.43
Erie	224,196	36.7	2.85
Genesee	127,508[a]	58.1	6.80
Niagara	148,108	44.9	4.29
Orleans	102,924	52.6	5.26
Wyoming[b]	156,246	50.2	6.60

| County | Cultivated land in the Holland Purchase 1845 | |
	Acres in crops	Percent of improved acres
Cattaraugus	50,317	32.0
Chautauqua	65,461	25.9
Erie	79,665	35.5
Niagara	74,610	50.4

| County | Unimproved farmland in Western New York in 1850 | |
	Unimproved farm woodland	Percent of total acres
Allegany	186,320	28.2
Cattaraugus	261,859	30.7
Chautauqua	281,581	40.0
Erie	191,832	28.0
Genesee	69,708	21.5
Niagara	102,128	28.6
Orleans	53,631	20.7
Wyoming	126,747	33.6

Sources: *Census of the State of New York for 1845* (Albany, N.Y., 1846); *The Seventh Census of the United States: 1850* (Washington, D.C., 1853); J. H. French, *Gazetteer of the State of New York* (1860; repr. Interlaken, N.Y., 1986).

[a]Includes Stafford, which is partially included in the Holland Purchase.

[b]Wyoming County was erected from Genesee and Allegany counties in 1841.

County, a major wheat-producing region by this time, 45 percent of the land was improved, but only 23 percent was under cultivation.[79]

79. Mitford M. Mathews, ed., *A Dictionary of Americanisms*, 2 vols. (Chicago, 1951), 1:864; J. D. B. De Bow, Sup't, *The Seventh Census of the United States: 1850* (Washington, D.C., 1853), xxiii. The calculations about improved land use are taken from the *Census of the State of New York, for 1845* (Albany, N.Y., 1846).

Improved land also included areas used for pasture or left fallow. The improvement of pasture lands often amounted to no more than cutting off the wood and turning out cattle to browse. After the timber was cut, these lands were neglected, and they quickly reverted to weeds, brush, and second-growth forest. Land left fallow underwent regeneration and plant succession just like pasture lands.[80]

The many acres of forest in the Holland Purchase chopped and burned over for potash must have been included in the tally of improved acres. Some idea of how much forest was cleared for potash can be gleaned from the United States Census of 1840. To make a ton of pearl ashes required chopping and burning the wood from up to ten acres of forest. The total output of pot and pearl ashes for the seven counties making up the Holland Purchase amounted to 1,794½ tons in 1840; hence almost 18,000 acres of forest may have been cut to produce a single year's output. Since ashes were usually made only from wood cut during the initial clearing process, presumably the output for 1840 represented only a fraction of what it must have been thirty years earlier, when settlements were just beginning. The manufacture of pot and pearl ashes diminished drastically during the next few years as the period of settlement came to an end.[81]

The progress of improving or clearing the forest in the Holland Land Purchase was steady and relentless. In 1825 (Table 4) the number of improved acres ranged from a low of 3 percent in Cattaraugus County to a high of 25 percent in Genesee County. By 1835 the figures had jumped to 11 percent in Cattaraugus County to 51 percent in Orleans County. And in 1845 (Table 5) the numbers varied from a low of 18.5 percent, again in Cattaraugus County, to a high of 58 percent for Genesee County. As significant as these numbers are, they do not tell the whole story of the ecological transformation that was under way.

In 1850 the federal census distinguished for the first time between improved and unimproved farmlands. The latter designation signified farm woodland, including grazed or ungrazed "farm wood lots or timber

---

80. Howard S. Russell, *A Long, Deep Furrow: Three Centuries of Farming in New England* (abridged ed.; Hanover, N.H., 1982), 276, 212.

81. *Compendium of the Enumeration of the Inhabitants and Statistics of the United States as Obtained from the Returns of the Sixth Census* (1841; rpr. New York, 1976), 122; Williams, "Products of the Forest," 12–14. Robert W. Silsby, "Credit and Creditors in the Phelps-Gorham Purchase" (Ph.D. diss., Cornell University, 1958), 23, calculates that ten acres might yield a ton of pearl ash. William Peacock, a subagent of the Holland Land Company, calculated that five acres "of hard timbered land" dominated by elm and sugar maple could yield twenty-five hundred pounds of black salts or one ton of pearl ash (William Peacock to Joseph Ellicott, April 10, 1819, JEC).

tracts, and cut over land with young growth." The large quantity of land designated as unimproved farm woodland can be taken as a rough measure of how many acres of the original old-growth beech, maple, and hemlock forest had been cut over and converted into second-growth forest. The figures for unimproved farm woodland range from 21 percent of the total acreage in Orleans County to 40 percent in Chautauqua County. Based on this general picture gleaned from the 1850 federal census, it seems clear that the settlers had brought about significant changes in the forest that existed at the time white settlement began, changing large portions of the old-growth forest into a patchwork of ecological zones ranging from small areas of cropland to much larger areas of brush pasture and semicultivated woodlots.[82]

ENVIRONMENTAL historians William Cronon, Donald Worster, and Timothy Silver have linked degradation of the environment with the advance of capitalism.[83] Viewed from their structural perspective, their conclusions have much validity. Yet their approach cannot explain very much about the specific links between settlers' aspirations and land use on the American frontier. Their structural view suggests that Euro-American settlers were the shock troops of capitalism. The environmental damage they wrought went hand in hand with a value system that made land a commodity and the forest a marketable resource. Still, the relation between the settlers' aspirations and how they used the land is more direct and essential than this approach acknowledges.[84]

The opportunity to mix labor with land in a frontier setting like western New York encouraged low-intensity use of resources. The logic of living in an environment where labor was the critical resource of production promoted husbanding of labor rather than conservation of nature. "The aim of farmers in this country," George Washington once explained in a letter to Arthur Young, an Englishman who was perplexed by the wasteful methods of land use he observed in America, "is, not to make the most

82. U.S. Bureau of the Census, *Historical Statistics of the United States, 1789–1945* (Washington, D.C., 1949), 115, 121.

83. Cronon, *Changes in the Land*, 161, 169; Donald Worster, *Dust Bowl: The Southern Plains in the 1930's* (New York, 1979), 5; Silver, *New Face on the Countryside*, 195–98; Worster, "Transformations of the Earth: Toward an Agroecological Perspective in History," *Journal of American History* 76 (March 1990), 1087–1106. Carolyn Merchant finds an important middle ground between Indian land use and what she calls the "capitalist ecological revolution." See her *Ecological Revolutions: Nature, Gender, and Science in New England* (Chapel Hill, N.C., 1989).

84. The phrase "shock troops" is from Alfred Crosby, *Ecological Imperialism: The Biological Expansion of Europe, 900–1900* (Cambridge, Eng., 1986), 295.

they can from the land [that is, per acre], which is, or has been cheap, but the most of the labour which is dear." In the Holland Purchase the early settlers expended labor primarily on resources that yielded an equity that could be readily harvested, exchanged, or carried to a new site. Since labor was the source of both economic value and individual liberty, the opportunity to convert wilderness into property undergirded every settler's striving to make a comfortable living and his claim to be a free man.[85]

85. Gray, *History of Agriculture,* 1:449.

3

"The Holland Land Purchase is overspread with woodchoppers"

The high ratio of land to labor constituted the main structural under-pinning of frontier settlement and land development in western New York. The great disparity between land and labor created a competition for settlers that plagued both private and public land developers from the mid-eighteenth to the mid-nineteenth century, forcing them to offer generous terms of lease and sale.[1] In the Holland Land Purchase the agents formulated an overall strategy that allowed settlers to take up possession of land with almost no conditions attached. The landlords were counting on these first settlers to supply the labor needed to clear the forests and make frontier farms. But this approach spawned two problems that the company was forced to address in 1821.

First, extending easy terms of credit to poor settlers whose short-term prospects precluded any reasonable expectation that they would be able to make regular payments of principal and interest required the landlords to carry a heavy mortgage debt. The second problem involved the ecological and economic impact of the settlers' land use, especially its destructive

1. The competition among private landlords to secure the labor needed for land development is examined in Irving Mark, *Agrarian Conflicts in Colonial New York, 1711–1775* (New York, 1940), 14, and Sung Bok Kim, *Landlord and Tenant in Colonial New York: Manorial Society, 1664–1775* (Chapel Hill, N.C., 1978), 219–20, 251, 223, 229. Public land policymakers also moved in the direction of granting preferential treatment to actual settlers, even though the outcome diverged sharply from the objective. See Thomas Le Duc, "History and Appraisal of U.S. Land Policy to 1862," in Howard W. Ottoson, ed., *Land Use Policy and Problems in the United States* (Lincoln, Neb., 1962), 3–27; Daniel Feller, *The Public Lands in Jacksonian Politics* (Madison, Wisc., 1984), 127; Paul W. Gates, *History of Public Land Law Development* (Washington, D.C., 1968), 219.

effect on the company's capital investment in wild land. The landlords became increasingly concerned about land, sold by article or under provisional terms, that might be damaged by the occupant and then left to revert to the company. There was equal concern for unsold land on which the old-growth timber was thinned or clear-cut by squatters. In either case the consequence was the same; partially cleared woodland that was abandoned to scrub vegetation and saplings ruined both the value and the appearance of the land. This chapter examines these problems and how the landlords tried to resolve them.

The Holland Land Company's agents were not alone, of course, in recognizing that carrying a large mortgage debt was a burden for any landlord. Albert Gallatin, secretary of the treasury and chief architect of Jeffersonian public land policy, had deep reservations about selling land on credit. He understood the problems and knew the difficulties of making new settlements in the western wilderness. He predicted that most settlers would fall into arrears with their land payments, and he knew that collecting this back debt was going to be a troublesome and potentially explosive business.[2]

Joseph Ellicott had forged a land development strategy that he believed could turn a rising land debt into a corporate safety net that protected the company against loss. Ellicott adopted the practice of assessing compound interest to make sure that the amount of unpaid land debt owed by the settlers was matched by the growing value of their improvements. Even if the first, second, or third settler never paid a dollar to the company, his labor expended in clearing the forests and building a farm, no matter if the improvement was primitive or unkempt, created a piece of property that could eventually be sold for an amount greater than the accumulated debt.

In his last annual report, dated September 16, 1820, Ellicott estimated that the debt due the Dutch landlords was $4,100,000. "This may appear a little extraordinary," he noted, "when it is known that there is now bonafide debts owing to the proprietors from their settlers, with their improvements for security, . . . a sum probably greater than the original purchase money and expenditures." The cash value of these articles and book sales, he conceded, was no more than 50 percent of their face value. He predicted that the cumulative land debt would continue to grow and that under existing circumstances the settlers could not keep up with their interest payments. His report showed that from the commencement of

2. Feller, *Public Lands*, 8, 10–12.

Table 6. Land sold and debt owed in the Holland Purchase

Year	Cumulative acres sold	Principal due	Cumulative debt
1812	554,220.52	$1,007,527.89	–
1814–15	612,894.72	1,114,440.44	–
1815–16	731,507.46	1,537,117.84	–
1816–17	812,758.78	1,904,253.06	–
1817–18	855,203.09	2,139,443.51	–
1818–19	883,386.73	2,322,441.37	–
1819–20	1,005,595.57	2,482,803.36	$4,100,000.00
1820–21	1,032,938.42	2,614,316.09	–
1821–22	1,061,631.75	2,718,797.69	4,405,713.71
1822	1,139,302.93	2,946,731.21	–
1823	1,219,505.20	3,161,869.00	–
1824	–	–	5,618,368.30
1825	–	–	5,839,909.10
1826	–	–	5,946,617.34
1827[a]	–	–	7,500,000.00

Sources: List of acreage of land sold in the Genesee Lands (M, O, P, Q, and H), Reel 178, Inventory no. 800, HLCP; Robert W. Bingham, ed., *Reports of Joseph Ellicott*, 2 vols. (Buffalo, N.Y., 1941), 2:1819, 282; 1821–22, 302; 1823, 344; 1824, 368; 1825, 388; 1826, 424.

[a]David Evans assumed the post of resident agent in March 1827 and calculated the cumulative debt in a letter to John J. Vanderkemp, June 12, 1827, Reel 173, HLCP.

sales in 1801 through March 1, 1820, precisely 1,005,595.57 acres had been sold for $3,122,994. The outstanding principal was $2,482,803.36. Unpaid interest and sales made on provisional terms accounted for the rest of the debt (Table 6).[3]

Underscoring his conviction that a sizable mortgage debt could be turned to the landlords' advantage, Ellicott's 1820 report boasted about "the progress of debt" achieved over the period from 1815 to 1820. More than 392,000 acres had been sold, and the cumulative debt had risen by almost $1.4 million. Ellicott's rules for making an "augmented price" were an important factor in the growth of the land debt because he usually collected only a few dollars at the time an expired contract was renewed. His practice of compounding interest added more than $921,000 to the cumulative debt. Meanwhile, he reintroduced provisional sales of land in Chautauqua and Cattaraugus counties, and these sales yielded, for the

3. Robert W. Bingham, ed., *Reports of Joseph Ellicott*, 2 vols. (Buffalo, N.Y., 1937–41), 2:1819, 267–87, 282, 270–71; cited hereafter as *RJE*. For the list of acreage sold in the Genesee lands, see Reel 178, Inventory no. 800, Holland Land Company Project, State University of New York College at Fredonia; cited hereafter as HLCP.

most part, no down payment at all. During the last years of his administration, these provisional sales disposed of 183,000 acres and increased the debt by more than $400,000.[4]

When Ellicott was fired in 1821 his successor, Jacob Otto, declared that the "accumulation of debt . . . is such that every reasonable attempt should be made to reduce it." Likewise, Paul Busti stressed the absolute necessity of reducing the debt and getting "what we can" from the settlers. Company officials blamed Ellicott for creating a land debt crisis.[5]

Otto condemned his predecessor's system of renewing land contracts because it had undermined the company's desired goal of selling "land to the real cultivators of the soil who expect to pay for it." Otto insisted that "the former system of renewing articles prevented rather than encouraged industry because the payments made by the settlers were absorbed in the increased price demanded, and at the end of many years of labour they were often more indebted and less likely to procure a deed than when their toils commenced." He also believed that Ellicott's system of renewing contracts discouraged the transition from pioneer to farmer that was central to the company's long-term strategy for developing wild lands. As the prospect for attaining fee simple possession diminished, pioneer settlers continued to dominate, raising cattle and stripping the land before abandoning it.[6]

Ellicott was fired in April 1821. The position of resident agent had made him the major power broker in the Holland Purchase. Using his power and authority as resident agent to set up new counties, lay out towns and villages, locate county seats, and decide where roads should be built, mills constructed, taverns established, and courthouses and jails put up, Ellicott was nearly omnipotent in setting policy for the Holland Purchase. But the control over local politics and economic development exercised by Ellicott and his circle of family and friends had also made him an envied and hated man.[7] When Otto took over at the Batavia office, he

4. *RJE,* 2:1819, 269–70; see also land sold in the Genesee Lands, Reel 178, no. 800, HLCP. Reports of David Evans in *RJE,* 2:1827, 439–40; Jacob Otto to Paul Busti, Jan. 18, 1822, Reel 171, HLCP; Reports of Jacob Otto in *RJE,* 2:1823, 344. Otto calculated how much compounding interest had added to the amount of principal on renewed articles for the period from the beginning of settlement in 1801 through Dec. 31, 1823 (Jacob Otto to John J. Vanderkemp, Feb. 9, 1822, Reel 171, HLCP).

5. Jacob Otto to Paul Busti, Oct. 29, 1821, Reel 171, HLCP.

6. Jacob Otto to William Peacock, April 10, 1822, Reel 171, HLCP; Reports of Jacob Otto, 1822, 324–25; ibid., 1823, 346.

7. For Ellicott's role as a power broker, see William Chazanof, *Joseph Ellicott and the Holland Land Company: The Opening of Western New York* (Syracuse, N.Y., 1970), 46–79, 144–47.

told Paul Busti that Ellicott had "ruled this place with an iron hand." "His enemies," Otto added, were willing to "go to any extent to redress themselves." Many in the Purchase believed, according to Otto, that Ellicott's erratic behavior was "produced by whiskey." Even Paul Busti, who had known and worked with Ellicott for twenty years, acknowledged "the queerness and eccentricity of Ellicott's temper."[8]

Settlers also accused Ellicott of reserving the best lands for his private speculation. Typical was an observation by the wife of Oliver Booth, who with her husband had settled in Orleans County. Expressing her belief that Ellicott had reserved the land around the mouth of Oak Orchard Creek for himself, she observed: "Oh, the old scamp thinks he will make his Jack out of it. He thinks some day there will be a city there, and he will survey the land into city lots and sell them. Ah," she sighed, "he is a long-headed old chap." When a local newspaper ran a series critical of the Holland Company and Joseph Ellicott in the fall of 1819, the complaints about Ellicott could no longer be ignored. At the time Jacob Otto replaced Ellicott, he reported widespread resentment over the former agent's alleged practice of reserving the best land for later speculation.[9]

The ultimate reason for Ellicott's dismissal was the urgent need to reduce the debt. To stem the tide of red ink, the Holland Company decided to get rid of the pioneer settlers or at the very least end their spendthrift use of land. This meant the company must promote, by incentive or coercion, if necessary, the settlers' desire to raise money by cultivating the soil. The improvements necessary for wheat and grain cultivation enhanced the value of the company's lands under contract and protected the landlords from the high number of delinquencies that had occurred in the early stages of frontier land development. By helping to create a market infrastructure for grain, the company hoped to foster the transition to the social class it was still depending on. At the same time, the company moved aggressively to disrupt the settlers' harvesting of local forest products. Making potash and cutting lumber were extractive industries that destroyed valuable timber resources not only on lands under contract but on adjacent unsold lots as well. The company wished to exercise greater

8. Jacob Otto to John J. Vanderkemp, Jan. 30, 1822, Reel 171, HLCP; see also Jacob Otto to John J. Vanderkemp, Feb. 7 and March 26, 1822, ibid.; Paul Busti to Jacob Otto, March 18, 1822, Reel 168, HLCP.

9. Arad Thomas, *Pioneer History of Orleans County* (Albion, N.Y., 1871), 254–55. See also Jacob Otto to Paul Busti, Jan. 15, 1822, Jacob Otto to John J. Vanderkemp, Feb. 11, 1822, and Jacob Otto to William Peacock, April 10, 1822, Reel 171, HLCP; Reports of Jacob Otto, 1821–22, 309. For the newspaper series on the Holland Land Company, see Chapter 5.

managerial control over how its land and productive resources were used and marketed.[10]

The federal government faced a similar land debt crisis during 1819–20. As Albert Gallatin had earlier predicted, the unpaid balance due on public land sales grew steadily after 1813. For the region north of the Ohio River the unpaid balance swelled from $1.4 million in 1813 to $9.8 million in 1819. In Alabama and Mississippi the unpaid balance skyrocketed from $630,274 in 1813 to over $12 million in 1819. The federal government moved swiftly to head off the debt crisis precipitated by the Panic of 1819. The Land Act of 1821 allowed debtors to give back some of the land they had bought on credit and have all payments previously made applied to whatever portion was kept. All accrued interest was forgiven. The Act of 1821 also gave hard-pressed debtors more time to pay. The Holland Land Company chose a different strategy for dealing with its debt crisis.[11]

"Encouraging the introduction . . . of men deserving the name of real farmers"

On July 9, 1821, Paul Busti announced the Holland Land Company's new strategy for encouraging settlement and promoting development of its lands. Busti's proclamation explained the company's new terms of sale, which included an opportunity for payment in kind. Discounts of 5 to 20 percent were offered, depending on the quantity of land purchased. To take advantage of this offer a buyer had to pay 5 percent at the time of purchase and agree to pay the rest during the next eight years. The period of credit was extended to ten years on sales made in the southern hill country, where the pace of settlement had lagged behind that in other regions of the Purchase. The company also offered to exempt first-time buyers from interest payments for two years. As an added bonus, the proclamation announced a 25 percent discount on cash purchases. The company proposed to renew contracts for the many delinquent settlers holding land under expired articles, calculating a new purchase price by adding the unpaid principal to the outstanding interest. Renewed articles required an immediate payment of 5 percent with the balance due in six annual installments. If a settler wished to take a deed, the company insisted that a bond and mortgage be given. As an additional incentive to get

10. Reports of Jacob Otto, 1824, 361.
11. Gates, *Public Land Law Development*, 136, 141.

the settlers to take their contracts more seriously, Busti offered a 20 percent discount on any contract on which the back interest was paid up at the time of renewal. Finally, the company agreed to accept wheat as payment for back interest. From the company's perspective, the new terms of sale and credit offered settlers an opportunity to put their land debt in order, but the new terms also signaled the company's determination to correct the mistakes of Ellicott's administration.[12]

Busti followed up his general address to the settlers of the Holland Purchase with detailed private instructions for the new resident agent, Jacob Otto. First, Busti admonished Otto to observe a strict neutrality "in politics and party feuds." "I feel it so highly important," he said, "for the Dutch owners to avoid giving umbrage to the suspicious spirit of Republicans, that if with any propriety I could take away from the Company's servants the privilege of voting, I would do it." Next, Busti described the company's renewed commitment to facilitate the social and economic transition from pioneer to farmer. "Admidst the desirable objects beneficial for the Company," he observed, "one that I wish you not to lose sight of, is, that of encouraging the introduction into the country of men deserving the name of real farmers. It is important in order to secure the payment of the debts, that lands held by mere improvers should pass in[to] better hands." Busti feared that a "pretty large" number of settlers "came into the country with no other aim than that of chopping down some timber, clear[ing] some few acres, build[ing] a cabin and after such slight improvements sell[ing] out." From the beginning of settlement, the company had operated on "a reasonable hope" that its practice of "indulgent liberality . . . would have inspired such improvers" to abandon "the miserable trade of woodchopper" and become "assiduous cultivators of the soil and good farmers." Popular thinking about social evolution held that "instances of such happy changes in the disposition of this kind of people have certainly occurred."[13]

The physical appearance of a frontier improvement, Busti explained, marked whether the occupant was a woodchopper or a good farmer. Additional buildings put up near the site of the original cabin and more acres cleared and fenced for crops testified to whether the transition from pioneer to farmer was under way. Busti told Otto to renew articles and grant deeds to farmers because their character and habits afforded "a good security that the amount of their debt, even if not yet partly paid,

12. *Buffalo Patriot,* July 24, 1821; *Buffalo Republican Press,* July 24, 1821.
13. Paul Busti to Jacob Otto, Sept. 30, 1821, Reel 168, HLCP.

will at a future day be recovered." The woodchoppers who persisted in "their old sluggish habits, satisfied to draw a scanty living from the few acres cleared around their hut," should be pressured to become farmers. Specifically Busti recommended renewing their contracts with stipulations. The company should declare its intention to forfeit their articles next time if they persisted in the "same slovenly way." In the meantime, the pioneers should be encouraged by whatever means to sell their lots to "more useful inhabitants."[14]

The company's characterization of a majority of the settlers as transient woodchoppers was of course a frontier stereotype. In fact, the company was objecting to the settlers' diversified woodland economy in which commercial agriculture played only a small role. The settlers' subsistence cultivation of the soil was supplemented in a vital way by small-scale commercial production of potash, lumber, and livestock. They were not the lazy deadbeats and shirkers that the woodchopper stereotype made them out to be. They had accepted Ellicott's practice of assessing compound interest, not because they were indifferent to paying their debts or acquiring fee simple ownership of land. Rather, they allowed themselves to become mired in debt because they too were counting on rising land values to protect their equity. Moreover, by investing labor only in property or commodities that provided an immediate return, they purposely chose not to make the improvements the company wanted. Given the uncertainty plaguing every settler's immediate and long-term prospects, some of which stemmed from the very real fear of ejectment, it made good sense for a settler not to invest much labor in the intensive improvements necessary for grain cultivation.

Getting the debt under control also required that the company give immediate attention to protecting its lands from further damage. The old-growth forests of the Holland Land Purchase were being rapidly converted into a second-growth woodland of small trees, brush, and undergrowth. This ecological change diminished the value of its property. "It is a known fact," Busti declared, "that half improved lands are less worth than the wild on account of the brushes and weeds by which after few years they are overspread." This ecological change left land "more difficult to prepare for cultivation." When these "badly improved" lots reverted to the company as a consequence of forfeiture or abandonment, resale was difficult.[15]

14. Ibid.
15. Jacob Otto to Paul Busti, Nov. 10, 1821, Reel 171, HLCP; Paul Busti to Jacob Otto, May 3, 1822, Reel 168, HLCP.

Incoming settlers showed little interest in these lands because "grubbing" the thickets of brush and small trees was more tedious and required more labor than chopping the mature trees of the original forest. A settler living near Olean in Cattaraugus County noted: "I would observe to you that these lands are not now worth . . . as much as in a state of nature being stripped of the timber and in place there of a growth of sprouts brier etc. together with the old tops and refuse timber which renders it more difficult tedious and expensive to put it in a state of cultivation so as to yield a compensation to the husbandman for his labour than if the land was in a state of nature with all the timber standing."[16]

The ecological consequences of settling the western New York frontier provide some perspective on recent criticism of Avery Craven's traditional interpretation of soil exhaustion. Recent studies point out that Craven was half right. Extensive cultivation of crops led to chronic soil depletion. Craven failed to appreciate, however, that farmers and planters exhausted arable fields, abandoned them to nature, and eventually cultivated these lands again after they had recovered their fertility. From New England to Virginia extensive agricultural practices created an ecological mosaic of cultivated land and old fields reverting to brush and second-growth forest. This knowledge has enriched our understanding of environmental change in early America, but there is more to this story. The emphasis placed on soil exhaustion exaggerates the proportion of land under tillage, and it ignores the ecological impact of open range grazing and clearing and burning woodlands for lumber, fuel, and potash. The spendthrift usage of land the Holland Land Company opposed was not primarily a consequence of soil exhaustion. The rhythm of slashing and burning by which the varied products of the forest were harvested left large amounts of land in some stage of reversion to second-growth forest.[17]

Judged by contemporary standards, reverting lands had been injured and their value was negligible. John Taylor, the Old Republican advocate

16. Jacob Otto to Paul Busti, Nov. 10, 1821, Reel 171, HLCP; Alexander Mills to Jacob Otto, Nov. 28, 1822, Reel 151, HLCP.

17. Avery Craven, *Soil Exhaustion as a Factor in the Agricultural History of Virginia and Maryland, 1606–1860* (1926; rpr. Gloucester, Mass., 1965); Abbot Payson Usher, "Soil Fertility, Soil Exhaustion, and Their Historical Significance," *Quarterly Journal of Economics* 37 (May 1923), 385–411; Carville V. Earle, *The Evolution of a Tidewater Settlement System: All Hallow's Parish, Maryland, 1650–1783* (Chicago, 1975), 18, 24–25; Timothy Silver, *A New Face on the Countryside: Indians, Colonists, and Slaves in South Atlantic Forests, 1500–1800* (Cambridge, Eng., 1990), 163–66. For the small amount of land under tillage, see my discussion in Chapter 2.

of agricultural reform, lamented that lands in their natural state were more valuable than those that had undergone "our habit of agriculture." He described the practice of abandoning land and using it for unlimited grazing as "our greatest agrarian calamity. Vast tracts of exhausted country are every where turned out, or left unenclosed, to recover what they can in their own way." Revisionist analysis of the Craven thesis also fails to link the problem of reverting lands with early American agrarian beliefs about access to land, control over productive resources, and enjoyment of individual liberty. The ecological transformation on the western New York frontier was in large measure a consequence of the ways small, independent producers chose to use land and resources in an environment that was land rich and labor poor.[18]

The most urgent ecological consequence of settlement, from the landlords' perspective, concerned what Busti called the "rapid destruction" of timber. Company officials expressed alarm as early as 1804, when Busti reported "that many trespasses" were being committed on company lands in the southern region of the Purchase. During the spring certain "clever fellows" cut the "best timber" they could find and rafted it down "to Pittsburgh by the Allegheny River." Busti predicted that the depredations would continue and become more serious as settlement progressed. As the demand for "planks and shingles" grew, the company's agents would have "to pay attention to the woods and by legal means put a stop to the trespasses."[19]

Throughout Ellicott's administration he counted every acre cleared for any purpose an act of improvement. Cutting trees and clearing forest contributed to the opening of new lands. But when Ellicott was fired and Jacob Otto took charge of the Batavia office, the attitude toward extensive agriculture and land use changed. As settlement increased and timber for building and fencing became an ever more critical resource, the company grew more concerned about the ongoing destruction of its forests. Vast stands of oak forest along the shore of Lake Ontario in the north and white pine forest on both sides of the Allegheny River in the south were being cut and milled by hundreds of small lumbermen for whom making planks and shingles to be sold in the market centers of Montreal and Pittsburgh constituted an essential part of their incomes.[20]

18. John Taylor, *Arator*, ed. M. E. Bradford (Indianapolis, Ind., 1977), 68–69, 244.

19. Paul Busti to Joseph Ellicott, June 20, 1804, Joseph Ellicott Collection, Buffalo and Erie County Historical Society, Buffalo, N.Y.; cited hereafter as JEC.

20. Horatio Gates Spafford, *A Gazetteer of the State of New York* (1824; rpr. Interlaken, N.Y., 1981), 367–68; Reports of Jacob Otto, 1825, 409–10.

"The great value of staves, for transportation, as well as for home consumption, and the usual demand for ship timber of every description in our large seaport towns, has produced within the last few years," Otto reported, "a numerous class of men all of whom do not reside in the country, who appear among us every Autumn, and remain until spring, during which time they are employed in cutting down valuable oak timber, from lots yet belonging to the Company." In the south of the Purchase Staley Clarke, subagent at Ellicottville in Cattaraugus County, reported that he had decided not to renew articles for land near the Allegheny River. The valuable white pine timber was being taken off. "Their only object," he declared, referring to the settlers living along the river, "is to get all the pine timber of any value."[21]

Company agents believed the forests of the Holland Land Purchase were being destroyed by "poor and worthless" settlers who made a living by cutting and selling timber rightfully owned by the Dutch landlords. The "unlawful plunder" was stripping away "the principal value of the land." In 1826 Jacob Otto declared that it had "become absolutely necessary to shield the property of the Company." To stop the illegal cutting, Otto regularly threatened and in some instances resorted to actions of trespass and suits of ejectment. Otto believed settlers had a right to cut timber only "for erecting necessary buildings, for the farm, and clearing a proper portion of the land." He felt they had no right to sell the valuable oak and pine timber "on their lots."[22]

"The Holland Land Purchase is overspread with woodchoppers," Busti lamented in 1822. It had been settled by "idle lazy people" who made neither improvements nor payments. Busti urged Otto to move against a few delinquent settlers in every part of the Purchase. Select the most prominent delinquencies arising from "indolence or unwillingness," Busti advised, "and apply the remedies of forfeiture and foreclosure." Yet he cautioned Otto to sustain the company's reputation for "liberality." "An indiscriminate severity" against all delinquent settlers "might produce serious injury" because the "quantity of badly improved lands reverting" to the Company would greatly multiply and these lots could be resold only at a permanent loss to the landlords.[23]

"A contract of a recent date is of great importance to the Company," Otto now believed, "for the longer these expired contracts remain unset-

21. Reports of Jacob Otto, 1825, 409; Staley Clarke to Jacob Otto, July 24, 1824, Reel 175, HLCP.
22. Reports of Jacob Otto, 1825, 411–12.
23. Paul Busti to Jacob Otto, June 5, 27, May 3, 1822, Reel 168, HLCP.

tled, the more unproductive they become . . . the more is the land injured by the possession of the occupant, and the greater will be the loss that the Company will sustain." Otto moved quickly to put the company's new policy into effect when he oversaw the creation of a new subagency at Buffalo in 1826. He instructed the new subagent, Robert Blossom, not to indulge the pioneer type of settler as had been the practice in the past. "Many persons in your County live on lots badly improved, and pay nothing; they also cut and destroy timber which is now becoming very valuable; even after the article has expired. Such persons will never do any good, they should be got rid of as soon as possible. In general, I have found," Otto explained, "that the threat of a prosecution will induce them to quit, or at all events, to give up possession to a new purchaser."[24]

During the summer of 1822 Busti approved of a plan proposed by Otto to inspect all land currently held under an expired contract. The object was to examine every delinquent settler's improvement to assess whether he was a woodchopper or a real farmer. Busti approved the plan, but he cautioned Otto to conduct these inspections in "a slow silent and imperceptible manner" to avoid arousing the "perfidious Agricola." Under the system adopted, settlers who agreed to act as informers for the company visited the improvements of settlers whose articles had expired and reported any "injury to the property." The reports detailed how much timber had been cut and evaluated the "general appearance of the place as to fences."[25]

Seth Wetmore, a small settler living in township 7, range 2, in Allegany County, became an informer for the company in 1825. Shortly afterward he submitted a list naming settlers in the town of Eagle who were guilty of cutting timber illegally. It reads:

Two brothers named Young cut three small pine trees drawed the logs to the mill and applied the boards on the School House.

Daniel Jackman cut one pine tree that was fell made use of a part of it for cooper stuff. Remainder lies in the swamp.

Randall cut one dry pine tree for cooper stuff. Used but a small part of it.

Elijah Hyde cut two green pines and two that was down. Sawed and made use of them to cover his buildings.

24. Reports of Jacob Otto, 1823, 348; ibid., 1825, 403.
25. Paul Busti to Jacob Otto, Aug. 7, 1822, Reel 168, HLCP; Reports of Jacob Otto, 1826, 421. "Agricola" was Albert Tracy, the young Buffalo congressman who attacked the Holland Land Company in the pages of a local newspaper in the fall of 1819. See Chapter 5.

Timothy Buckland cut two green pines and one dry one. Made use of them to cover his buildings.

Hills, Anson Hills, Hiram Humphrey cut in company between thirty and forty pine logs. Drawed them out of the swamp but not made use of them any farther.

Levine Rathbun in company with his father and brother cut from a pine tree that was down enough to make 2500 shingles.

All those above names live in the town of Eagle and are willing to settle for the trespass and with some trusty person appointed to ascertain the value and to save being put to cost.[26]

Similarly, Nathan Freeman reported to the company that he had seen "Warren Wellman drawing logs with three yoke of oxen and two hands cutting timber. . . . I should judge," Freeman added, "that twelve or fifteen acres had been gone over or pretended to be cleared and that I should think there was not over one hundred and fifty rails on the lot." In another statement Freeman said that his neighbor Jacob Young's improvements consisted of fourteen acres "not well fenced." Still another inspection of Young's lot found that "the fence is principally brush and logs. . . . I also examined the timber land and found a number of logs cut on the ground. I saw something like a hundred logs in the creek." In each of these instances the informers testified about other settlers who were cutting and using timber, and in the latter cases they also described the flimsy fences put up by the occupants. For the landlords the collective picture drawn by these reports stigmatized the settlers being investigated as woodchoppers from whom little payment or real improvement could be expected.[27]

The degree to which the company's interpretation of these reports was guided by its desire to push the transition from woodchopper to farmer can be seen in a case involving the subagent at Ellicottville. Staley Clarke received a report that Joseph Hook, a squatter on lot 5 in township 1, range 9, was cutting timber. Clarke called on an attorney and the under sheriff to stop the depredation and "take possession of any lumber" found on "the spot." Several weeks later, however, Clarke decided Hook was not trespassing on company land. He was a squatter, but further investigation revealed evidence of his industry and character. "He has built a frame

26. Statement of the amount of timber cut on vacant lands in the town of Eagle, Allegany County, March 19, 1825, Reel 152, HLCP.
27. Statement from Nathan Freeman given to Judge Samuel Carter, June 6, 1828, Statement of Abraham Crandall to Judge Samuel Carter, June 6, 1828, and Statement of Josiah Little to Judge Samuel Carter, no date, Reel 153, HLCP.

house," Clarke noted, "and has raised a frame barn . . . and has seven or eight acres of Improvement." This was clear evidence to Clarke that Hook was on the way to becoming a good farmer whose improvements would secure the company against permanent loss.[28]

The greatest number of reports received from around the Purchase concerned the unlawful plunder of timber. Bates Cooke reported on the "stave getters" active along Lake Ontario "during the winter season." It was difficult to stop them because they usually managed to escape before a local magistrate could arrest them. "But they are as sure to return," Cooke noted, "as they are to quit." Likewise, L. Bepal complained about the destruction of valuable oak timber in the "vicinity of the canal" and "on the bank of the Tonewanta Creek." In the northern township of Wilson, Jeremiah Whipple reported in December 1826 that the woods were full of stave makers and the timber was "falling fast." The destruction ruined "the looks of the land," rendered it "unsaleable," and stripped away its most valuable attribute. He estimated that at least one hundred thousand staves had been made from these woodlands during the last two years.[29]

The company's informers were a mixed lot; their motivation varied from the expectation of gain to the fear of reprisal. Bates Cooke, for example, supplied the company with information about timber cutting and agrarian meetings organized in his region. In return for such cooperation, Cooke asked Jacob Otto in January 1827 for a loan of $10,000 to help rebuild a flour mill destroyed by fire. Perhaps to remind Otto of his usefulness to the company, Cooke reported on a recent agrarian meeting held at Lockport and promised to keep him informed. The company also paid for information concerning the identity and activities of woodchoppers and stave getters. Abel Parker, a settler living in township 11, range 2, southwest of company headquarters in Batavia, was employed to travel around the townships of Allegany County to report on trespassers. Parker received one dollar for each person who agreed to settle out of court and five dollars for every successful conviction in court. During the early

28. Staley Clarke to Jacob Otto, Jan. 24, Feb. 4, 1824, Reel 175, HLCP.
29. Bates Cooke to Jacob Otto, Jan. 28, 1822, Reel 151, HLCP; L. Bepal to Jacob Otto, Nov. 16, 1826, and J. Whipple to Jacob Otto, Dec. 2, 1826, Reel 153, HLCP. For other reports about timber cutting, see Conrad Zittle and Thomas Clevelin to Jacob Otto, Dec. 22, 1824, Reel 152, HLCP; unknown to David Evans, April 17, 1828, David Maxwell to David Evans, March 4, 1828, Joshua Parish to David Evans, Feb. 4, 1828, Benjamin Barton to David Evans, Nov. 11, 1827, Conrad Zittle to Jacob Otto, Dec. 9, 1826, Jonathan Dolph to Jacob Otto, Feb. 3, 1827, and M. Cowell to David Evans, March 14, 1828, Reel 153, HLCP.

summer of 1825, Parker reported on forty-two alleged trespassers and received eighteen dollars for his service.[30]

Some settlers became informers as a consequence of the company's leverage over them. Seth Wetmore, who provided the company with the names of woodchoppers active in the town of Eagle, had been coerced into making his statement. Wetmore's original article had expired but was renewed in November 1819. At the time of renewal he paid one dollar on an outstanding debt of $428.00. When he agreed to snitch on his neighbors in March 1825, his renewed article was just six months away from expiration. He still owed $427.00 plus back interest on the same one hundred acres first articled in November 1811. But his problem with the Holland Land Company extended beyond his delinquency because he too was guilty of trespass. Wetmore "admitted that he had cut pine trees to make eight logs." The company struck a deal with him, granting him permission to use the logs to rebuild a cabin recently destroyed by fire in return for his pledge "to report any trespasses which shall be committed by others under his observations." Theodore Talbot, the company attorney who arranged this deal, declared that "such occasional instances of indulgence may perhaps operate advantageously and appear to me worthy at any rate of experiment."[31]

Another instance of apparent coercion occurred in the case of Samuel Lindley and John Clark. In December 1825 they reported that James Ferguson was "cutting down the timber" on an adjoining lot. Otto had previously told Clark that he would be held responsible for any illegal cutting that took place in the vicinity of his farm. Making Clark responsible for helping to protect the timber on adjoining lots forced him to act as an informer.[32]

To protect its property the company could resort to legal action through suits of ejectment, trespass, or replevin, and it did so in some instances. Yet examination of company records and surviving local court dockets turned up very few actual cases. As Otto indicated in his instructions to Robert Blossom, the new subagent at Buffalo, the "threat of prosecution" was usually sufficient to change a settler's behavior. The threat of eject-

30. Bates Cooke to Jacob Otto, Jan. 27, 1827, Reel 153, HLCP; Theodore Talbot to Jacob Otto, July 5, 1825, Reel 152, HLCP.
31. The information about Seth Wetmore's land contract is taken from the Register of the buyers of the lots of tracts M, O, P, Q, H, W, T, and R with statement of the surface area of the land, purchase price, and amount paid, 1802–27, Reels 178–79, Inventory no. 802, HLCP. Theodore Talbot to Jacob Otto, Aug. 8, 1825, Reel 152, HLCP.
32. Samuel Lindley and John Clark to Jacob Otto, Dec. 5, 1825, Reel 152, HLCP.

ment served "to convince many settlers . . . who have lived a great many years without paying one farthing into the Office, that such conduct can no longer be submitted to by the owners of the soil." Indeed, the threat of ejectment underlay the system of informers who investigated lots held under expired articles. When the report was favorable, it became the basis for further company "indulgence." When it was not, "the idle and intemperate" were told they could not stay much longer on land they neither improved nor purchased.[33]

Suits for trespass were more common, yet here again the company often threatened legal action but only rarely resorted to it. "In many instances compromises have been made for trespass," Otto conceded in 1825. In the case involving the trespassers fingered by Seth Wetmore, the accused agreed to pay damages rather than face formal legal action. Some settlers who had been caught cutting timber on the company's lands avoided being cited for trespass by agreeing to pay for the timber they took.[34]

"Mere support is unworthy of their exertions"

Getting rid of the woodchoppers while protecting the company's property from further injury went hand in hand with new efforts to encourage "industrious" farmers. The company wanted wheat and grain cultivation because this improvement required a fairly heavy investment of labor, and it created a valuable equity which the improver was reluctant to give up or abandon without full compensation. The farmer thus became more vulnerable to the landlords' control, especially the ever-present threat of ejectment. Moreover, the value of the grain farmer's improvement secured the article of agreement under which the property had been conveyed. The company wanted grain production and a market network for its sale and distribution because the landlords desired to reestablish the hierarchical control over land and market development they had enjoyed, at least on paper, from the beginning of settlement. But, as we have seen, real control over land and development of resources had been given over to the settlers. It was the price the landlords had to pay to encourage settlement and development in an environment where the ratio of land to labor gave labor a big advantage.

33. Reports of Jacob Otto, 1825, 403, 410, 391, 411.
34. Ibid., 410; Bates Cooke to Jacob Otto, Feb. 2, 1825, Reel 152, HLCP; Joshua Parish to David Evans, Feb. 4, 1828, Reel 153, HLCP.

In effect, the company tried to establish a market infrastructure during the 1820s that could successfully compete with a flourishing local market, already in existence, which traded in the products of the forest and was controlled by the woodchopper types the company wished to discourage. The landlords' market network was built on a program of payment in kind that promised to put enough money in every settler's pocket, if he worked hard and saved faithfully, to exchange his old article for a deed in fee. "The purchasers of lands labor under great difficulty to make payments in money from the want of a market to sell their produce at such prices as reward them for their labor," Jacob Otto explained in 1825. The market incentives proposed by the company were designed to correct this problem.[35]

As part of the company shake-up surrounding Ellicott's dismissal in 1821, Busti introduced a policy under which the company agreed to accept wheat, cattle, and pork as payment for back interest. This was not the company's first experiment with payments in kind. In 1807 Busti proposed receiving grain and cattle from the settlers for payment of interest. Ellicott acknowledged the merit of the idea, but he warned Busti that its implementation would be difficult. He explained that the company must sell grain it received from the settlers in the "Atlantic markets." "The freight would amount to as much as the grain would bring at market," and the company would "be saddled with all the trouble for nothing."[36]

Ellicott experimented with accepting payments in kind, receiving limited quantities of wheat, cattle, and pork. Just as he predicted, however, marketing these commodities proved difficult. In addition to the high cost of freight, grain was perishable, becoming musty and often spoiling before it reached an eastern market. Cattle could be driven to market, but the "going price" for livestock in the Purchase was higher "than the market price in Philadelphia." If the company paid the higher price, it suffered a loss when the animals were sold. This temporary experiment with payments in kind convinced Ellicott it was a bad idea and was unnecessary because the settlers' improvements secured their land debt. In 1810 he abandoned the idea.[37]

When Busti reintroduced a payment in kind policy in 1821, the com-

35. Reports of Jacob Otto, 1825, 411; ibid., 1824, 364; ibid., 1821–22, 299.

36. Busti's announcement to the settlers, dated July 9, 1821, appeared in local newspapers in Buffalo and throughout the Purchase. See *Buffalo Patriot*, July 24, 1821; Joseph Ellicott to Paul Busti, July 9, 1807, JEC. See also Paul Evans, *The Holland Land Company* (Buffalo, N.Y., 1924), 313–16.

37. Joseph Ellicott to Paul Busti, Aug. 21, July 9, Sept. 25, 1807, JEC.

pany's general agent had three objectives in mind. Something had to be done about the growing debt, which by 1821 had reached $4.4 million. Even at simple interest, the principal increased by $308,000 that year. Busti's second objective concerned encouraging commercial agriculture, particularly cultivation of wheat. His third objective entailed promoting surplus production for the market in general.[38]

Wheat was a product of great potential value in western New York and one that the company desperately wished to promote. Wheat was the most important crop of the commercial agricultural boom that had begun during the last third of the eighteenth century, when American farmers responded to higher prices and growing European demand for wheat, flour, beef, and pork. Company agents appreciated that the "wheat boom" had introduced many farm households to the dynamics of market production for sale and profit. Growing wheat also represented a more intensive use of land that augmented rather than injured the company's property. Cultivating wheat required that "the soil must be well cleared" and enclosed by a legal fence to protect the crop from roving livestock. A Robert Frost character once said that "good fences make good neighbors." The Holland Land Company believed that good fences signified good settlers, steady, hardworking cultivators of the soil. Good fences also marked good improvements, just as the absence of fences or poorly constructed ones usually signified badly improved lots cut over and abandoned to nature.[39]

The cultivation of wheat also produced a commodity high in value and always in demand. Wheat was one of only a few commodities produced on the western New York frontier that could withstand the high cost of transportation to market. As more farmers settled, grew wheat for market, and received cash in exchange to pay for their farms, the company expected the problem of delinquent contracts and badly improved lots to diminish in both scope and magnitude.

The company believed the prospects for growing wheat on a commer-

38. Reports of Jacob Otto, 1821–22, 302.
39. Joyce Appleby, "Commercial Farming and the 'Agrarian Myth' in the Early Republic," *Journal of American History* 68 (March 1982), 831–48; James T. Lemon, "Household Consumption in Eighteenth-Century America and Its Relationship to Production and Trade: The Situation among Farmers in Southeastern Pennsylvania," *Agricultural History* 41 (1967), 59–70; Lemon, *The Best Poor Man's Country: A Geographical Study of Early Southeastern Pennsylvania* (Baltimore, 1972), 27, 180–81; Charles Sellers, *The Market Revolution: Jacksonian America, 1815–1846* (New York, 1991), 15–16; Reports of Jacob Otto, 1824, 374. The Robert Frost character is quoted in J. Crawford King, Jr., "The Closing of the Southern Range: An Exploratory Study," *Journal of Southern History* 48 (Feb. 1982), 53.

cial basis in western New York were very good. The "newness" of the country meant that a deep accumulation of rich organic soil covered the ground. This layer of decaying organic material produced "abundant crops of wheat" without the expense and labor "of manuring." "Our general average rate of production for the first years after the lands are cleared, is from 30 to 35 bushels of wheat per acre . . . while the farms of our Atlantic States, generally will not produce more than half that amount," Jacob Otto boasted. The fertility of new lands greatly enhanced their value, but like other attributes of the company's property this one was vulnerable to injury by squatters. First occupancy and use of woodlands usually featured cutting, burning, and grazing, activities that destroyed or reduced the crucial top layer of organic soil.[40]

But if the prospects of growing wheat for market were very good, actual production was hampered by the absence of dependable markets. To make matters worse, the market price of wheat fell precipitously as a result of the Panic of 1819. "The three last years past," Otto noted in the spring of 1822, "have been unusually trying to the whole people of America, and more especially to remote districts where labour owing to the abundance and low price of produce has afforded the people no adequate reward. This depression of price, particularly as respects that most important object the production of wheat, has diminished the inducements and retarded the cultivation of the earth."[41]

The company encouraged production of wheat through its payment in kind policy, accepting this grain as payment for overdue interest. The company used "storekeepers and millers in the different parts of the territory" as collection agents. Otto instructed them to credit "the debtors" in the "full amount of the goods . . . delivered in their hands." To win the cooperation of local storekeepers and millers, the company subsidized them because they refused to accept the settlers' produce at the prices the company offered. Storekeepers were accustomed to exact "18 pence worth of produce" for "6 pence worth of goods" in their transactions with the settlers. The company had to offer more generous terms.[42]

Local merchants and millers actively sought to participate in this program. Robert McKay, for instance, solicited the company's favor by proposing: "I will receive your wheat and deliver to you at the Genesee River one barrel super-fine flour for every six bushels wheat of the first quality

40. Reports of Jacob Otto, 1823, 339–40.
41. Reports of Jacob Otto, 1821–22, 294.
42. Paul Busti to Jacob Otto, Sept. 30, 1821, Reel 168, HLCP; Jacob Otto to Paul Busti, Nov. 29, 1821, Reel 171, HLCP.

and one barrel fine flour for every five and a half bushels and will guarantee the inspection either in New York or Montreal." McKay's pledge of a guarantee was important because Otto feared that the fraud and dishonesty practiced by storekeepers and settlers alike would misrepresent the value and quality of the produce received by the company as payment in kind. "Most men in a new country are adventurers without property," he complained, "and very many without principle." Careful bookkeeping was imperative. Every product received on behalf of the company should be carefully checked and credited to the settler who deposited it. Produce put up in barrels should be sold, Otto instructed, only by "an agent or factor of known responsibility" in New York or Montreal.[43]

In 1825 the new general agent, J. J. Vanderkemp, strengthened the program by offering to pay a premium of twelve cents in addition to the current market price for every bushel of wheat delivered and accepted by millers in Batavia and Leroy. But the new incentive did not produce the desired effect. The amount of wheat received by the company remained small. In 1826 the total value of wheat collected and credited to the settlers' accounts was only $3,369.14.[44]

The low price of wheat was largely responsible for the small amounts received. The price dropped to .37½ cents per bushel in 1826. "When wheat is at so low a price as during the past year," Otto explained, "the settler scarcely knows how to spare any thing for his land, and what he can raise is barely sufficient to discharge his annual family debts." Otto predicted that surplus production of wheat would remain small as long as the price stayed below a dollar per bushel.[45]

Under the payment in kind policy implemented in 1821 cattle and pork were also accepted as payment for back interest. Although the company disapproved by this time of the woodland herdsmen who neither cultivated nor paid for the land they used, it realized that livestock represented the principal wealth of many settlers. Large portions of the Purchase, especially in the southern counties, were better suited for grazing livestock than for growing wheat. With this in mind, company agents used the new policy to encourage livestock production for market while at the same time offering settlers a way to reduce their enormous debt.

43. Robert McKay to Jacob Otto, March 18, 1822, Reel 151, HLCP; Lyman Spaulding to Jacob Otto, Nov. 13, 1826, Reel 153, HLCP; Jacob Otto to Paul Busti, Dec. 23, 1821, Reel 171, HLCP.

44. Reports of Jacob Otto, 1825, 393; ibid., 1826, 430.

45. Reports of Jacob Otto, 1826, 430; ibid., 1825, 394.

To market the cattle received from the settlers, Busti proposed pasturing the animals on "2000 acres of upland and flats" along the Genesee River. Specifically he proposed leasing some of this land to settlers in return for their pledges to clear and fence it for pasture. The leases carried the obligation to pay taxes on the land, but no rent was demanded. Busti found enough tenants, but in September 1822 he reconsidered the decision to receive cattle throughout the spring and summer. The trouble and cost of keeping "those wild animals" persuaded him the company should collect and receive cattle only "at stated periods." From then on, the company employed agents in every part of the territory to take cattle from the settlers at announced times and places.[46]

At first, Jacob Otto praised the company's decision to receive cattle. "Large herds were readily collected in a short period of time," and "the good effects of taking cattle and produce from the settlers" were paying off, especially among "the most backward." "They are now animated," Otto proclaimed, "with the prospect of being rewarded for their industry by being able to pay for their farms." The future looked bright, he believed: "The present success renders it certain that the same exertions may be expected every year and we may reasonably suppose that an augmentation will occur, for in a country naturally rich attention is all that is required to enlarge droves to any moderate extent."[47]

During the first year, however, the program lost money. "About 11 dollars per head were lost in the operation," Otto admitted. Yet he thought the loss represented a onetime event. "It was the first attempt ever made on this purchase and of course all the unruly, old and lean cattle were put off. It is probable," he added, "that such a collection of animals will never again be made and the loss was owing, to the impossibility of disposing of the old cattle, which were not fitted for the grazier." Company graziers told Otto that in the future the company should not accept any animal over three years old.[48]

In 1823 Otto began to change his mind about accepting cattle. He received 1,581 head of cattle and could have taken many more if market conditions had warranted. The company again sustained a loss, amounting to $8.87 per head. To make matters worse, the policy itself became a

46. Paul Busti to Jacob Otto, Sept. 30, 1821, Feb. 12, Sept. 4, 1822, Reel 168, HLCP; Jacob Otto to Paul Busti, May 18, 1822, Reel 171, HLCP; *Buffalo Patriot*, Oct. 7, 1823.

47. Jacob Otto to Paul Busti, Oct. 29, 1821, Reel 171, HLCP; Reports of Jacob Otto, 1822, 323.

48. Reports of Jacob Otto, 1822, 323–24; E. W. Rumsey to Jacob Otto, Sept. 23, 1822, Reel 151, HLCP.

source of grumbling among many settlers who believed the price allowed for cattle was too low. "Ever since the late war," Otto explained, "cattle have been made overrated in value; for our army, being stationed on this frontier, derived their principal supplies of beef from the surrounding country, which greatly diminished the stock; and this has had a tendency to keep up the prices; but since that period there has been a gradual increase and we may now be said to abound in cattle."[49]

Otto's greatest objection concerned the conduct of the agents employed by the company to gather the cattle. Some of the buyers were ignorant about the business, purchasing too many "woods cattle" and paying too high a price for them. These men, an experienced herdsman told Otto, knew "no more about cattle than a child and not half as much as my son which is only twelve years old." The graziers also accepted animals in poor health; many were "too weak to drive." "I have found," Otto complained, "that men in this country who trade in stock, and are supposed to be good judges of their value, are so difficult to discipline, that during the last season it was found to be the most troublesome and vexatious of all my business."[50]

Given the "endless troubles, vexations and disappointment" connected with the cattle trade, Otto recommended restricting it "to the Southern parts of the Purchase." It was not necessary to "receive cattle from the Northern parts" because the extent of settlement and improvement there offered "ample security for final payment of the debt." Conditions in the southern part of the Purchase were different. The settlements were new and "the progress of improvements" was inconsiderable. The settlers there had paid little or nothing for their land, and cattle constituted the principal property they owned. To receive cattle from them was better than getting nothing at all.[51]

The cattle trade continued to lose money for the company in 1824 and 1825. The loss amounted to $6.41 per head in 1824 and $5.29 per head in 1825. Philadelphia remained the primary market for western New York cattle. It was a highly competitive market that included stock raised in Ohio and Kentucky, where the climate was milder. Expenses incidental to cattle drives from western New York also added to company losses. Some animals were lost along the way; others became "sore footed" and had to be left behind. Additional expenses were incurred for turnpike tolls and

49. Reports of Jacob Otto, 1823, 335.
50. B. Churchman to Jacob Otto, Sept. 28, 1824, Reel 152, HLCP; Reports of Jacob Otto, 1822, 325; Reports of Jacob Otto, 1825, 396; Reports of Jacob Otto, 1823, 337.
51. Reports of Jacob Otto, 1823, 334, 336.

damages that resulted when the half-wild cattle broke through lawful fences and injured property along the route.[52]

The payment in kind program also included pork. Unlike cattle, hogs were slaughtered, salted, and "put up" in barrels rather than driven to eastern markets. The company received 251 barrels in 1823, but some of these spoiled and could not be shipped to market. Salt of "inferior quality" had failed to preserve the barreled pork. Otto expected to resolve this problem with the aid of state authorities who were taking action to protect the quality of salt produced at the Onondaga Works in central New York.[53]

Although pork was an important commodity in the economy of western New York, marketing it outside the area was difficult. The problem of spoilage continued to make receiving pork a risky business. Otto attributed the spoilage to the fact that barrels were constructed in a "careless manner." Too many of the locally made barrels used to pack the pork leaked, and when the brine escaped the pork spoiled. The problem of spoilage was particularly bad during the summer season. To reduce the company's loss, Otto decided to receive pork only at Batavia, where he or one of his clerks could supervise the "salting and packing" process. But overall the high demand for pork left little to spare, and it never became an important commodity in the payment in kind program. From 1822 to 1825 the company received only a small amount from the settlers, and in 1826 it abandoned this part of the program.[54]

THE Holland Land Company fired Joseph Ellicott because the landlords knew their business investment was in trouble. It had failed to yield the return that the Dutch capitalists expected when they invested in the wild lands of America at the end of the eighteenth century. After more than twenty years of development, the company was forced to carry a heavy land debt that only seemed to be getting worse. The Holland Purchase had attracted far too many transient woodchoppers and herdsmen who seemed utterly indifferent to paying their land debt or acquiring title. The company was finally coming to grips with the settlers' agrarian culture and its challenge to the landlords' corporate aspirations. The company's desire to assert hierarchical control over land development ran headlong

52. Ibid., 1824, 366; ibid., 1825, 396–97; Paul C. Henlein, *Cattle Kingdom in the Ohio Valley, 1783–1860* (Lexington, Ky., 1959); Nicholas Bond to Jacob Otto, Sept. 15, 1822, and James Ganson to Jacob Otto, Sept. 11, 1822, Reel 151, HLCP.
53. Reports of Jacob Otto, 1823, 332–33.
54. Ibid.; Evans, *Holland Land Company,* 324.

into the settlers' egalitarian sentiments about individual managerial dominion over the resources of subsistence and production.

The company's general agent in America, Paul Busti, appointed a successor to Ellicott and moved aggressively to correct past mistakes. Both Busti and the new resident agent, Jacob Otto, proceeded on two fronts. While trying to stop the destruction of valuable timber resources and rid the Purchase of the most notorious delinquents, Busti and Otto also introduced new market incentives for wheat, beef, and pork. The payment in kind policy was designed to help the settlers pay their land debts, but it was also aimed at drawing the settlers into market agriculture. The company had to regain control over the region's economic and social destiny. Protection of the region's valuable forests and stockholders' demands for a return on their long-standing investment demanded that immediate action be taken.

4

Labor, Land, and Property Rights

As the Holland Land Company struggled to save its investment in the years after 1821, the land debt continued to grow. In 1827 company agents counted 5,071 expired contracts spread throughout the Purchase but concentrated in the rolling hill country lying between the sixth and the eleventh tier of townships (Map 2). These expired contracts encompassed 605,650 acres or 27 percent of all land sold through December 31, 1826. David Evans estimated that "at least eight thousand families" were living in the Purchase on lands for which the contracts had expired. These eight thousand families probably comprised at least forty thousand persons. When this figure is measured against the population of the Holland Land Purchase in 1825, the magnitude of the debt problem for both the company and the settlers becomes apparent. Of a total population of 111,906, over 35 percent lived on land that was covered by an overdue contract. And this does not measure the full extent of the problem because it ignores many contracts not yet expired but for which considerably less than full payment had been received.[1]

How and why had so many settlers failed to pay for their land and farms? The settlers' debt crisis was rooted in the frontier economy and persistent stagnation that followed the Panic of 1819. But there were

1. The figure for the number of expired contracts is taken from the Register of the buyers of the lots of tracts M, O, P, Q, H, W, T, and R with statement of the surface area of the land, purchase price, and amount paid, 1802–27, Reels 178–79, Inventory no. 802, Holland Land Company Project, State University of New York College at Fredonia; cited hereafter as HLCP. See the Reports of Jacob Otto in Robert W. Bingham, ed., *Reports of Joseph Ellicott*, 2 vols. (Buffalo, N.Y., 1941), 2:1826, 424, for the amount of land sold through December 31, 1826.

other factors too. The minimum price of federal government lands was reduced to $1.25 per acre in 1820, and a major shift in the migration highway through the Holland Land Purchase deepened the crisis. And of course the practice of compounding interest and renewing contracts by adding unpaid principal to the outstanding interest left many settlers owing more than their land and improvements were worth. Finally, company restrictions on selling or trading articles threatened to close the safety valve that protected most settlers from losing their equity.

Making a farm in the Holland Land Purchase required heavy inputs of labor. Clearing, fencing, building, and planting were labor-intensive projects. Some capital was needed for building and purchasing livestock and tools. Charles Williamson, an early promoter of the Genesee Country, itemized the cost of establishing a frontier farm in 1798. He calculated that the minimum cost was $100 for a good log house with two rooms, "if made by hired men"; $70 for a team of oxen and $15 for a cow; and $20 for farming utensils, including a plow, a harrow, two chains, two axes, and a hoe. The total cost was $205. Of course, many settlers did not hire someone to build their cabin. Whatever the actual cost of establishing a frontier farm, however, a settler was left with little or no capital. Ellicott knew that the money received from a settler at the time of purchase constituted the only payment the company was likely to receive for the first three or four years. The large number of expired contracts counted in 1827 indicates that Ellicott's three or four years often stretched to ten years and sometimes even longer.[2]

In the Holland Purchase it took five to eight years to make the improvements—clearing land, putting up fences, and raising livestock—that constituted "the most available means of capital formation" and the basis for achieving the "comfortable subsistence" to which frontier farm households aspired. An industrious settler aided by family labor might clear up to twenty acres during this time. Ellicott appreciated the effort involved. He estimated that the cost of labor required to clear and fence an acre of land was sixteen dollars. Charles Williamson said the cost of

2. Charles Williamson, *Description of the Genesee Country, in the State of New York* (Albany, N.Y., 1798), 32; Helen I. Cowan, *Charles Williamson: Genesee Promoter, Friend of Anglo-American Rapprochement* (1941; rpr. Clifton, N.J., 1973), 157; Robert W. Bingham, ed., *Reports of Joseph Ellicott*, 2 vols. (Buffalo, N.Y., 1937–41), 1:1803, 237; cited hereafter as *RJE*. For other discussions of the cost of pioneer farm making, see Michael Williams, *Americans and Their Forests: A Historical Geography* (Cambridge, Eng., 1989), 113–14; Clarence Danof, *Change in Agriculture: The Northern United States, 1820–1860* (Cambridge, Mass., 1969), 114–15; Paul W. Gates, *The Farmer's Age: Agriculture, 1815–1860* (New York, 1960), 34.

MAP 2. Number of expired contracts in the Holland Purchase by township and range in 1827.

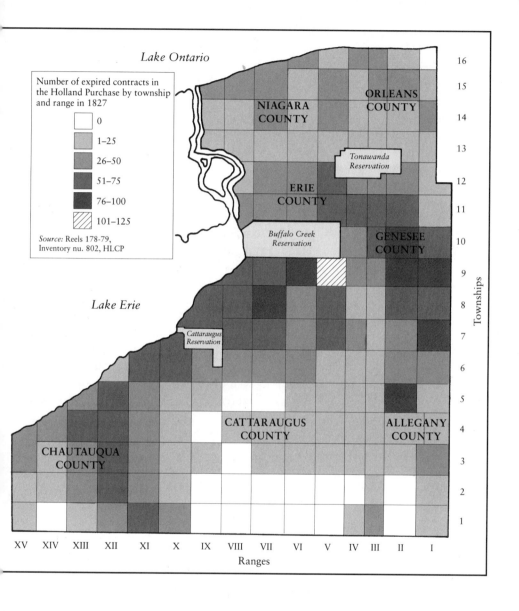

Lake Ontario

Number of expired contracts in
the Holland Purchase by township
and range in 1827

☐ 0

⬜ 1–25

▨ 26–50

▨ 51–75

■ 76–100

▨ 101–125

Source: Reels 178-79,
Inventory nu. 802, HLCP

ORLEANS
COUNTY

NIAGARA
COUNTY

*Tonawanda
Reservation*

ERIE
COUNTY

*Buffalo Creek
Reservation*

GENESEE
COUNTY

Lake Erie

*Cattaraugus
Reservation*

CATTARAUGUS
COUNTY

ALLEGANY
COUNTY

CHAUTAUQUA
COUNTY

16
15
14
13
12
11
10
9
8
7
6
5
4
3
2
1

Townships

XV   XIV   XIII   XII   XI   X   IX   VIII   VII   VI   V   IV   III   II   I

Ranges

converting an acre of "well timbered" land into a field of wheat was fourteen dollars. Albert Tracy projected the cost of improvement at eighteen dollars per acre, and William Cooper fixed it at twenty-five dollars per acre. The cost of starting a farm, calculated in terms of the labor necessary to bring wild land under improvement, remained high even during the 1820s, two decades after settlement began. The high cost of labor kept agriculture in "a rude state." "Several years must elapse in a new country like this," Jacob Otto complained in 1822, "before grain can be raised beyond what is required for the necessities of a family, and in the outset but little can be spared for sale."[3]

How much land, particularly improved land, was needed for a frontier farm household to achieve the comfort and relative security of subsistence surplus agriculture? Various studies of the New England countryside during the eighteenth century offer some estimates that are useful in assessing land needs in the Holland Land Purchase. Percy Bidwell and John Falconer's classic study estimated that a farm household needed four to six acres of cropland, roughly twenty acres of upland grass and meadow, and another seventy to eighty acres of pasture and woodland. The distinction between pasture and woodland was minor because livestock were put out to graze in woodlands and old agricultural fields that had been abandoned to nature.[4]

Charles Grant's study of Kent, Connecticut, found that about five acres of tillage land and thirty-five acres of other land was enough for a farm family to subsist. Robert Gross figured it took twenty-five acres of improved land, eight to ten acres of tillage, and fourteen to sixteen acres of pasture and meadow to meet the subsistence needs of a middle-class farm family of six. Gregory Nobles's study of Hampshire County in western Massachusetts concluded that fourteen acres of plowed land and seventy-five acres of pasture and meadow were required to keep a farm family "safely above the level of subsistence." Christopher Jedrey has provided some figures for the land requirements of communities engaged prin-

3. *RJE*, 2:1818, 164; Stephen Innes, *Labor in a New Land: Economy and Society in Seventeenth-Century Springfield* (Princeton, N.J., 1983), 50; William Wyckoff, *The Developer's Frontier: The Making of the Western New York Landscape* (New Haven, Conn., 1988), 157; *RJE*, 2:1809, 29; Williamson, *Description of the Genesee Country*, 25–26; Albert Tracy estimated the cost of clearing and improvement in the second installment of his "Agricola" series, *Niagara Journal* (Buffalo, N.Y.), Oct. 12, 1819; William Cooper, *A Guide in the Wilderness; or the History of the First Settlement in the Western Counties of New York* (Dublin, 1810), 32; Reports of Jacob Otto, 1824, 364; ibid., 1821–22, 303.

4. Percy W. Bidwell and John I. Falconer, *History of Agriculture in the Northern United States, 1620–1860* (Washington, D.C., 1925), 119–21.

cipally in stock raising. A family of five needed six to eight acres of crop land, including a kitchen garden and orchard; fifteen acres of pasture and fallow; plus fifteen to twenty acres of meadow. This added up to about forty acres of improved land plus enough woodland for land rotation and domestic fuel needs.[5]

William Wyckoff has calculated that in the Holland Land Purchase, "most farms before 1815 had fewer than 20 or 25 acres of cleared land," Many settlers, he adds, "supported themselves on fewer than 15 acres." Median farm sizes ranged "from 165 acres in 1804 to 120 acres in 1811." The situation had not changed much by 1824. With the exception of a narrow corridor along the Buffalo Road, the number of improved acres per farm household was still under 20. It was 14.59 for Allegany County, 16.97 for Chautauqua County, 17.16 for Erie County, and 13.18 for Genesee County. In the eighth, ninth, and tenth tier of townships, where the greatest concentration of expired contracts was found, the number of improved acres per farmer was generally less than 15. In the township of Attica the average frontier farm had 11.72 improved acres. In Orangeville, located to the south, the figure was 10.06. In the township of Holland the average frontier farm had only 6.7 acres of improved land. By 1824 settlement in these townships had been under way for more than a decade. In the town of Attica, for example, the first land sales had occurred between 1799 and 1802.[6]

If many settlers had less than fifteen acres of improved land, the actual number of tillable acres was probably less than five. Improved land in the Holland Purchase referred in general to land that had been cleared of trees. But clearings cut for potash or lumber were usually abandoned to brush pasture. These half-cleared, half-wild frontier farms provided but a marginal standard of living. Taking the rough estimates of Bidwell, Falconer, Grant, Nobles, Gross, and Jedrey as benchmarks, it appears that settlers in the Holland Purchase for the most part had failed to attain the minimal standards of security and comfort that rural folk associated with

---

5. These comparative estimates are found in Gregory H. Nobles, *Divisions Throughout the Whole: Politics and Society in Hampshire County, Massachusetts, 1740–1775* (Cambridge, Eng., 1983), 118; see also Charles S. Grant, *Democracy in the Connecticut Frontier Town of Kent* (New York, 1961), 31–39; Robert Gross, *The Minutemen and Their World* (New York, 1976), 213–14 n. 35; Christopher Jedrey, *The World of John Cleaveland: Family and Community in Eighteenth-Century New England* (New York, 1979), 63.

6. Wyckoff, *Developer's Frontier*, 157, 120, 124. The number of improved acres per farm household in 1824 is drawn from Horatio G. Spafford, *A Gazetteer of the State of New York* (1824; rpr. Interlaken, N.Y., 1981). The figures for Genesee and Allegany counties include only those townships located within the Purchase. Spafford counted farmers and "persons employed in agriculture" interchangeably.

the achievement of household independence and autonomy. When Jacob Otto observed in 1824 that "we have, on this extensive Tract of Country, a great many settlers so very poor, and their improvements so inconsiderable, that they are barely able to supply their families with the necessaries of life," he identified the chief reason why so many of the Holland Company's settlers were delinquent in their land payments.[7]

The Holland Land Company was not the only creditor to whom the settlers were indebted. "The whole of this Community is Debtor and Creditor and Creditor and Debtor," Joseph Ellicott grumbled, "all pressing upon each other." New settlers quickly became indebted to local storekeepers and spent years working to extinguish these debts. During the decade or more of struggle it took to make a frontier farm self-sustaining, the purchase of provisions, clothing, and tools put the settler in debt to the local storekeeper. His article of agreement was often pledged as security. Since the article represented the only color of title a settler possessed, all payment of cash or trade went to redeem the article. The company received nothing until the settler paid these debts. "I would observe that many of the unfulfilled articles," Joseph Ellicott complained, "particularly those where little or no payments have been made on them are held by storekeepers as collateral security for debts owing by the settler, and all the money such settler can rake and scrape goes to pay the trader." Ellicott's successor, Jacob Otto, explained that the local merchant's hold on the settler's industry was owing largely to the scarcity of markets. "The time has been," Otto remarked, "when a number of small stores scattered over the country received the proceeds of his industry. Having no other market his necessities compelled him to dispose of his produce to them at reduced prices, and in exchange he received goods at a high price, by which means he has found himself as poor at the end as at the commencement of the year, or rather indeed more reduced by the accumulated debt due to the Company."[8]

Local merchants and shopkeepers extended credit that sometimes went unsettled for many years. For instance, Peter Tower, operator of a tavern and store in Niagara County, extended credit to Chester Moss from October 5, 1824, to November 15, 1833, when Moss settled the debt. Similarly, Samuel Smith, a cooper in the town of Porter, sold tubs, barrels, pails, and firkins to Amassa Wilder for nine years until the account was

    7. Reports of Jacob Otto, 1824, 361.
    8. *RJE*, 2:1818, 244–45; Reports of David Evans in *RJE*, 2:1827, 438–39; Reports of Jacob Otto, 1823, 347; Jacob Otto to Paul Busti, June 22, 1822, Reel 171, HLCP; Reports of Jacob Otto, 1821–22, 296, 300. *RJE*, 2:1817, 229.

settled on June 5, 1829. If a settler was unable to redeem his article by settling his debts, the storekeeper might rent the land out for "a portion of the annual produce," transforming the settler into a tenant.[9]

Because cash was scarce in the Holland Purchase, many farmers settled accounts in provisions. James Omsbee helped to settle his account with Samuel Smith by paying him with mutton, hay, and onions. Omsbee also fed Smith's sorrel mare for eight weeks during the winter of 1829–30. In Chautauqua County, Arvin Clark settled an account with the local tanner by bartering various provisions and by working for him. Credited to Clark's account were a calf, some butter, a half day's work hoeing, and a day's work digging potatoes. Clark also butchered a cow and several hogs for Alexander Brown. John Peters, a farmer living in Chautauqua County, helped to settle an account with local storekeepers by running logs down the creek and shaving shingles. For this work he received a credit of $46.25. Although these barter and credit arrangements were essential, the exchange of produce for store goods worked to the decided advantage of local merchants and artisans. The high cost of credit made it difficult to pay off debts and redeem the article of agreement that so often served as collateral security.[10]

Local mills also did business by barter and credit. Grain mill operators received a portion of the grain they ground into flour as payment for the critical service they performed. Their share was usually every tenth bushel processed into flour. Sawmill operators received payment in the form of lumber cut from the logs that settlers brought to mill. This practice shows up in the account books of early lumber mills in the form of credit given to settlers. A great deal of trade done by barter and credit also occurred between the settlers themselves. In the town of Shelby in northern Genesee County, "Abner Hunt threshed wheat for John Burt, for every tenth Bushel." In 1818 Henry Bidelman cleared six acres of land for A. A. Ellicott and received enough flour for his family that season. Bidelman cleared another five acres for Elijah Bent and received one hundred pounds of pork in return.[11]

9. Day Book of Peter Tower and Day Book of Samuel Smith, Town of Porter Historical Society; Reports of Jacob Otto, 1823, 347, *RJE;* 2:1817, 229.

10. Day Book of Samuel Smith, Town of Porter Historical Society; Tannery Day Book of Alexander Brown, and Account Book of John Peters, Fenton Historical Center, Jamestown, N.Y.; Jacob Otto to Paul Busti, Nov. 29, 1821, Reel 171, HLCP.

11. Jared Van Wagenen, Jr., *The Golden Age of Homespun* (1953; rpr. New York, 1963), 137; William Forbes Lumber Book, Dec. 31, 1827 to Dec. 13, 1828, Fenton Historical Center, Jamestown, N.Y.; Arad Thomas, *Pioneer History of Orleans County* (Albion, N.Y., 1871), 379, 243.

How should the historian assess the widespread indebtedness in the Holland Purchase? Should a critical distinction be made between what settlers owed to local storekeepers and to one another against what they owed to the Holland Land Company? Were these local debts any less onerous? Clearly, credit and debt were essential to land development and the operation of the frontier economy. But a crucial distinction must be drawn between debt that is constructive and "the kind of chronic, disabling indebtedness" which ultimately results in the loss of farm and land. Until the landlords began to press the settlers for payment, the land debt had been constructive. The company's policy of encouraging improvements made it a part of the rural network of credit and debt that facilitated the face-to-face exchanges of goods and services that occurred throughout the frontier economy. But when the company began to press for payments, threatening the settlers' property in improvements and their means of subsistence, the land debt became an instrument of oppression.[12]

"In this remote region the want of a market will always be experienced"

"The three last years past have been unusually trying to the whole people of America," Jacob Otto said in 1822, "and more especially to remote districts, where labour owing to the abundance and low price of produce has afforded the people no adequate reward." The persistent economic stagnation resulting from the Panic of 1819 referred to by Otto exacerbated the chronic problem of distant markets and too little money in circulation which plagued the landlords' development strategy. Even before the Panic struck, Joseph Ellicott had noted that "in this remote region the want of a market will always be experienced, and money a scarce article." Ellicott believed these problems would continue "until the grand navigable canal uniting the tide of the Hudson with that of the great lakes is accomplished." As Ellicott knew, many of the settlers were still semisubsistence farmers who depended on the woodland as a source of income. The difficulty and cost of reaching distant markets along with the high ratio of land to labor encouraged production of extractive commodities with high value that could withstand the expense of shipment to market. These included cattle, potash, and lumber. The high value of potash and lumber notwithstanding, successful marketing of even these products depended on easy access to cheap water transportation. In the

12. Innes, *Labor in a New Land*, 64–65.

northern region of the Purchase, with its access to Lake Ontario, Montreal became an important market for potash, lumber, and other provisions. In the south of the Purchase, the Allegheny River provided cheap transportation to the market center at Pittsburgh.[13]

For the landlocked interior of the Holland Purchase access to even local market centers was a serious problem. A petition to company agents from a group of settlers in Allegany County complaining about the lack of roads in the hinterland explained: "There is a very respectable settlement of industrious settlers . . . who have, like resolute pioneers, broke the way far into the thick forest—and having no mills or other publick accommodations within a great distance, they are under the necessity of travelling far, thro very bad roads or rather paths, for those accommodating—and the intervening hills and gulphs are such as to make it very expensive, much more than the individuals are able to bear." Local agricultural products could not bear the cost of more than half a day's transport to market. Roads were generally so impassable that farmers delayed "bringing their produce to market until winter, with the intention of improving the sleighing." In some areas of the interior, settlers could rely on nearby local markets created by the seasonal movement or temporary concentration of new settlers, westward bound migrants, and soldiers.[14]

Provisioning newly arrived settlers until they could get their farms started constituted an important local market for frontier farmers. The newcomers purchased or exchanged their labor for a variety of items, including butter, cheese, milk, veal, pigs, poultry, and garden and field vegetables. The most active of these local markets flourished along the major roads penetrating the Purchase. The Buffalo Road, running west from Batavia through the twelfth tier of townships and terminating at Buffalo Creek, attracted land buyers as well as local trade and commerce. Slowed by the war, the tide of western migration swelled again in 1815. More than twelve thousand new settlers arrived in the Holland Purchase during the year following the end of the war. As a result, the demand for provisions increased prices dramatically. Pork sold for thirty dollars a barrel, and "almost every other article of provision" rose in price. When the "cold summer" of 1816 ruined crops throughout the Purchase, any farmer with a surplus to sell could get just about any price he asked.[15]

13. Reports of Jacob Otto, 1821–22, 294, 299; *RJE*, 2:1819, 268; *RJE*, 2:1817, 214–15.
14. Petition from settlers in T2, R2, and T3, R2 to David Evans, June 25, 1827, Reel 153, HLCP; *Buffalo Emporium and General Advertiser*, Feb. 21, 1828.
15. *RJE*, 2:1815, 177–79.

In the south of the Purchase an important local market center grew up near the headwaters of the Allegheny River. The village of Olean became the jumping-off point in 1809 for emigrants bound for the Ohio River country. During the spring of 1818 more than three thousand emigrants gathered to await the opening of the river. Local farmers sold provisions and built, or supplied timber for, the arks and rafts that carried the emigrants down the river. Tavern keepers gave lodging to those who could afford it, while poorer emigrants stayed in private houses or "were obliged to erect tents and shantees to live in." If spring was late in coming, provisions could become scarce and prices exorbitant. Flour sold for "as high as 25 dollars per barrel, pork for $50." But these seasonal or temporary markets were volatile and unpredictable. The construction and completion of the western end of the Erie Canal, for instance, ended this particular local market by shifting the major emigration route through the Holland Purchase to the north. After 1825, Buffalo replaced Olean as the major point of embarkation to the West.[16]

The concentration of troops along the Niagara River during the War of 1812 also created a temporary market boom. Buffalo and several other communities were destroyed during the war. Emigration dropped off to a trickle and new land sales virtually stopped. Still, the concentration of troops created market opportunities. The army needed food and supplies. Nearby settlers enjoyed "a cash market for . . . provisions, produce, and forage." The pay received by both regular army and militia soldiers put money into local circulation. As valuable as these seasonal and temporary market booms were for some settlers, they did not transform the frontier farm economy. Expanding the external market network for grain and other agricultural products was a complex process that occurred slowly and unevenly over time. Unable to count on a steady market for surplus farm goods, the settlers continued to rely on the external market for forest products.[17]

This frontier economy was also burdened by the scarcity of money. "The scarcity of a circulating medium is universally felt here at present," Jacob Otto conceded in 1826, "and the balance of trade is so much against our western country owing to the profusion of manufactures of every kind, brought among us for sale; the low price of our natural productions for many years past being little more than sufficient to satisfy debts due the merchants." Otto was pointing to the trade imbalance be-

16. Orsamus Turner, *Pioneer History of the Holland Purchase* (1850; rpr. Geneseo, N.Y., 1974), 506–7.

17. *RJE*, 2:1812, 104; *RJE*, 2:1814, 149.

tween the Holland Purchase and the commercial centers of Albany, New York, and Philadelphia. What little money there was flowed to the market centers of the East as payment for manufactures and provisions. Clearly, the local economy depended on barter and credit exchanges in part out of necessity. Yet the company also exacerbated the trade imbalance by demanding cash payments for land.[18]

"I have improvements on it and hate to leave it"

The most urgent of the structural problems underlying the settlers' land debt crisis concerned the accumulation of debt to a point exceeding the value of the land with improvements. Company agents recognized the problem, reporting that many settlers sought to renegotiate old, expired articles in the hope of saving their equity. In September 1822 Jacob Otto told his subagent in Ellicottville that he too was importuned by requests to "change or alter the value of the land." Daniel Raymond made such a request in November 1823. A settler in the township of Cuba in Allegany County, Raymond held one hundred acres under an article that had expired two years earlier. He had bought his land in 1815, but after eight years of farm making and improvements he had to face the harsh truth that he owed more than the farm was worth. Raymond wanted a new article, yet his willingness to take one depended on renegotiating the terms. This settler explained that some of his neighbors had abandoned their lots because falling land prices and growing indebtedness had destroyed their equity. Raymond concluded by saying that he had a friend who would loan him money to make a down payment of 5 percent on a new article if the price was fair.[19]

Daniel Raymond was not alone; many other settlers shared the same problem by the early 1820s. The roots of their problem could be traced to the practice of compounding interest, to the economic crisis of 1819 that had reduced land prices, and finally to the competition of cheap federal government lands in the western territories which made the rough-hewn farms of the Holland Purchase less attractive to emigrants.

The way compound interest could raise the price of land can be assessed by examining an individual case. Elisha Dagget came to the northeast

18. Reports of Jacob Otto, 1826, 421.
19. David Evans to John J. Vanderkemp, May 11, 1827, Reel 173, HLCP; Jacob Otto to Staley Clarke, Sept. 11, 1822, Reel 171, HLCP; Daniel Raymond to Jacob Otto, Nov. 28, 1823, Reel 151, HLCP.

corner of Cattaraugus County in 1811. Dagget and fellow emigrants from New Hampshire and Vermont were the first settlers in this part of the Holland Purchase. Dagget took an article of agreement on January 25, 1811, for two hundred acres at a price of $2.25 per acre. Dagget's contract expired ten years later with an outstanding balance still due. Dagget had paid $223.82 in principal and $248.67 in interest, which exceeded the original purchase price of $450 by $22.49. Ellicott's procedure for renewing articles of agreement involved computing a new selling price based on compound interest. In this case compounding the interest raised the purchase price from $2.25 per acre to $3.87 per acre, leaving an unpaid principal after ten years of toil and payments of $301.51. At simple interest, the new purchase price would have been $3.51 per acre, a difference of $.36 per acre. Multiplying by two hundred acres, the practice of compounding the interest increased the price of Dagget's land by $72. This contract was not renewed. Available records do not tell why it was not renewed, but it seems apparent that with federal government land selling at $1.25 per acre, the market value of Dagget's land was far less than the $3.87 per acre Ellicott might have charged to renew the contract.[20]

Dagget's case illustrates how a settler's land debt could pile up, and he was more energetic than most. Dagget paid over $470, whereas the other twenty-two delinquent settlers living in township 6, range 4, had paid on average only $40.30 per contract. The outstanding debt on these contracts was $3.48 per acre.[21]

Falling land prices prompted by the Panic of 1819 and the Land Act of 1820 left settlers who had purchased at higher prices mired in debt. Settlers in the south of the Purchase protested that they had paid too much for their land, which many of them had bought during the speculative surge of 1816–19. The story of two settlers, Harlowe Butler and Harvey Parmele, who purchased land in township 3, range 8, on July 8, 1819, is a case in point. A region of steep hills and deep valleys, this township was still a wilderness in 1819. The first store did not appear until 1826; the first sawmill was erected in 1829. "There was no road to this place," Butler and Parmele wrote to Jacob Otto, "we followed a line most of the way for ten miles marked by two or three who have got here before us and were building habitations for their families; but discouraged by the loneli-

---

20. The information about Elisha Dagget's contract was gleaned from the Register of buyers, 1802–27. J. H. French, *Gazetteer of the State of New York* (1860; rpr. Interlaken, N.Y., 1980), 190.
21. Register of buyers, 1802–27.

ness of the place and the difficulty of getting in provisions all but one of them gave up the idea of effecting a settlement here."[22]

After three years of making improvements, the two settlers were able to raise their own provisions. Among the first to settle this remote township, Butler and Parmele purchased lot 51 when land was selling at $4.00 per acre. Just a year later, the price dropped to an average of $2.88 an acre when the speculative surge in land prices that followed the War of 1812 suddenly collapsed. They protested to Otto that as the first settlers they endured more hardship, yet the latecomers were buying for about one-third less per acre. "Two or three hundred dollars more or less would little distress a person in affluent circumstances especially where long credit is given," Butler and Parmele explained. "But with us who have no way to meet the payments but by the produce of our land that sum with the interest increasing . . . adds greatly to our distress. This consideration . . . after incurring so much more expense, and after undergoing much more hardship and fatigue than our neighbors we must labor hard for three or four years more than they to pay for our land tends greatly to discourage even industry itself."[23]

Butler and Parmele told the company they desired "to make the payments and take deeds at the expiration" of their articles. But the newness of their farms, the continuing hard times, and the high land prices made it difficult to pay even the interest that regularly came due. These two settlers asked Otto for a reduction in price and for additional time to pay. They felt trapped, unable to extinguish this land debt by their own means. "Should we neglect making payments till we have larger improvements or till better times, the interest already becoming due would increase the sum at such a rate as to be equally discouraging." A growing number of settlers faced a similar dilemma, despairing of ever attaining title to the property their labor had created.[24]

In the last annual report he submitted to Paul Busti, Joseph Ellicott observed that "an immense extent of new lands" had just been offered for sale by the United States "at the rate of $1.25 per acre." The Michigan territory lay immediately to the west of the Holland Purchase and was

22. French, *Gazetteer* (1860), 193; Harlowe Butler and Harvey Parmele to Paul Busti, Jan. 19, March 8, 1822, Reel 151, HLCP.

23. *RJE*, 2:1818, 266; *RJE*, 2:1819, 286; Harlowe Butler and Harvey Parmele to Paul Busti, Jan. 19, March 8, 1822, Reel 151, HLCP. As of March 1, 1822, Butler owed the company $636.38 in principal and $28.17 in interest on 178.5 acres while Parmele owed $638.25 in principal and $28.35 in interest on 179 acres. See Reel 123, Inventory no. 557, HLCP.

24. Harlowe Butler and Harvey Parmele, March 8, 1822, Reel 151, HLCP.

"said to be of a very superior quality." Ellicott concluded that "the low-ness of price" of these new lands together with other circumstances had "greatly reduced the actual value of the lands" in the Holland Purchase. Ellicott was referring to the Land Act of 1820, which reduced the minimal purchase unit to eighty acres and the price to $1.25 per acre. Credit purchases were eliminated, but the proliferation of state and local banks meant that new lands could be bought with a loan of only $100.[25]

From the company's perspective, the volatility of the land market un-dercut its "expectations . . . of realizing great profits on this property." From the settlers' perspective, the combined effects of accumulating debt, falling land prices, and stiff competition from government lands threat-ened the opportunity to recover their equity by selling out. "In the early process of the settlement and down to the year 1816," David Evans re-called, "the first settlers made clearings and sold their possession to a more wealthy class that succeeded them and by that means obtained fair compensation for their labor." But cheap government lands for sale in Michigan diminished this trade throughout the Holland Purchase. The fact that "in too many cases" the amount of debt encumbering a settler's land exceeded "the actual value of the property" made it increasingly difficult to sell out. Under these circumstances, a prospective buyer had to compensate the occupant for his improvement and then purchase the land from the company at a price that included the accumulated debt run up by the previous occupants. This situation made land in the eighth, ninth, and tenth tier of townships, where the greatest number of expired contracts was held, virtually unsellable. These lands were encumbered with an out-standing debt of between $3.00 and $4.99 per acre (Map 3). These im-proved lands with their tangle of small trees and underbrush, a product of the settlers' extensive agriculture and use of woodlands for potash, lum-ber, and pasture, were uninviting to emigrants. Other land in the northern third of the Purchase was encumbered with even more debt per acre, but the advance of the Erie Canal secured these debts and rendered property there a good deal more marketable.[26]

As the market for improved lands in the Holland Purchase diminished, closing the safety valve that permitted settlers to receive a fair compensa-tion for their labor, Jacob Otto put even more pressure on settlers by changing "the words of the contract, so that the settler could not sell, or

25. *RJE,* 2:1819, 271. See also Reports of David Evans, 1827, 441.
26. *RJE,* 2:1819, 271; David Evans to John J. Vanderkemp, June 12, 1827, Reel 173, HLCP; Reports of David Evans, 1827, 439–41. The figures on outstanding debt per acre are drawn from the Register of buyers, 1802–27.

transfer his right in it," unless Otto gave explicit permission in writing. The opportunity to exchange or sell an article constituted an important expression of individual market freedom in the Purchase because it served as the collateral security that allowed many settlers to borrow money. Throughout the first twenty years of settlement, articles of agreement were traded, exchanged, and transferred frequently. When Jacob Otto was appointed to replace Joseph Ellicott, Busti told his new resident agent that the practice of merchandising articles should be stopped. Otto followed Busti's advice but was surprised at the extent of the problem.

> The traffic in articles constitutes a large portion of the trade of this country. . . . Since the first settlement of this country it is probable that more money has passed between individuals in this transfer of contracts than has been received by the Company in the payment of lands. . . . An article has lately been shown to me, which has been transferred as good security for a debt of $2000 and the improvements of the land are fully worth the money, although this office has never received but 25 dollars, and that sum many years ago, when the article was first granted.[27]

The company intended that the new contractual stipulation, requiring the landlords' consent to any sale or transfer of land under contract, would help to correct the mistakes of Ellicott's administration. But it came at the worst possible time for the settlers when growing numbers of them despaired of ever gaining fee simple title to their farms. These settlers also worried that if they had to leave the Holland Purchase, they must abandon their improvements without receiving compensation for their labor.

"I think it my right . . . to get something for my improvement"

The Holland Company's efforts to reduce the land debt, rid the Purchase of woodchoppers, and protect its property from further ecological injury while encouraging intensive agriculture and commercial production for sale and profit sparked an open conflict between diverging conceptions of land and property. The landlords' commercial and entrepreneurial vision made land a cash-valued commodity like any other product of the Market Revolution. Land was a way to make money, an instrument

27. Reports of Jacob Otto, 1824, 372; Paul Busti to Jacob Otto, Sept. 30, 1821, Reel 168, HLCP; Reports of Jacob Otto, 1821–22, 304.

MAP 3. Outstanding dept per acre on land held under expired contracts in the Holland Purchase in 1827.

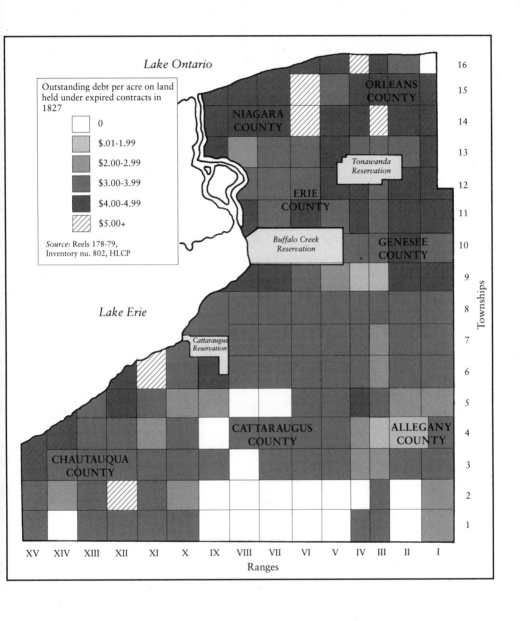

Lake Ontario

Outstanding debt per acre on land
held under expired contracts in
1827

	0
	$.01-1.99
	$2.00-2.99
	$3.00-3.99
	$4.00-4.99
	$5.00+

Source: Reels 178-79,
Inventory nu. 802, HLCP

ORLEANS
COUNTY

NIAGARA
COUNTY

Tonawanda
Reservation

ERIE
COUNTY

Buffalo Creek
Reservation

GENESEE
COUNTY

Lake Erie

Cattaraugus
Reservation

CATTARAUGUS
COUNTY

ALLEGANY
COUNTY

CHAUTAUQUA
COUNTY

16
15
14
13
12
11
10
9
8
7
6
5
4
3
2
1

Townships

XV XIV XIII XII XI X IX VIII VII VI V IV III II I

Ranges

of capital accumulation in the burgeoning market economy of the early nineteenth century. The settlers' agrarian conception viewed individual dominion over land as the basis of personal liberty and equality. The existence and perpetuation of the rural family household depended on a direct and essential relationship with land and the means of subsistence. These potentially contradictory conceptions of land coexisted for the first twenty years of settlement, the latent conflict submerged by the spirit of joint enterprise and cooperation that linked landlords and settlers in the Holland Purchase. But the company's new policies pressed the settlers for payments that were hard to come by in a cash-poor economy plagued by persistent stagnation made worse by the Panic of 1819.[28]

When the company began to press the settlers for payment, they accused it of trying to monopolize the flow of cash, believing this was part of the landlords' strategy to limit the individual managerial control they exercised as independent producers. When renewing an expired article, the landlords insisted on cash payment of 5 percent of the new purchase price. Despite its recently introduced payment in kind policy, the company refused to accept anything but cash as payment of principal.

Jacob Otto first detected the settlers' resentment following Busti's general address to them on July 9, 1821, when the company authorized "a deduction of 20 per cent" on all cash payments applied to current land contracts. Under this provision, if a settler paid fifty dollars, for instance, he was credited with sixty dollars. "It is a principle," Otto explained, "not calculated to produce any beneficial results to the poor, who, not being able to command cash, are unable to avail themselves of these advantages. Their land debts continue to accumulate and with that accumulation their articles are renewed; while the affluent settler, who is well qualified to pay, without any allowance of discount, all that is due on this land, enjoys exclusively, the benefits which the possession of cash confers." Otto concluded: "This grant of exclusive privileges has excited much discontent; for all want those benefits, which at present are only confined to a few."[29]

Agrarian philosophy held that privilege was the antithesis of equal rights. Privilege undercut equality and liberty by subjecting the many to the coercion of the few. Money was an instrument of privilege in a cash-

---

28. Christopher Clark, *The Roots of Rural Capitalism: Western Massachusetts, 1780–1860* (Ithaca, N.Y., 1990), 21–58; Charles Sellers, *The Market Revolution: Jacksonian America, 1815–1846* (New York, 1991), 165.

29. For company agents' demand for cash payments, see Jacob Otto to Paul Busti, June 22, 1822, Reel 171, HLCP; Staley Clarke to Jacob Otto, Dec. 26, 1822, Reel 175, HLCP; Reports of Jacob Otto, 1823, 349–50.

poor economy. Still, money had no intrinsic value; it had value only as it represented property. The landlords' income, like that of all interests dependent on the "nominal value of money," derived from payment received for principal and interest. In a frontier economy, where money was always scarce, the landlords' demand for cash kept the nominal value of money high and the actual price of labor and agricultural produce low. The settlers believed that the operation of a money economy under these circumstances deprived them of a fair return for their labor and property. As a grant of exclusive privileges for the few, the practice of allowing discounts for cash payments constituted an assault on the equality and liberty of the majority to whom this benefit was denied.[30]

It is important to emphasize that these rural people did not object to a cash economy per se; rather, they opposed the decided advantage that was handed to individuals who controlled the flow of cash in an economy in which it was in short supply. This fact helps to explain rural people's position on paper money. In general, they preferred hard money because it accorded with their agrarian belief that labor was the source of all economic value. But as the rhythm of market activity intensified and the demand for the use of cash became more widespread, rural people supported paper money as a remedy for protecting the labor and property of small producers. In the Holland Purchase the settlers believed they had two choices. They could protest the company's demands for cash payments or they could stand behind local leaders who favored distribution of paper money in amounts and on terms that would give their labor and property a fair exchange or market value. At times they did both.[31]

30. My discussion of agrarian values, money, and special privilege is based on Samuel Eliot Morison, ed., "William Manning's 'The Key of Libberty,'" *William and Mary Quarterly* 13 (1956), 218–19. See also Gordon S. Wood, *The Radicalism of the American Revolution* (New York, 1992), 279–80. See discussion of agrarian opposition to monopoly in Lawrence Frederick Kohl, *The Politics of Individualism: Parties and the American Character in the Jacksonian Era* (New York, 1989), 28–34. Christopher Clark has said that increasing use of cash in rural society constituted a key step in the development of rural capitalism (*Roots of Rural Capitalism*, 224–27).

31. The attitude of rural people toward paper money was complex and ambiguous, as Bray Hammond has pointed out. See his classic *Banks and Politics in America: From the Revolution to the Civil War* (Princeton, N.J., 1957), 628–29. In the Holland Purchase the settlers resisted the company's demands for cash payments because money was scarce, but they also supported Albert Tracy, who served three terms in Congress "riding the hobby" of two popular issues. Tracy criticized the only bank in the region because it was a tool of Joseph Ellicott and the Holland Land Company, and he criticized the company itself, alleging that the landlords intended to expropriate the settlers' labor and property. Tracy later served as a member of the first board of directors of the branch office of the Bank of the United States established at Buffalo in 1826. Tracy, like the settlers he represented, recog-

Moreover, demands for payment disrupted relations between the land-lord and settlers in the Holland Purchase. For two decades these relations were, for the most part, cooperative and conciliatory. Both sides appreci-ated that settlement of wild land was a joint venture in which the burdens and benefits were shared by landlords and settlers alike. Paul Busti and Joseph Ellicott viewed their relation with the settlers through one of the dominant metaphors of the age—patriarchal authority and responsibility. Both agents agreed that the company should practice "a kind of parental aid." Successful settlement and development required that the company exercise a firm but gentle hand, urging and directing the settlers to become good farmers.[32]

No doubt the patriarchal metaphor shaped the "liberality and lenient measures" for which the company was known. These measures included easy credit terms for settlers and company-subsidized construction of roads as well as grain and sawmills. Ellicott also helped secure the vital services of physicians and artisans for Batavia and other frontier com-munities in the Holland Purchase. But the settlers were not simply passive agents in their relationship with the company. During his long tenure as the company's general agent, Paul Busti admonished Ellicott again and again to treat the settlers kindly and fairly. He did so, in part, because he had a keen sense of the settlers' character; they were touchy and proud and quick to defend their birthright of liberty and equality. Busti knew they would not contenanace any transgression of their rights and espe-cially not at the hands of foreign landlords. Busti often received reports from Ellicott describing the settlers' readiness to take offense.[33]

In 1807, for instance, some Federalists in the Purchase challenged other settlers' right to vote because they were suspected of being Republicans. Many of the settlers in the Purchase, Ellicott told Busti, came from Ver-mont, "where the people are principally Republican and from the nature of their constitution almost every person is qualified for an elector." Despite the restrictions placed on the right to vote by the New York

---

nized the need for local banks as the regional economy became more complex. One Buffalo newspaper put it this way: "The business of this village, and of the surrounding region, upon every side, are hourly subjected to the most discouraging impediments to their advancement from the want of banking facilities" (*Buffalo Journal*, Feb. 10, 1829). For Albert Tracy, see DeAlva Stanwood Alexander, *A Political History of the State of New York*, 3 vols. (New York, 1906), 1:372–73, 397–98.

32. *RJE*, 1:1803, 238.

33. Paul Busti to Joseph Ellicott, Dec. 19, 1805, Joseph Ellicott Collection, Buffalo and Erie County Historical Society, Buffalo, N.Y.; cited hereafter as JEC; Joseph Ellicott to Paul Busti, May 22, 1807, JEC.

constitution of 1777, most of the early settlers holding land under an article of agreement were still allowed to vote. Consequently, when settlers from the surrounding countryside came to vote at Batavia in April 1807, having traveled in some instances up to twenty miles, and found their right to vote challenged, their tempers flared. Fights erupted outside the polling place, punches flew, and "bloody noses and black eyes" testified to the seriousness of this affront to liberty and equality.[34]

Pressing the settlers for cash payments also subverted traditional patterns of rural indebtedness in the western New York countryside. Household production for home consumption and local exchange created networks of obligation that blended into the reciprocity and interdependence of rural life. As settlers bartered and exchanged both goods and services, they became indebted to one another. Although historians must resist the temptation to sentimentalize these networks of obligation, the prosaic rhythm of creating new debts and paying old ones was governed by a widely shared and clearly understood ethic. This rural exchange ethic, as Christopher Clark points out, held "that debts would be paid as means were available and that legal action circumvented the normal processes of negotiation and accommodation that should occur between creditor and debtor."[35]

The agrarian ethic governing relations between creditor and debtor was rooted in a keen awareness of human frailty. The settlers of the Holland Purchase knew firsthand the capricious reality of misfortune and disaster—a crop destroyed by hail, a barn set afire by a bolt of lightning, a young child suddenly overtaken by fever and death. The frontier households of the Holland Purchase lived on the margin between achieving a comfortable subsistence and experiencing the deprivation of scarcity and want. Theirs was a world in which the uncertainty and unpredictability of nature's forces buffeted the lives and prospects of all human beings. Therefore, when a settler told the company he could not pay because of

---

34. Joseph Ellicott to Paul Busti, May 22, 1807, JEC.

35. Clark, *Roots of Rural Capitalism*, 33, 37–38, 47; Wood, *Radicalism of the American Revolution*, 67–68; Peter J. Coleman, *Debtors and Creditors in America: Insolvency, Imprisonment for Debt, and Bankruptcy, 1607–1900* (Madison, Wisc., 1974), 111–12; Bruce H. Mann, *Neighbors and Strangers: Law and Community in Early Connecticut* (Chapel Hill, N.C., 1987); David P. Szatmary, *Shays' Rebellion: The Making of an Agrarian Insurrection* (Amherst, Mass., 1980), 19–36; George Dangerfield, *Chancellor Robert R. Livingston of New York, 1746–1813* (New York, 1960), 200–201; David M. Ellis, *Landlords and Farmers in the Hudson-Mohawk Region, 1790–1850* (Ithaca, N.Y., 1946), 88–90; Neil A. McNall, *An Agricultural History of the Genesee Valley, 1790–1860* (Philadelphia, 1952), 17–51, 60, 102–3, 210–27; Sung Bok Kim, *Landlord and Tenant in Colonial New York: Manorial Society, 1664–1775* (Chapel Hill, N.C., 1978), 219–20.

sickness, injury, crop failure, or hard times, he or she expected the agent to take those circumstances into consideration. They were part of life, and creditors were obligated to adjust demands and expectations of payment accordingly.

Even when the Holland Land Company dismissed Ellicott and decided the settlers had enjoyed "sufficient indulgence" and that it was now time to insist that they "fulfill their engagements," the settlers continued the agrarian tradition of appealing to and negotiating with company agents over the terms of their land contracts. From the township of China in southern Genesee County, Lemuel Paul asked company agents for more time to pay in December 1824. He acknowledged that he had possessed his lot for ten years and "nothing is paid but the five percent." "My intention is to do all I can," he explained, despite the "disappointments so common to many." Another settler, Mylo Warner, had possession of a lot articled to someone else that was about to be resold. He conceded "the propriety and justice of . . . demands of interest and the obligation of those in possession of lands to pay arrearages that have been so long due. But my misfortunes and embarrassments have been such," he noted, "that I have been unable to pay." Warner anticipated selling "a pair or two of oxen" and some grain "in the course of another season" and told Otto to expect payment then.[36]

In November 1824 Polly Pattison pleaded with Jacob Otto to save her small farm in the township of Royalton in Niagara County. Her husband had recently sold it "for a trifling consideration." Norman Pattison was drunk at the time. "I do humbly trust you will not suffer me and my children to be turned out of door to the mercy of the world," she wrote. Four of Mrs. Pattison's neighbors corroborated her story, confirming that Norman Pattison was a drunk and a wife beater and that he had sold his article "for much less than its real value."[37]

Similarly, four settlers from Franklinville in Cattaraugus County wrote Otto to "represent the case of Mrs. Betsy Rawson." A widow, Mrs. Rawson faced ejectment unless she made some payment by January 1, 1825. She had six small children "wholly dependent on her exertions for support." Otto was asked to issue a new contract for six or eight years, enough time for the children to reach "suitable ages to put out to trades and obtain a livelihood for themselves." Mrs. Rawson's farm had twenty acres cleared and "a good log house all of which she must lose on the

36. Reports of Jacob Otto, 1821–22, 296; Lemuel Paul to Jacob Otto, Dec. 25, 1824, and Mylo Warner to Jacob Otto, Dec. 27, 1824, Reel 152, HLCP.

37. Polly Pattison to Jacob Otto, Nov. 23, 1824, and John Garsy, Samuel White, Levi Bixby, and Benjamin Hale to whom it may concern, Sept. 29, 1824, Reel 152, HLCP.

account of not being able to pay any part of either principal or interest." The case of Mrs. Rawson points to the primary source of the settlers' rising discontent and anger after 1821. Even though the company threatened legal action against delinquent settlers more often than it resorted to actual proceedings, the mere threat of ejectment and losing one's possessions challenged fundamental agrarian beliefs about liberty, labor, and property. Settlers feared the landlords' coercion because it threatened their livelihood and their status as free people. In the male-dominated patriarchal society of Jacksonian America, to be coerced or dominated by another white man was slavery.[38]

The bountiful person-to-land ratio of early America, agrarians believed, was the great counterweight offsetting the power and privilege of the few who sought to control government for their own selfish purposes. The generous ratio of land to labor gave labor a dignity and worth that was truly dynamic. Labor was no longer a badge of servility or a consequence of divine punishment or even something most human beings did only to subsist. The opportunity to take a portion of land and natural resources from the common stock of wilderness, a claim that was established and validated by labor and sometimes by violence against Native Americans, became the foundation of liberty and equality in early nineteenth-century America.[39]

In the Holland Land Purchase, the right to dominion over the land one's labor improved undergirded the settlers' rebellions of 1836 and 1844–45. But even before popular violence erupted, company efforts to coerce land payments elicited individual assertions of the right of improvement. Faced with the threat of ejectment in August 1825, Ezekiel Taylor told the company he would not leave until he received compensation for his labor. "I think it my right to hold and try to get something for my improvement." In Niagara County a dispute between Samuel Lindley and James Ferguson over an article of agreement prompted the latter to swear that neither Lindley nor the Holland Land Company "could ever get him off until he was paid for the betterments." In Cattaraugus County, Benjamin Waterman could not pay for his land, yet he refused to surrender the lot without compensation of "some kind" for his improvement. When another settler spoke with Otto about taking an article on this lot,

38. Elias Haskins, Charles Howell, Joseph Beebe, Seth Markam, and John Tracy to Jacob Otto, Sept. 17, 1824, ibid. See also William Mitchell, Joseph Gastland, and Chester Moffett to Jacob Otto, Oct. 20, 1823, Reel 151, HLCP.
39. Wood, *Radicalism of the American Revolution*, 170–71, 413 n. 50; Alan Taylor, *Liberty Men and Great Proprietors: The Revolutionary Settlement on the Maine Frontier, 1760–1820* (Chapel Hill, N.C., 1990), 25, 28. See also my discussion of labor in the Introduction, esp. note 13.

Waterman became incensed. "B. Waterman . . . was very angry with me,"
Kellogg Vosburgh told Jacob Otto, "because I called on you on the subject of the lot which he is on and swears that I should not have a foot
of the land on any conditions." In May 1824 Samuel Cleveland protested
that his land had been transferred by the company's agent for Chautauqua
County to Cleveland's father. "After a man has spent the best of his
days and strength to change the wilderness into fruitful fields," he ex-
claimed, "and if after he has labored fourteen years to have it taken a way
from him by fraud and lies without ever having a hearing it is as much
as I can bear." Cleveland ended by warning that God's justice would
triumph in the end. "For vengeance is mine and I will repay saith the
Lord."[40]

Historians and theorists of private property have found that whenever
property has been evenly distributed among independent artisans and
farmers, the idea that labor was the source of all economic value and
property gained wide acceptance. Equally important if less appreciated is
the fact that in the early American republic this labor theory of property
operated in tandem with a new view of labor. Labor became the primary
agent of liberty and equality. Together these agrarian conceptions of land
and property and labor and liberty encouraged land use practices and
privatism of resource use that led to soil exhaustion, deforestation, and
what many environmentalists today characterize as ecological degradation. But in the Holland Purchase during the early nineteenth century
these agrarian ideas transformed battles over the use and meaning of land
into a greater struggle to sustain the personal liberty and economic independence of small producers. The Market Revolution with its massive
concentrations of wealth and power, its entrepreneurial conception of
land, and its capitalist doctrine of private property threatened to separate
small settlers from managerial control over the means of subsistence and
production.[41]

The right to property did not have a single or precise meaning in early
America. It referred, for instance, to the procedural safeguards of the Fifth
Amendment. The right of property was also linked to enfranchisement.
The Pennsylvania constitution of 1776 recognized "certain natural, inher-

40. Ezekiel Taylor to Samuel Haight, Aug. 14, 1825, and Samuel Haight to Jacob Otto,
Aug. 14, 1825, Reel 152, HLCP; Sam Lindley to Jacob Otto, April 2, 1827, Benjamin
Waterman to Jacob Otto, Nov. 25, 1826, and Kellogg Vosburgh to Jacob Otto, Jan. 29,
1827, Reel 153, HLCP; Samuel Cleveland to Jacob Otto, May 27, 1824, Reel 151, HLCP.
41. Richard Schlatter, *Private Property: The History of an Idea* (London, 1951), 160. For
frontier land use and environmental historians, see Chapter 2.

ent, and unalienable rights" belonging to all men. These included "enjoying and defending life and liberty, acquiring, possessing, and protecting
property." By the early nineteenth century, as we have seen in the Holland
Purchase, the right of property meant the fair and equal opportunity of
free white men to become independent patriarchal farmers. Thomas Hart
Benton expressed this ideal for the nation when proclaiming that "the
lands belong to the people."[42]

Creating an independent rural household in the Holland Purchase required access to and control over large amounts of fresh or fully regenerated land because the internal dynamics of this agrarian culture rested on
family labor, extensive agricultural practices, and transmission to the next
generation of the resources needed to carry forward. Property was the
essential objective, but the agrarian conception of property required that
land and other means of subsistence and production remain under the
complete managerial control of individual proprietors. No free person's
access to the means of subsistence and production should depend on the
authority and consent of another.[43]

Agrarian culture made a crucial distinction between property with use
value and that having only exchange or market value. "Genuine" property
combined both values. Such property had immediate use and subsistence
value, but it also could be sold or exchanged in the marketplace. This form
of property made a man free by giving him full managerial control over
the means necessary to earn a decent living. Neither his life nor his liberty
depended on the consent or power of another. Property that possessed
only market value left and individual at the mercy of the "prices current"
column of the local newspaper.[44]

42. William B. Scott, *In Pursuit of Happiness: American Conceptions of Property from
the Seventeenth to the Twentieth Century* (Bloomington, Ind., 1977), 53. The Pennsylvania
constitution of 1776 is quoted in Francis S. Philbrick, "Changing Conceptions of Property in
Law," *University of Pennsylvania Law Review* 86 (May 1938), 714. Benton is quoted in
Daniel Feller, *The Public Lands in Jacksonian Politics* (Madison, Wisc., 1984), 77. Thomas
Le Duc has said: "It was Benton who perfected, if he did not conceive, the doctrine that since
the national resources belonged to the people, any one of those people had a moral right to
appropriate permanently timber, minerals or land surface" (Le Duc, "History and Appraisal
of U.S. Land Policy to 1862," in Howard W. Ottoson, ed., *Land Use Policy and Problems in
the United States* [Lincoln, Neb., 1962], 12).
43. See Paul Conkin's discussion of the agrarian proprietary ideal in Conkin, *The Southern Agrarians* (Knoxville, Tenn., 1988), 106–25.
44. Allen Tate, "Notes on Liberty and Property," in Herbert Agar and Allen Tate, eds.,
Who Owns America? A New Declaration of Independence (Boston, 1936), 80–93; Scott, *In
Pursuit of Happiness*, 194–96. See also G. Edward White, *The Marshall Court and Cultural
Change, 1815–1835*, vols. 3–4 of the *History of the Supreme Court of the United States*, ed.
Paul Freund and Stanley Katz (New York, 1988), 755.

In the Holland Purchase cattle fit the description of "genuine" property. Cattle constituted the principal property of a majority of the settlers. They were raised for drawing loads and pulling farm implements, but they were also a vital source of milk, cheese, butter, and beef. Their use and subsistence value was clear, yet they had a market value too. Local storekeepers accepted cattle for cash or trade. Even the Holland Land Company received cattle as payment for land. Because these animals had both use and market value, their owners had the relatively free choice between keeping their livestock and selling or "turning out" a few during the fall after the main work season had passed.[45]

THE conflict between the landlords' capitalist ideas of land use and property rights and the settlers' agrarian sentiments was analyzed by Jacob Otto in his first annual report. Otto divided the settlers into two classes. The first group consisted of settlers with "sober industrious habits." Their lands featured "good buildings" and "well cultivated fields" that were protected from roving livestock by "lawful" fences. "The second class of settlers are those who remain on the land originally taken up by them without the hope of ever being able to pay for it," Otto explained. "Their improvements are inconsiderable and in many instances scarcely deserve the name."[46]

The distinction drawn by Otto points to the new moral value of productive labor. The first group of settlers were "sober" and "industrious," possessing "lands considerably improved," whereas the second group were lazy and miserably poor. Their "inconsiderable" improvements testified to their aversion for hard work. Otto used the age's new attitude toward productive labor to stigmatize delinquent settlers for not working hard enough, but he was really declaring the landlords' preference for wheat farming and commercial agriculture over an extractive economy that harvested the varied resources of the forest. For the company to receive regular land payments, the settlers had to produce an agricultural surplus. This meant bringing their frontier farm households into the market economy, and experience showed that wheat was the commodity that brought small farmers into the marketplace.[47]

After a settler "fitted" his fields for cultivation of wheat, Otto believed it would be easy for him to pay for his land. The soil was fertile and fairly easy to till. Coercing or luring settlers out of their mixed woodland econ-

---

45. Wyckoff, *Developer's Frontier,* 161; Paul Busti to Joseph Ellicott, Oct. 24, 1804, JEC.
46. Reports of Jacob Otto, 1821–22, 295–96, 298.
47. Ibid., 295; Sellers, *Market Revolution,* 16.

omy, both tactics the company tried, was clearly the key. "In a new country few men are affluent," Otto observed, "and almost every man labours for the support and comfort of his family. My leading object has been to demonstrate to them that mere support is unworthy of their exertions; and that by a judicious occupation of the soil it will yield them, beyond all doubt, an annual surplus, which, in a short time, would suffice to pay for the land on which they reside."[48]

Not all the settlers shared the company's convictions about the region's potential for wheat farming. Some openly disagreed with its assessment. "Dear Sir—What kind of respectability," a settler named C. Joselyn wrote to the company, "do you suppose is necessary for me to bury myself in the wilds of *Cattaraugus*? I have been assessed by a knave, and you have been credulous enough to believe him." Apparently Josslyn's lot and improvements had become the subject of an informer's report to the company, and as a consequence he was judged a woodchopper and told that he must pay up or leave. Joselyn's sarcastic note pointed out that from the settler's perspective the company's expectations about wheat farming, for at least most of the Purchase, were unrealistic. Furthermore, its expectations directly interfered with a settler's freedom to choose and manage his own livelihood.[49]

It was widely believed that the hilly uplands of the Holland Purchase were better adapted for pasturing livestock, making maple sugar, manufacturing potash, and milling lumber than for commercial horticulture. Haratio G. Spafford's popular *Gazetteer of the State of New York* (1824), for example, praised the region's suitability for raising livestock. Spafford described the township of China, in the southwestern corner of Genesee County, as "better adapted to the growth of grass than grain." He described the township of Sheldon, situated just to the north, as being "heavily timbered: a beech and maple country better for grass than grain, but excellent for stock and dairy farming." The township of Concord in Erie County was "a good grazing country." Nearby Collins, just to the west, was rated "a good country for dairy farmers, from Yankee-land but miserable for the horse-keeping, grain farmers of the Mohawk country."[50]

With a few exceptions, the Holland Purchase lacked, according to contemporary evaluations, the rich alluvial bottomlands characteristic of good grain country. Consequently, most farm lots did not include the

48. Reports of Jacob Otto, 1824, 364.
49. C. Josslyn to Jacob Otto, Oct. 13, 1824, Reel 152, HLCP.
50. Spafford, *Gazetteer* (1824), 113, 489, 128, 124.

desirable mix of arable bottomland or intervale to go along with upland meadows, pastures, and woodlands. The elevated table lands of Genesee, Erie, Cattaraugus, and Chautauqua counties yielded sufficient grain for home consumption but not enough for full-scale market production.[51]

The settlers valued the woodland resources of the upland because they were, for most part, ready to harvest. The old-growth woodlands could be grazed by livestock and tapped for maple sugar with little labor. Exploiting the timber for potash and lumber required more effort but not as much as wheat or other field crops. Before wheat could be sown, cultivated, and harvested, fields had to be cleared and fenced. And local fencing regulations put the burden of fencing out livestock on the owners of cultivated fields. Fencing was a labor problem because construction and maintenance of "lawful" enclosures required heavy inputs of labor. The problem with more intensive agriculture, then, was not so much the lack of capital but the scarcity of labor. Most settlers had been drawn to the Genesee Country by the bounty of woodland resources found there, and they built a frontier economy that took advantage of nature's abundance.

While agrarian concern for individual managerial control over the means of subsistence and resources of production encouraged the settlers to invest their energy in goods and property that had subsistence as well as market value, it also promoted the idea of common use property. Even though the Holland Land Company had legal title to over 3.3 million acres of land in western New York, common use practices governed actual settlement of the region. Just as settlers pastured their livestock on any land not enclosed by a fence, they also organized communal work parties known as bees to harvest timber from vacant land, using it to build cabins, barns, schools, and meetinghouses. They also gathered timber on and off their farms to craft the wooden tools, containers, and household implements needed for subsistence and local exchange.[52]

Where the settlers saw reasonable use of a resource properly held and enjoyed in common the company saw acts of trespass and depredation. When Seth Wetmore reported from Allegany County on the amount of timber taken from vacant lands, the company threatened the offenders with suits of trespass. But the use of timber documented by Wetmore's statement was perfectly in keeping with the settlers' agrarian tradition of common use rights. Two brothers named Young had used the lumber made from three small pine trees to help build a schoolhouse. Daniel

51. Ibid., 124; Elisa Smith to Jacob Otto, March 8, 1823, Reel 151, HLCP.
52. T. R. Clark to David Evans, Nov. 24, 1827, Reel 153, HLCP; Van Wagenen, *Golden Age of Homespun*, 103–11, 141–60.

Jackman had used the timber from a fallen pine tree "for cooper stuff." Elijah Hyde and Timothy Buckland had harvested several pine trees and "made use of them to cover [their] buildings."[53]

The settlers freely conceded, however, that in some instances timber was being cut recklessly. The critical distinction they made concerned how the timber was used. William Campbell has employed some men "in cutting oak timber and working it into staves," a settler reported to David Evans in April 1828. The informant saw "heaps of staves" along the Ridge Road; Campbell's "workmen and teams" could be seen "passing daily." This anonymous settler reported that Campbell boasted he was not afraid of the Holland Land Company or any suit it might bring. In the town of Porter, Conrad Zittle and Thomas Clevelin charged that timber destruction was the work of a "gang of Canadians." "We feel very sorry to have our country robbed of so good a lot of timber as that is."[54]

Similarly, David Maxwell reported to company agents in March 1828 that "stave stealers have commenced cutting all the oak timber off of the lot where I live," complaining, "they have got a great many trees down." Maxwell volunteered to stop the illegal cutting if the company authorized him to act. "I will do it cheerfully without any fee or reward. . . . It is too bad," he added, "to have all the rail timber stolen let it belong to whom it will." Maxwell made an interesting distinction here. The "stave stealers" were criminals because they sold the timber for cash to contractors on the canal. Common use rights belonged only to resident settlers who cut timber for improvements on the farm or in the local community. The unfenced timber resources should be reserved for settlers who operated as small independent producers.[55]

A settler named Bepal complained about the destruction of valuable oak timber in the "vicinity of the canal." "There are instances of whole companies of people from other towns and even distant counties cutting timber and making staves at a great rate on lots where they pretend to have obtained a purchase of some old article or a right to cut timber from some non resident holder of an article without so much as clearing . . . a garden." Bepal reported that a man named Cavy cut oak timber and sold it to "stave makers from a distance at a low rate for cash." Similarly, some settlers from Cambria in Niagara County condemned Jervais Rose for

53. Statement of the amount of timber cut on vacant lands in the town of Eagle, Allegany County, March 19, 1825, Reel 152, HLCP.
54. Settler to David Evans, April 17, 1828, Reel 153, HLCP; Conrad Zittle and Thomas Clevelin to Jacob Otto, Dec. 22, 1824, Reel 152, HLCP.
55. David Maxwell to David Evans, March 4, 1828, Reel 153, HLCP.

cutting timber and recommended that the land should go to a settler named William Merchant. Rose is "cutting and selling the pine timber," they explained, ". . . without any intention of paying for said lot and that he is converting the profits arising there from to other purposes than to the improvement of the said lot." Conversely, William Merchant had lived on the lot for a year, paid taxes, and made some improvements. "He has not cut nor destroyed the timber [which meant he used timber only for actual settlement purposes]. We therefore pray . . . let the said Merchant have the lot that Justice may be done on the premises."[56]

The settlers' hostility toward the so-called stave stealers was complex and somewhat contradictory. They were angry partly because many of these woodcutters were nonresidents, but some of the resentment seems to have been based on the fact that their operations were commercial. Yet many of the settlers engaged in small-scale lumber production for the external markets at Montreal and Pittsburgh. The ambiguity inherent in these condemnations of the stave stealers is deeply revealing. The agrarian conception of land and productive resources contained a set of elements that were wide enough to foster a spirit of both resistance and accommodation to the Market Revolution.[57]

The rising conflict for control of the unfenced woodland resources in the Holland Purchase was actually a struggle over property rights. Specifically, it was a fight between a tradition recognizing an absolute right of private property only when land was enclosed by a fence and in actual use and the emerging capitalist doctrine. Even though land lost its status as a special form of property under the latter doctrine, the right of property promoted by the Market Revolution became more absolute, moving toward the triumphant liberal notion that made property a private zone of freedom and autonomy beyond the reach of government or community imposition. This triumphant liberal notion ultimately justified the hierarchical domination of small producers that the earlier tradition of property rights had stood firmly against.[58]

56. L. Bepal to Jacob Otto, Nov. 16, 1826, Charles Deefoe, Amos Phillips, Truman Beach, and David Allen to the Agents for the Holland Land Company, Feb. 23, 1827; see also Jeremiah Whipple to Jacob Otto, Dec. 2, 1826, Reel 153, HLCP.

57. See Paul Goodman, "The Emergence of Homestead Exemption in the United States: Accommodation and Resistance to the Market Revolution, 1840–1880," *Journal of American History* 80 (Sept. 1993), 470–98.

58. Elizabeth Mensch, "The Colonial Origins of Liberal Property Rights," *Buffalo Law Review* 31 (Fall 1982), 735. For common use rights, see Stephen Hahn, "Hunting, Fishing, and Foraging: Common Rights and Class Relations in the Postbellum South," *Radical History Review* 26 (Oct. 1982), 37–64.

Throughout the early American countryside fences marked the boundary between common use resources and those that could be set aside for the exclusive enjoyment of truly private ownership. Symbolically and juridically, fences cordoned off the property that was enclosed, protecting it from intrusion by domestic livestock or anyone else. Rules of trespass in colonial New York, for instance, required a plaintiff to show a fence. By the mid-eighteenth century these rules no longer required a fence, but without one an owner was likely to recover minimal damages. Although the common use tradition of cutting timber on another person's property also became more limited as the eighteenth century progressed, this was in part owing to the special status accorded pine trees because of the crown's interest in naval stores.[59]

The tradition of property featured throughout the countryside was an outgrowth of the munificent person-to-land ratio of early America. It was a tradition that encouraged labor, cultivation, and improvement. It was thus ideally suited for a new country where the need to promote agriculture and economic development justified some intrusions on the right of property. "The sense of property is graciously bestowed on mankind," Chancellor James Kent observed in his *Commentaries on American Law,* "for the purpose of rousing them from sloth, and stimulating them to action." Encouraging cultivation and creation of property in early America, where the ratio of land to labor was high, required that the law protect labor's claim to any improvements it made. "We have a statute in New York relative to lands," Kent explained, "in what was formerly called the military tract, which declares that the settler on those lands, under colour of a bona fide purchase, should not be divested of his possession or recovery, by the real owner, until the former had been paid the value of his improvements made on the land."[60]

The high ratio of land to labor formed the demographic context in which Paul Busti and Joseph Ellicott had crafted their strategy for settling the Holland Purchase. Busti and Ellicott appreciated how the great ex-

---

59. Mensch, "Colonial Origins of Liberal Property Rights," 674–75, 725, 726.

60. James Kent, *Commentaries on American Law,* 4 vols. (New York, 1840), 2:319, 335–37. The improvement law to which Kent refers is found in *Laws of New York,* April 8, 1813, chap. 80. For a discussion of improvement laws, see Paul W. Gates, "Tenants of the Log Cabin," *Mississippi Valley Historical Review* 49 (June 1962), 3–31. The conflict over property rights and the right of improvement was at issue in the Supreme Court case of *Green v. Biddle* (1823). See *Green v. Biddle,* 8 Wheaton 1, (1823), 57, and Charles Warren, *The Supreme Court in United States History,* 2 vols. (rev. ed.; Boston, 1926), 1:637–42. For an examination of Maine's Betterment Acts, see Taylor, *Liberty Men and Great Proprietors,* 220–25, 226, 227, 228, 230, 235, 242, 358 n. 33, 362 n. 2, 366 n. 17.

panse of unsettled land in America complicated their task. As they considered changes in company policy during the first years of settlement, they often doubted whether any strategy could overcome the great disparity between land and settlers. Nevertheless, Ellicott worked to attract as many settlers as possible to the Holland Purchase. But attracting yeomen farm families depended on the landlords' ability to treat the settlers with "a lenient hand" for as long as it took to get the territory "pretty well settled." Aside from not "crowding" the settlers "for their payments," pursuing the necessary "lenient measures" also meant accommodating the settlers' common use land practices and agrarian system of property rights.[61]

The problem was that settlers' agrarian ideas about labor, land, and property rights were not ultimately compatible with the landlords' desire to establish hierarchical control over land and its commercial development. These traditions were necessary in a new country, but as intrusions upon the right of property, landlords and jurists wished to discard them as soon as a critical mass of settlement and development was reached. When the Holland Land Company set about in 1821 to change its administration of the Purchase, the landlords signaled their belief that critical mass had been achieved. Yet the transition to a purely market conception of land use and property rights, which the landlords desired, was more complicated and difficult than they seemed to allow. It entailed a great deal more than cultivating a few additional acres and putting up good fences. At issue was a fight between capitalists and agrarians to control the use and meaning of land.[62]

"The immense debt now due to the Holland Company"

The company's efforts to make the settlers pay, rid the Purchase of woodchoppers, and lure or coerce them into commercial agriculture caught the settlers at a difficult time. As the company tired to impose greater control over land use and the buying and selling of possession claims, growing debt and slumping land values impeded the settlers' principal goal of creating new property while enjoying the opportunity to keep or sell their improvements as they chose. At the same time, the company's

    61. Paul Busti to Joseph Ellicott, March 9, 1802, June 5, 1804, JEC; *RJE*, 1:1804, 261; *RJE*, 2:1809, 28.
    62. Kent, *Commentaries on American Law,* 2:337.

strong encouragement of grain cultivation interfered with the settlers' commitment to operate as independent producers. The settlers' problems were particularly acute in the middle and southern hill country of the Purchase.

The most comprehensive statement of these settlers' grievances appeared in a memorial sent to the company's general agent, John J. Vanderkemp. Meeting at Ellicottville on February 21, 1834, where they drafted a memorial describing "the deplorable condition of this portion of the Purchase," the settlers petitioned for whatever relief their condition warranted and the agents' authority might provide. The memorial explained that the settlers' woodland economy did not generate enough cash to accommodate the landlords' demand for payment, nor could it be transformed into the farmland economy of wheat and grain production that the landlords wanted. "If the present state of things must continue, the nominal amount of the debt must be increased instead of diminished and the hope is but a doubtful one that any considerable number of our farmers can ever extinguish their land debt from their agricultural pursuits in tilling the soil."[63]

Cattaraugus County, with its steep hills and narrow valleys, was not well suited for tillage. The growing season was short and unpredictable. "The great elevation of the country and its blighting and blasting frosts have become proverbial," the settlers explained, "but among the most serious inconveniences under which we labor is the general variableness and instability of our climate, by operation of which nearly one half of the useful time of the farmer is forever lost." Wheat could not be cultivated and was early abandoned as a general crop. Potatoes and oats were better adapted to the growing conditions of Cattaraugus County, but neither had any real market value. The potential of the region for raising cattle had also been exaggerated. "Woods cattle" could survive on the "scanty pittance" provided by native pastures, but these animals had limited value in the livestock markets of Philadelphia.[64]

The completion of the Erie Canal in 1825 brought a market "nearer than before," the memorial continued, but its impact was limited because the settlers "had no productions of the earth to sell." In fact, the Erie Canal had made the settlers' struggle in Cattaraugus even harder. "The construction of that canal has operated injuriously upon us," the hill country settlers complained. The lure of the canal had drawn labor and

63. Memorial from Cattaraugus settlers to J. J. Vanderkemp and the local subagents, Reel 90, HLCP.
64. Ibid.; B. Churchman to Jacob Otto, Sept. 28, 1824, Reel 152, HLCP.

capital away from Cattaraugus County. Moreover, the produce of the county was not sufficient to pay for the merchandise imported and consumed by the settlers. The isolation of Cattaraugus made it more costly to transport store goods from the Genesee River than to move the same property from New York to the Genesee River. Subsistence farming persisted in Cattaraugus "not withstanding the settlement of this country had been some twenty years in progress." The settlers still labored under "the ordinary disadvantages attending the settlement of a new country."[65]

But if the settlers of Cattaraugus could not meet the landlords' expectations about land development, of much greater seriousness, they could no longer fulfill the expectations they had set for themselves. They could no longer mix their labor with wilderness secure in the knowledge that as free men they enjoyed full dominion over the fruits of their labor. The "immense debt" owed to the company had effectively destroyed a large portion of the material gains that the opportunity to mix labor with land had once provided. "The whole country," the settlers explained, "is embarrassed and opposed by the depression of the times, as well as the conviction that unless some relief shall be extended to it, it will be beyond the power of the settlers to extricate themselves from their embarrassments, and that conviction itself is daily producing results disastrous to the prosperity of the country." Land prices had sunk so low that farms could be sold for only half what they were worth. "At this moment," the settlers asserted, "nothing but the impossibility of disposing of their property here, consisting of their possessions and improvements, prevents a general and alarming depopulation of the country." Too many settlers had lost their incentive to work and improve their farms. The memorial called upon the company to cancel part of each settler's land debt.[66]

Company agents for the most part accepted the memorial's conclusions, yet they did not fully understand the implications. "The memorial . . . fully and accurately sets forth the true situation of the County," the local subagent wrote. David Evans, the resident agent at Batavia, sent a copy of the memorial to company officials in Philadelphia, along with some remarks. "It has for some time past appeared quite evident to my mind," Evans noted, "that a very considerable portion of the present inhabitants can never pay for the land they occupy." Settlers living in "a great part" of Cattaraugus, Allegany, along with "the south parts of Genesee and Erie and a small portion of Chautauqua," were "similarly situated." The Hol-

65. Memorial from Cattaraugus settlers.
66. Ibid.

land Purchase, particularly the hill country townships south of the village of Buffalo Creek, had become a mecca for "the poorer classes" who could not afford to pay cash for cheaper federal government lands in Michigan territory and the states of Indiana and Illinois. But the poverty of these settlers was their own fault. Contrary to the Cattaraugus memorial's allegations about the deficiency of the climate and growing conditions, Evans argued that the land could be "made good for grazing." If it was "well cleared and cultivated," the land yielded hay, oats, peas, potatoes, and turnips. Similarly, "sufficient wheat, rye and Indian corn" could be produced. The "principal cause of the failure to grow sufficient grain" for home consumption with enough left over to cover annual debts, including land debt, was the persistent habit of "appropriating more land than labor to the object." Evans concluded that the Cattaraugus settlers were poor and would likely remain so because their economic culture was based on the logic of conserving labor rather than land.[67]

With these comments, Evans touched upon the fundamental conflict between the company's corporate culture and the settlers' agrarian and egalitarian culture. The landlords' corporate expectations of profit required that the settlers produce an annual surplus, a portion of which could be paid to the company as principal and interest. Producing such a surplus depended on the cultivation of wheat; it also depended on fields that were well cleared, tilled, and enclosed by good fences to protect the valuable grain. The principal resource needed to make an annual surplus of grain was heavy and intensive inputs of labor.

Evans stigmatized the hill country settlers for being lazy and not working hard enough. His condemnation was ironic because the settlers viewed the opportunity to labor as the cornerstone of their equality and liberty. In fact, there was little disagreement between this company agent and the settlers concerning the value of productive labor. All agreed that labor was the source of property and economic value. But this consensus did not resolve the problem of who owned the property that labor created. The settlers' agrarian beliefs warned that the landlords, like all moneyed capitalists, desired to live without labor; hence they were wholly dependent upon appropriating a portion of the settlers' annual produce. The conflict between landlord and settler also involved the question of managerial control over land and productive resources. Should small amounts of labor be applied to large areas of land or should labor and capital be

67. Staley Clarke to David Evans, March 8, 1834, Reel 175, HLCP; Reports of David Evans, 1834, 505–6.

invested more intensively? The settlers saw this as principally a matter of control over the means of subsistence. Because these small producers generally lacked the capacity to increase productivity through a greater expenditure of labor and capital, company efforts to promote higher levels of productivity undercut their goals of economic independence and individual proprietary dominion. In the Holland Land Purchase the company's hierarchical market objectives were on a collision course with an agrarian culture that had been molded by the land-labor ratios of early America.[68]

68. See Schlatter, *Private Property*, 182–85.

5

The Agrarian Convention of 1827

Not only small producers held agrarian sentiments or opposed the
hierarchical domination of the Holland Land Company. Agrarian
culture was complex and ambiguous; by the early nineteenth century its
conception of land and property rights was an admixture of market ideas
and more traditional rural notions. Its producer ideology operated in
concert with changes in the law of property that encouraged putting land
into actual use over leaving it idle. But its commitment to keeping the
nation a society of small producers and property holders was not compatible with the concentration of wealth and property an open and mobile
capitalist economy was sure to create.[1]

During the early nineteenth century, agrarian sentiments served a wide
diversity of interests. John Taylor and his fellow Virginia Old Republicans
ultimately used agrarian ideas about government and the exercise of authority to bolster states' rights and their defense of slavery. William Manning, an uneducated New England farmer and tavern keeper, like count-
less other yeomen and small producers, appealed to agrarian principles to
shield themselves from economic degradation and oppression. Meanwhile, politicians exploited the agrarian dread of moneyed aristocrats and
nonproducers to woo voters and win elections. "Politicians sought con-

---

1. For a provocative discussion of how the traditional agrarian conception of land as
family security and economic independence could be given statutory protection during the
age of the Market Revolution in a way that embodied both accommodation and resistance to
capitalist transformation, see Paul Goodman, "The Emergence of Homestead Exemption in
the United States: Accommodation and Resistance to the Market Revolution, 1840–1880,"
Journal of American History 80 (Sept. 1993), 470–98.

stantly to 'ride a hobby,' as they said: to locate and exploit a popular issue." The favorite target of popular political attacks was often some concentration of power, public or private, that allegedly manipulated government for its own selfish purposes or accumulated wealth without "the ordinary process of mental and physical labor."[2]

In the Holland Land Purchase local political and entrepreneurial elites appealed to agrarian sentiments and ideas in their struggle with the foreign landlords for control of the region. Agrarians of every persuasion believed that moneyed men used their political power to bend government and the marketplace to their own selfish ends. These few oppressed and exploited the producing majority by expropriating a portion of the property and economic value that labor created. The expropriation took the form of interest payments, taxes, and legal fees and even extended to control over the money supply and medium of exchange. But the ultimate objective was always the same. The moneyed few wished to reap profit without expending any actual labor.[3]

This chapter examines how two local politicians and developers in the Purchase used agrarian sentiments to promote their own vision of economic development. Living in an age when government promotion of economic growth became the central dynamic of American politics, both Albert Tracy and Peter B. Porter sought to build a political alliance that could effectively foster the rise of the West. Both men concluded that the

---

2. Charles Sellers, *The Market Revolution: Jacksonian America, 1815–1846* (New York, 1991), 120, 138–39, 166; Samuel Eliot Morison, ed., "William Manning's 'The Key of Libberty,'" *William and Mary Quarterly* 13 (1956), 202–54; Michael Merrill and Sean Wilentz, "'The Key of Libberty,' William Manning and Plebeian Democracy, 1747–1814," in Alfred F. Young, ed., *Beyond the American Revolution: Explorations in the History of American Radicalism* (DeKalb, Ill., 1993), 246–82; Michael Merrill and Sean Wilentz, *The Key of Liberty: The Life and Democratic Writings of William Manning, "A Laborer," 1747–1814* (Cambridge, Mass., 1993); Ruth Bogin, "Petitioning and the New Moral Economy of Post-Revolutionary America," *William and Mary Quarterly* 45 (1988), 391–425. The quotes are taken from J. Mills Thornton III, *Politics and Power in a Slave Society: Alabama, 1800–1860* (Baton Rouge, 1978), 71–72.

3. The labor theory of value was the cornerstone of small producers' values and beliefs. For plebeian expressions of the labor theory of value, see Alfred F. Young, "Afterward: How Radical Was the American Revolution?" in Young, ed., *Beyond the American Revolution*, 319–20; Michael Merrill and Sean Wilentz, "'Key of Libberty,'" 248, 254; Richard L. Bushman, "Massachusetts Farmers and the Revolution," in Richard M. Jellison, ed., *Society, Freedom and Conscience* (New York, 1976), 77–124; Bushman, *King and People in Provincial Massachusetts* (Chapel Hill, N.C., 1985), chap. 5. For the political and constitutional expression of the labor theory of value, see Isaac Kramnick, *Republicanism and Bourgeois Radicalism: Political Ideology in Late Eighteenth-Century England and America* (Ithaca, N.Y., 1990), 190–96, and Gordon Wood, *The Radicalism of the American Revolution* (New York, 1992), 278–79.

Holland Land Company had impeded rather than advanced land and market development in western New York. The company was interested, they believed, only in corporate profits that could be obtained by skimming off some of the wealth created by productive labor. In 1827, their combined opposition to the company culminated in the organization of the Agrarian Convention. Delegates from around the Purchase met at Buffalo to denounce the company's policies. The delegates criticized the company mainly for establishing policies that submerged the settlers in debt while curtailing their individual managerial freedom to make improvements and dispose of the equity as they saw fit. The company stood in the way, the delegates resolved, of a free and open market for land.[4]

IN the fall of 1819, Albert Tracy, a freshman congressman from Buffalo, attacked the Dutch landlords in a local newspaper. Western New York, he said, had fallen under the rule of an aristocratic "system of management." For two decades "these lordly proprietors" and their "pampered agents" had grown richer and fatter, their "ill gotten wealth" squeezed from the "patient industry" and "persevering enterprise" of the settlers. The conflict between landlords and settlers, he argued, was a struggle of "aristocratic landholders" against "actual occupants" and "improvers of the land." The foreign proprietors had lured small farmers and herdsmen to western New York with a policy of easy credit and little or no down payment. But the landlords' promise of "agricultural ease and independence" concealed their true interests. The Dutch landlords were speculators, according to Tracy, men more interested in a good rate of return on their investment than in the welfare or liberty of the settlers. Development of wild land could succeed only by attracting settlers willing to use and improve the company's property without ever securing fee simple title to it. By keeping land prices high and compounding interest whenever a settler asked for more time to pay, the landlords ensnared many settlers in

4. For government promotion of economic growth in the early Republic, see Sellers, *Market Revolution,* 32. The point of convergence between Albert Tracy's or Peter B. Porter's commitment to agrarian sentiments and the labor theory of value and the small settlers' commitment occurred at the juncture formed by both groups' shared understanding of the rudiments of political economy. Hierarchical dominion over land and market development was an outgrowth of political power. The producing majority had to stand guard at all times against the moneyed few who sought to dominate and exploit them. For an important discussion of how modern usage of the term "capitalism" has been divorced from the historical context of political economy that emphasized the political power of moneyed men, see Merrill and Wilentz, "'Key of Libberty,'" 273–74 n. 5. See also Michael Merrill, "The Anticapitalist Origins of the United States," *Review: A Journal of the Fernand Braudel Center* 13 (Fall 1990), 465–97.

a tangle of debt. The landlords had not pressed for payment, Tracy charged, because the value of the settlers' labor and improvements did not yet equal the debt they owed. When the settlers' equity covered the debt, the landlords would press them for payment, evict them, and then expropriate the value of their labor and improvements.[5]

Albert Tracy was wellborn and well-educated, the son of a distinguished New England physician. After studying medicine for a brief period, Tracy became a lawyer and moved to the frontier village of Buffalo in 1815. He quickly became allied with an aggressive group of entrepreneurs dubbed the Kremlinites, who were ultimately responsible for building a harbor and making Buffalo the western terminus of the Erie Canal.[6]

Tracy's challenge to the Holland Land Company marked the beginning of the second party system in the Purchase. His appeal to agrarian and egalitarian ideals formed part of a calculated effort by an aspiring entrepreneurial elite to displace the entrenched privilege and power of Joseph Ellicott. Even though Ellicott and the company had little real authority over the actual process of land development, Ellicott, aided by his inner circle of family and friends, exercised tight control over local politics. His power was such that he "could almost 'play God' with the purchase," in the words of one historian. That power gave Ellicott and his family and friends important economic advantages that became a potent source of jealousy and resentment among local boosters who did not enjoy Ellicott's friendship and patronage.[7]

A good example of Ellicott's control and the opposition it could generate occurred over the issue of chartering and operating the only bank in the region. The Bank of Niagara was given a public charter in 1816, but like other banks of this era it primarily served its chief stockholders and investors. Ellicott explained the "mysterious business" of banking to Paul Busti in February 1817: "It is in reality nothing more than authorizing by law ABC to receive interest on other peoples' property for the mere loan of the name of their institution. Suppose Paul Busti and Joseph Ellicott wished to put $10,000 of their property in circulation in current notes.

5. Tracy used the pen name "Agricola" in a four-part series that appeared in the *Niagara Journal* (Buffalo, N.Y.), on Sept. 28, Oct. 12, Oct. 19, and Nov. 2, 1819.

6. DeAlva Stanwood Alexander, *A Political History of the State of New York*, 3 vols. (New York, 1906), 1:372–73, 397–98.

7. For Ellicott's political power in the Holland Purchase, see William Chazanof, *Joseph Ellicott and the Holland Land Company: The Opening of Western New York* (Syracuse, N.Y., 1970), chaps. 3–4. The quote is found on page 144.

They offer their own note to a Bank for that amount. The Bank in return issues to the said PB and JE the official notes of their Institution to that amount less the interest."[8]

The ease and facility with which a board member or principal stockholder could obtain a loan or convert some of his property into capital simply by giving a personal note made the control of banks an important financial asset, especially in a frontier economy where money was always scarce. Ellicott supervised the organization of the Bank of Niagara and became its president in July 1818. Just as Ellicott understood and coveted the advantages which his control of the bank secured him, Albert Tracy and his Kremlin allies resented the exclusive and private nature of those advantages. When Tracy openly criticized the bank in April 1818, his argument appealed to agrarian sentiments, yet John C. Spencer was close to the truth when he told his young friend that "I think I perceive in your remarks on the Bank a little regret that you could not have had a finger in the pie."[9]

Tracy and his Kremlin group became strong supporters of Governor DeWitt Clinton in 1818 because they endorsed his entrepreneurial vision of the West. The governor's commitment to the Erie Canal made him enormously popular with local developers in Buffalo, Black Rock, and Lockport who dreamed about the great western emporium the canal promised to create. Albert Tracy attacked Ellicott's bank and his operation of the company's land office because he blamed Ellicott's policies for the persistent frontier poverty and underdevelopment that plagued the Purchase. Ellicott's political break with Governor Clinton in the spring of 1819 affirmed Tracy's growing conviction that the foreign capitalists whom Ellicott represented were in league with the commercial and carrying interests of the East that conspired to keep the West down.[10]

---

8. Joseph Ellicott to Paul Busti, Feb. 12, 1817, Joseph Ellicott Collection, Buffalo and Erie County Historical Society, Buffalo, N.Y.; cited hereafter as JEC.

9. For an examination of the Bank of Niagara controversy, see Chazanof, *Joseph Ellicott,* chap. 8, and Charles E. Brooks, "Economic Change and Agrarian Conflict in the Holland Land Purchase of Western New York, 1800–1845" (Ph.D. diss., State University of New York at Buffalo, 1988), chap. 4. John C. Spencer to Albert Tracy, Jan. 29, 1819, Albert H. Tracy Papers, New York State Library, Albany. For the operation of banks during the early nineteenth century, see Naomi R. Lamoreaux, "Banks, Kinship, and Economic Development: The New England Case," *Journal of Economic History* 46 (1986), 647–67. The classic study of banking in this era is, of course, Bray Hammond, *Banks and Politics in America: From the Revolution to the Civil War* (Princeton, N.J., 1957).

10. Brooks, "Economic Change and Agrarian Conflict," chap. 4. For a discussion of early sectional consciousness based on the perceived conflict between the commercial East and the producing West, see Drew R. McCoy, "James Madison and Visions of American Nationality

Western agrarian resentment of eastern market elites that used political power to establish centralized control over economic growth was persistent and long-standing in western New York. The resentment turned on class as well as sectional interests. The ill will harbored by westerners was expressed by Congressman Peter B. Porter in 1810. He reminded the Eleventh Congress that "the people" of the United States were divided by geography into "two great and distinct sections." The Appalachian Mountains separated the nation into east and west. To the east of these mountains the people were merchants, manufacturers, and "agriculturists," but the "mercantile interest" was dominant. But to the west of the mountains small farmers held the advantage. Notwithstanding the existence of these two great interests, Porter argued, Congress seemed "exclusively occupied" with "the protection and security of commerce." Appealing to agrarian sentiments, yet in a way that anticipated the home market argument of the American System, Porter denounced the national government because it actively supported commerce but did nothing for agriculture. It could charter banks for the benefit of the merchant but could not build canals to help the farmer. The consequence of this neglect was to keep the West poor. Small frontier farmers in the Holland Purchase were being denied the incentive necessary to spur productive labor because there were no markets to buy the surplus their active labor might produce. Spending too large a "part of their time in idleness and dissipation," western settlers would stay poor because the transforming hand of commerce was being withheld by the government.[11]

A graduate of Yale, Peter B. Porter moved to the western New York frontier in 1793. A few years later, he opened a law practice in the village of Canandaigua. Porter supported the Jeffersonian Republicans, and in 1797 he was appointed to serve as the clerk of Ontario County. His political fortunes continued to rise, as he won a seat in the state assembly in 1802, then six years later was elected to Congress. Porter made Black rock his home in 1810 and along with his brother Augustus established the shipping firm of Porter, Barton, and Company. The Porter brothers' firm controlled the portage business around Niagara Falls. Centered at Black Rock, three miles downriver from Buffalo and the eastern end of Lake Erie, their firm oversaw a fledgling western trade, supplying military

in the Confederation Period: A Regional Perspective," in Richard Beeman, Stephen Botein, and Edward C. Carter II, eds., *Beyond Confederation: Origins of the Constitution and American National Identity* (Chapel Hill, N.C., 1987), 236–37.

11. *Annals of Congress, 11th Cong., 1st and 2nd sess., Part 2, 1810* (Washington, D.C., 1853), 1386–88, 1400.

forts at Detroit and Michilimackinac with beef, flour, whiskey, and especially salt. By 1816 lake schooners were being built at Black Rock, and two years later the first steamboat to ply the waters of Lake Erie was launched from there. The *Walk-in-the-Water* operated out of Black Rock, sailing every Friday for Detroit during the three years it was in service. Directing commercial activity along the Niagara River portage, the Porters dreamed of making Black Rock a major western trade center through which the produce of the West and the manufactures of the East would pass.[12]

On October 26, 1825, the Erie Canal was formally opened with great pomp and fanfare. The official ceremonies began in Buffalo amid a flurry of speechmaking and booming cannons and ended in New York City, where a keg of water taken from Lake Erie and carried on board the canal boat *Seneca Chief* was poured into the harbor symbolizing the "wedding of the waters." The importance of this event for the Holland Purchase was underscored by the bitter rivalry that had taken place between the villages of Buffalo and Black Rock over where the canal should terminate. Albert Tracy and the Kremlin faction had championed Buffalo's cause while Peter B. Porter led Black Rock's effort. Oliver Forward, a prominent member of the Kremlin faction, explained in 1821 that winning the canal was "a question on which the future prosperity of this village entirely depends." Likewise, James Barton spoke for the Black Rock entrepreneurs when he said: "I, with all the rest of our citizens, thought we had a right to retain this commerce if we could."[13]

The battle for the canal raged for six years before Buffalo finally claimed the prize. During these years, the fierce commercial rivalry spilled over into local politics. During Tracy's campaign for reelection to Congress in 1821 and 1823, the rhetoric became heated and bitter. The *Niagara Journal*, the Kremlin group's newspaper, launched a scathing public attack against Porter during and after the campaign of 1821 be-

12. Joseph Grande, "The Political Career of Peter Buell Porter, 1797–1829" (Ph.D. diss., University of Notre Dame, 1971); Joseph Grande, *Peter B. Porter and the Buffalo–Black Rock Rivalry* (Buffalo, N.Y., 1982), 7–13.

13. For the opening of the Erie Canal, see Ronald Shaw, *Erie Water West: A History of the Erie Canal, 1792–1854* (Lexington, Ky., 1966), 181–94; Eric Brunger and Lionel Wyld, *The Grand Canal: New York's First Thruway* (Buffalo, N.Y., 1964), 9. The Buffalo–Black Rock controversy can be traced in a collection of letters by DeWitt Clinton, Joseph Ellicott, Peter B. Porter, and others found in Frank H. Severance, ed., *The Holland Land Co. and Canal Construction in Western New York; Buffalo–Black Rock Harbor Papers; Journal and Documents* (Buffalo, N.Y., 1910). See also Grande, *Peter B. Porter.* Oliver Forward is quoted in Shaw, *Erie Water West,* 156; James Barton is quoted in Brunger, *Grand Canal,* 6.

cause reports circulated throughout the Purchase that Porter had worked against Tracy's reelection. The paper charged that Porter was a friend and associate of Joseph Ellicott, the "Land Office Nabob." Both men enjoyed the "fostering hand" of monopoly and special privilege; both were members of an "odious aristocracy" that lived without labor. In 1823 Tracy faced Augustus Porter, Peter Porter's older brother, in his bid for reelection. When Tracy's supporters alleged that Porter had plundered private property during his military service as commander of a contingent of militia which he had raised and led during the War of 1812, Porter sued for libel. Tracy later apologized for his part in the war of words.[14]

By 1826 the battle between Buffalo and Black Rock was over, and the canal was in full operation, sparking wide interest in a host of other internal improvement projects under consideration within the Purchase. Meanwhile, Tracy had lost his seat in Congress, and the path was now clear for Tracy and Porter to join forces against the antidevelopment policies of the Holland Land Company. As the burden of land debt in the Purchased continued to grow while land prices slumped, Tracy and Porter concluded that canals and roads would not be enough to get the Purchase moving again. The Holland Land Company's policies were largely responsible, they believed, for the crisis that had overtaken the settlers of the Purchase.

The Agrarian Convention of the Holland Land Purchase

In early January 1827, Peter B. Porter and his business partner Benjamin Barton set in motion a political challenge to the Holland Land Company that seized upon the agrarian grievances of small producers as well as the entrepreneurial dreams and frustrations of more commercially oriented settlers like themselves. The promise of growth and prosperity brought by the canal spurred the dreams and ambition of local boosters and developers, but these dreams were frustrated by the continuing reality of frontier isolation and government policies that always seemed to favor the eastern commercial elites. Every proposed internal improvement or bank to benefit the Purchase that was ignored, rejected, or interminably

14. Grande, "Political Career of Peter Buell Porter," 120–22, 130–67; Grande, *Peter B. Porter*, 21; *Niagara Journal* (Buffalo, N.Y.), April 24, 1821; *Buffalo Patriot*, Dec. 24, 1822, April 29, May 6, 1823; Shaw, *Erie Water West*, 155, 158–61.

delayed was construed by entrepreneurs like Porter as evidence of a deliberate policy to keep the west down.

During the crisis of the 1820s, the small settlers and producers of the Holland Purchase drew upon a vernacular agrarian culture that could be traced back far into the eighteenth century. Based on the labor theory of value, this culture was strengthened and fortified by evangelical Christianity and a deep-seated plebeian tradition associated with the rights and liberties of Englishmen. In the Holland Purchase the actual experience of frontier settlement and land development played as great a role as culture in shaping the values and beliefs that small settlers called upon to sustain themselves during difficult times. More influential and ambitious settlers like Porter and Tracy, by contrast, were the heirs of an agrarian political and constitutional tradition that was used by aspiring elites in both the city and the countryside to cast themselves as members of the producing majority who were drawn up in battle against the privilege and power of the moneyed few. In 1827 these two independent and divergent expressions of agrarianism converged in western New York. Porter and Tracy helped to organize the Agrarian Convention movement representing both sides of agrarianism. The dichotomy offered here is useful for understanding the complex relationship between small producers' beliefs and the political and constitutional dynamic that underlay the development of the second party system in the Holland Purchase, but it also blurs the nuanced and subtle overlapping that joined these two instincts. In reality, a mixture of agrarian concerns and entrepreneurial ambition formed part of every settler's character, no matter where he lived or how poor or well off he was.[15]

On January 2, 1827, two hundred delegates from Erie and Niagara County gathered at the Washington House in Lockport to consider "the course of policy pursued by the Holland Company, in the sale and settlement of their lands." Benjamin Barton, Porter's partner in the transportation firm of Porter, Barton and Company, was appointed chairman. The delegates organized a committee to draft resolutions and prepare an address to the settlers of the Holland Land Purchase. Lawyers and entrepreneurs dominated the committee. The committee included Ebenezer Wal-

15. For other studies that emphasize a basic dichotomy in American character during this era, see Lawrence Frederick Kohl, *The Politics of Individualism: Parties and the American Character in the Jacksonian Era* (New York, 1989); John Ashworth, *"Agrarians" & "Aristocrats": Party Political Ideology in the United States, 1837–1846* (1983; rpr. Cambridge, Mass., 1987), 7–131; Richard E. Ellis, *The Jeffersonian Crisis: Courts and Politics in the Young Republic* (New York, 1971), 250–84; Sellers, *Market Revolution.*

den, an attorney and land speculator who had invested heavily in Buffalo real estate; Bates Cooke, a lawyer and mill operator at Lewiston; James Mason and Hiram Gardner, lawyers from Lockport; James Van Horn, proprietor of an early gristmill on Eighteen Mile Creek in the town of Newfane; and Gad Pierce, an innkeeper and farmer from Niagara Falls. This committee embodied the rising tide of expectations encouraged by the commercial boom and the Erie Canal in particular. That the Agrarian Convention began in Lockport underscores the commercial orientation of the men who sparked an open political challenge to the Holland Land Company and the state government that fostered it. Lockport, in the words of Horatio Spafford's *Gazetteer,* was "one of the creations of the Erie Canal." In 1821 there were only two buildings there. Two years later the place had been transformed; it was a boom town with a population of twelve hundred and three hundred buildings, including a printing office and weekly newspaper, twelve stores, twenty-four mechanics' shops, five law offices, eight physicians, eight inns, four schools, a Quaker meeting-house, and plans for a Baptist church. The overnight transformation of Lockport from a frontier crossroads to a bustling canal town prefigured the wondrous growth that could transform the entire region if the Holland Land Company and the state government removed the obstacles to progress.[16]

Porter's committee reported its resolutions and submitted an "Address to the Inhabitants of the Holland Purchase" when the Lockport meeting reconvened at six o'clock in the evening on January 3. Repeating the key charge made by Albert Tracy eight years earlier, the resolutions charged that the company continued to follow a policy "calculated to retard and discourage the growth and improvement of the country." The Holland Company continued to sell its lands "at the highest possible prices on a

16. The names of the delegates attending the Lockport meeting are listed in *Proceedings of the Meeting Held at Lockport, on the 2nd and 3rd of January 1827; and of the Convention of Delegates from the Several Counties on the Holland Purchase Held at Buffalo, on the 7th and 8th of February 1827, to Consider the Relations Subsisting between the Holland Company and the Settlers on Said Purchase, and to Propose Some Remedy by Which the Condition of the Settlers May Be Alleviated* (Buffalo, N.Y., 1827), 3-4; cited hereafter as *Proceedings at Lockport and Buffalo.* John Theodore Horton, Edward T. Williams, and Harry S. Douglass, *History of Northwestern New York: Erie, Niagara, Wyoming, Genesee and Orleans Counties,* 2 vols. (New York, 1947); Orsamus Turner, *Pioneer History of the Holland Purchase* (1850; rpr. Geneseo, N.Y., 1974); *History of Niagara County, New York* (New York, 1878); Merton Wilner, *History of the Niagara Frontier,* 4 vols. (Chicago, 1931); and *Historical Album of Orleans County* (New York, 1879) were helpful in identifying the occupations of the delegates. Horatio G. Spafford, *Gazetteer of the State of New York* (1824; rpr. Interlaken, N.Y., 1981), 290-91.

long credit," while exacting an "annual interest of seven per cent" on thousands of land contracts. By increasing the price of lands adjoining the more settled areas of the Purchase and "by occasionally suspending sales altogether in particular places for purposes of speculation," the company profited from the value that the settlers' improvements added to the Purchase. The company also exhibited "the total want of liberality" in helping to build roads, bridges, and "every other species of public improvement." Rather than investing in the economic infrastructure of the region, the agents of the company sent the "whole of their annual collections" to Europe. As a consequence, the Purchase lacked the "manufactories and . . . other establishments" that a newly settled region required for its "growth and prosperity."[17]

Under the company's current policy, the "ruin of at least two thirds of the settlers" was inevitable. Only a radical modification of company policy or immediate tax relief from the state legislature could save the settlers, who were unable to keep up with their annual payments of interest and principal. The "constantly accumulating debt" foretold the certainty of an enforced collection by the company that "must be expected to take place in the course of a few years." The Lockport resolutions concluded by calling for a general convention of agrarian representatives from every county and township in the Purchase to meet in Buffalo. The prospective convention was urged to consider the critical "state of the country as regards its relations with the Holland Company."[18]

The Lockport address to the settlers described and analyzed the persistent stagnation of the Purchase. The region remained in a backcountry condition, it argued, because the company refused to invest the capital required for economic development. Labor and capital were "the great sources of individual and national prosperity." The address defined capital as "inanimate labor, or the operations of property vested in commerce, manufactures, or other profitable employments." The labor of isolated individuals could never bring a region out of subsistence culture. Capital was needed, particularly its power to combine the efforts of many individuals. "If the whole Purchase were brought to the condition of a garden, capable of yielding agricultural products to any given extent," the address maintained, "it might be the means of affording a very comfortable support for the inhabitants, but would never enable them to pay for their farms, until capital is invested in rearing towns and manufactories, to

17. *Proceedings at Lockport and Buffalo*, 4–5.
18. Ibid., 5.

purchase and consume the surplus products, and thus react upon the value of the land."[19]

The Holland Land Company was ignorant of, or at least indifferent to, the useful principles guiding the policy of other large landholders in western New York. Pointing to the land business practices of Oliver Phelps and Charles Williamson during a former period and to those of William Wadsworth and Philip Church at the present time, the address emphasized that "these gentlemen" actively encouraged and subsidized "mills, manufactories, warehouses, lumber and slaughter yards, and other facilities for receiving and depositing of the products of the country." A portion of the capital they took from their settlers in the form of interest and principal was reinvested "to foster and encourage the growth of the country."[20]

The address proposed two possible remedies. One was directed at the company while the other constituted an appeal to the state legislature for help. The address entreated the Dutch landlords to consider what the federal government had done in 1820. Confronted with a public land debt of $23 million, Congress made major changes in federal land policy. It abolished the credit system and reduced the minimum price of public lands to $1.25 per acre. A year later Congress permitted buyers to renegotiate their purchases, allowing them to retain all improved land and repurchase it at the reduced prices. The changes in federal land policy proved "not less beneficial to the government than to the settlers themselves." New settlements "in Michigan, Ohio and other western states," areas carved out from federal territory and settled under the provisions of the government's new land policy, showed the wisdom of these changes.[21]

The other proposed remedy enjoined the state legislature to modify the "system of taxation." It reminded the settlers of the role the state had played in creating the current dilemma. The legislature conferred upon these foreign landowners exemptions and privileges that were denied to New York's own citizens, the effect of which was "to place one of the fairest portions of the state in the condition of pecuniary vassalage to a set of European Bankers." Because the legislature had created the problem, it should grant the hard-pressed settlers some relief by easing their tax burden. The "most onerous" tax paid by the settlers was that "raised for the construction and repair of roads and bridges and for building school

19. Ibid., 6–7. For an analysis of the entrepreneurial view of capital and economic diversification during the age of Jackson, see Kohl, *Politics of Individualism,* 119.

20. *Proceedings at Lockport and Buffalo,* 7.

21. Murray Rothbard, *The Panic of 1819: Reactions and Policies* (New York, 1962), 24–26; *Proceedings at Lockport and Buffalo,* 9–10.

houses and support of teachers." Every man in the Purchase, including the "itinerant laborer and mechanic" who stayed only a few months, was compelled to work on the highways, in fact paying a poll tax. The Holland Company paid neither highway nor school taxes, yet the value of its unsold lands advanced as a direct consequence of these improvements. To correct this obvious injustice, the Lockport address called upon the legislature to modify the highway tax system. All property in the Purchase, "whether owned by citizens or foreigners," should share the cost as well as the benefit of public improvements.[22]

The Agrarian Convention at Buffalo

Peter B. Porter dominated the Buffalo convention even more than he had the Lockport meeting. It was primarily his leadership that guided the Agrarian Convention's political challenge to the Holland Land Company in 1827. Albert Tracy, Porter's chief rival and author of the "Agricola letters" in 1819, would also play a prominent part in the convention's deliberations and was appointed along with Porter to serve on its Committee of Petitions and Correspondence.

Who attended the Buffalo convention? The most complete records about the rank-and-file delegates document the representatives from Chautauqua County. This county was a microcosm of the Holland Purchase, encompassing lowland plains with easy access to Lake Erie transportation as well as isolated hill country townships dominated by small independent producers. The "turbulent spirits" who lived in these hills demolished the Holland Land Company's office at Mayville in February 1836.[23]

There were seventeen delegates from Chautauqua County. Mini-biographies exist for all but one of them. Without exception, they were lawyers, entrepreneurs, and state and local public officials. Five were practicing attorneys. Four were local businessmen, including Obed Edson, who ran a semiweekly line of stages between Fredonia, Jamestown, and Warren, Pennsylvania. Theron Bly, a delegate from the town of Harmony, built and operated a cloth dressing factory. Six of the delegates were town supervisors. Among the politicians were both Bucktails and

22. *Proceedings at Lockport and Buffalo,* 10–11.
23. William H. Seward used the phrase "turbulent spirits" to characterize the settlers of the back towns after the rebellion of 1836. See Frederick W. Seward, *William H. Seward: An Autobiography,* 2 vols. (New York, 1891), 1:306.

Clintonians. Two of the delegates, Nathan Mixer and Philo Orton, had run for the state assembly the previous November. Mixer ran as a Bucktail and Orton as a Clintonian, and both were defeated.[24]

Records for delegates from the other counties are less complete, but the overall profile corresponds to that in Chautauqua County. Genesee County had some of the poorest settlers in the Purchase, but the delegates tended to be storekeepers or professionals. In the township of Attica, for instance, there were eighty-three expired contracts, covering 8,857½ acres or roughly 40 percent of all land in the town; yet Attica was represented by David Scott, who operated a store in Cowlesville before establishing the town's first newspaper, the *Attica Republican*. Similarly, the town of Alexander, where there were seventy-three expired contracts, was represented by Henry Hawkins, a merchant, farmer, and trustee of the town's first public library. When he died in October 1845, he left a $5,000 endowment for the Genesee and Wyoming Seminary. Few ordinary settlers attended the first Agrarian Convention in Buffalo. The primary reason seems to have been poverty. As one Cattaraugus settler later explained: "We are most confounded poor—it is as much as we can do to live without spending money on conventions."[25]

24. The mini-biographies are drawn from Andrew W. Young, *History of Chautauqua County, New York* (1875; rpr. Bowie, Md., 1990).

25. County histories are very useful for identifying the delegates. See Turner, *Pioneer History of the Holland Purchase*; Horton et al., *History of Northwestern New York*; Young, *History of Chautauqua County; Centennial History of Chautauqua County*, 2 vols. (Jamestown, N.Y., 1904); Obed Edson, *History of Chautauqua County*, 2 vols. (Boston, 1894); Franklin Ellis, *History of Cattaraugus County, N.Y.* (Philadelphia, 1879); John Manley, *Original Portraits and Biographies of the Old Pioneers and Congressmen of Cattaraugus County* (Little Valley, N.Y., 1857); John Minard, *Allegany County and Its People* (Alfred, N.Y., 1896); Crisfield Johnson, *Centennial History of Erie County, New York* (Buffalo, 1876); Josephus Nelson Larned, *A History of Buffalo*, 2 vols. (New York, 1911); F. W. Beers, ed., *Gazetteer and Biographical Record of Genesee County, New York* (Syracuse, N.Y., 1890); Beers, ed., *History of Wyoming County, New York, 1841–1880* (New York, 1880); Safford E. North, ed., *Our County and Its People: A Descriptive and Biographical Record of Genesee County, New York* (Boston, 1890). The number of expired contracts for these two townships is calculated from the Register of the buyers of the lots of tracts M, O, P, Q, H, W, T, and R with statement of the surface area of the land, purchase price, and amount paid, 1802–27, Reels 178–79, Inventory no. 802, Holland Land Company Project, State University of New York College at Fredonia; cited hereafter as HLCP. The anonymous settler is quoted in the *Cattaraugus Republican* (Ellicottville, N.Y.), Sept. 25, 1839. This settler's observation notwithstanding, many historians point to the persistence of deferential politics that made it natural for settlers to turn for leadership to "established local professionals and businessmen." See Kathleen Smith Kutolowski, "Antimasonry Reexamined: Social Bases of the Grass-Roots Party," *Journal of American History* 71 (Sept. 1984), 269–93; the above quote is found on page 286. See also Kutolowski, "The Janus Face of New York's Local Parties: Genesee County, 1821–1827," *New York History* 59 (April 1978), 145–72; Ronald

When the convention came to order Wednesday morning, February 7, its first business was administrative. Peter B. Porter was called to the chair and a committee was set up, consisting of three members from each county, plus Porter and the two secretaries, Simeon Cumings and John Dexter. Albert Tracy was one of three delegates representing Erie County. When the convention reconvened the next morning, the committee submitted a formal report. Returning to the principal themes outlined by the Lockport address, it explained the relation between the settlers' land debt and the absence of markets. Citing the case of a typical settler who arrived in the Purchase "twelve or fifteen years ago," it explained how his original debt of $800 had increased "to 1000 or 1200 dollars." His growing indebtedness was directly related to the chronic underdevelopment of the Purchase. "His only means, in prospect, for the discharge of his land debt, are dependent on the sale of the few products of his farm that will bear transportation to market," the report noted, "and generally speaking, the distance to this market is so great, and the state of the roads so wretched, that he often fails to realize from sales of his beef, pork, wheat, corn, oats, flax, and wool, which are staple commodities of the country, more than the actual cost of their production."[26]

The fault lay with the Holland Land Company's policy. Easy credit had brought many settlers to the Purchase, but their efforts to clear and cultivate the soil could never bring the region "to a state of prosperity and independence." Only a "policy of providing a market for the advantageous disposal" of the settlers' surplus products could do that.[27]

The report expressed the committee's unanimous belief that the settlers did not "possess the means" to pay even half of what they owed. Yet the company resorted to "expelling by legal process, whole families from land and possessions on which they spent years of labor." If the company persisted in pushing settlers off the land, it risked creating "a state of feeling and excitement dangerous to the tranquility, as well as subversive of the prosperity of the country."[28]

The report appealed to the self-interest of the company. The general physical appearance of the Purchase pointed to "the radical error in the system of this Company." Buildings were falling down, fields reverted to

---

P. Formisano, "Deferential Participant Politics: The Early Republic's Political Culture, 1789–1840," *American Political Science Review* 68 (June 1974), 473–87.

26. *Proceedings at Lockport and Buffalo*, 14–16; for the Buffalo convention proceedings, see also *Black Rock Gazette*, Feb. 17, 1827, and *Fredonia Censor*, Feb. 21, 1827.

27. *Proceedings at Lockport and Buffalo*, 17.

28. Ibid., 18.

weeds and woodlands, and farms were abandoned. As settlers realized they could never pay "their land debt," they lost their ambition and relaxed their exertions. If this situation continued, the company could never hope to receive "payment of any part of the debt" owed by the settlers. Hence the report called upon the company to reduce "the prices of its unsold lands" and to "relinquish a part of the nominal debt due from each settler." The reduced price of land would stop the flow of emigrants and capital to the West and "give new life and vigor to our settlements." The reforms also would enable many of the poorer settlers to sell all or "a portion of their lots and improvements." This option might enable settlers to recover their equity and leave the Purchase or give up some land, keep the improved portion, and stay in western New York.[29]

Finally, the Agrarian Convention's report argued that if the company could be made aware of the desperate condition of the settlers, it might be persuaded to institute some of the changes adopted by the federal government in 1820–21. But if the foreign proprietors had become "so blinded to their interests as to refuse a compromise," the settlers should appeal to the legislature. That appeal should emphasize the justice of modifying the highway tax law. Under the existing law, as both the "Agricola" series and the Lockport address pointed out, the settlers paid highway taxes, sometimes amounting "to an assessment of 40 days labor to a single person." In addition, a supplemental road tax authorized any town to raise an additional $250 through a levy on all property within the town. Since the majority of settlers did not hold deeds, this latter tax was added to the debt they owed to the company.[30]

Before adjourning, the delegates declared themselves "The Agrarian Convention of the Holland Purchase" and agreed to meet annually on the first Wednesday of January until they achieved their objectives. The delegates appointed a Committee of Petitions and Correspondence that included Peter B. Porter, Benjamin Barton, and Albert Tracy, directing it to prepare a petition to the state legislature concerning the "unequal and oppressive system of taxation." This committee was also to inform "the principals or agents of the Holland Land Company" about "the depressed and embarrassed condition of the settlers." Finally, the delegates established a Committee of Finance and Accounts to raise money to cover the cost of the Buffalo meeting as well as any future expenses resulting from the activities of the Committee of Petitions and Correspondence.[31]

29. Ibid., 19.
30. Ibid., 20–21.
31. Ibid., 21–23.

The principal theme of the Agrarian Convention of 1827 was its belief that diversified economic growth was necessary to free the settlers from their oppressive land debt. The frontier farm economy that prevailed throughout much of the Purchase could never generate sufficient profit to pay off the land debt. The commercial and entrepreneurial orientation of the convention clearly shaped its key objectives: diversify the regional economy, free the majority of settlers from a debilitating land debt, and encourage an open and mobile market for land. The latter objective represents a crucial point of convergence between the entrepreneurial dreams and frustrations of the more commercially oriented settlers and the agrarian grievances of the poorer hill country settlers. When the convention called upon the company to reduce land prices "to countervail the effects" of the new federal land policy, the rationale was based on the need to revitalize an open market for land in the Purchase. The combination of high prices and badly improved land encumbered by debt had strangled the land market. As a consequence, the tide of emigrants and capital that flowed through the Purchase was lost to the West. But this entrepreneurial concern with an open land market overlapped agrarian resentment of the company's decision to make all articles unassignable. As a later statement issued by the convention made clear, making articles unassignable struck at the heart of agrarian independence. Since most settlers still held their land under an article of agreement, making articles unassignable meant that improvements could no longer be used as collateral security to obtain the credit from local storekeepers that was necessary to get poorer settlers through the year. Putting a stop to the buying and selling of possession claims also made it more difficult for a settler to sell his improvement and recover the value of his equity. It also interfered with a settler's managerial freedom to mix labor and land as he saw fit.[32]

But did the Agrarian Convention present a true picture of the settlers' problems? The answer is yes and no. The debt problem was serious and getting worse. The company's own figures pointed to a steadily rising debt. In fact, as we have seen, the company's concern about the rising accumulation of debt prompted the general shake-up that began with Ellicott's dismissal. The steady accumulation of debt, particularly after 1819, coupled with persistent economic stagnation and competition from cheap federal government lands had created a crisis. The convention's

32. The later "Grounds of Complaint" statement referred to here appeared in the *Black Rock Gazette,* May 12, 1827.

conclusion that a majority of settlers lacked the means to pay their land debt was accurate.

The company itself recognized the seriousness of the settlers' debt problem. In May and June of 1827, Evans acknowledged privately to the company's general agent that many settlers were in deep trouble. If Evans needed further convincing, it came from settlers' letters and petitions. Samuel King wrote from the township of Friendship in Allegany County that the settlers were "much . . . discouraged." "The interest on their contracts is fast accumulating," he explained, "and they can raise nothing that they can turn without a sacrifice to pay for their lands." Settlers in the town of Rushford asked Evans for the company's help in opening a road "through Rushford, China and Aurora to Buffalo." "Unless some encouragement is given," these settlers urged, "more than has been heretofore— many are abandoning their articles and offering them for a trifle where the improvements have cost more than the land with them will now sell for— this country exhibits but a melancholy picture after being settled sixteen years."[33]

Even the areas of the Purchase serviced by the Erie Canal were not immediately transformed by prosperity. Up until 1826, the greatest economic impact of the canal came from construction work. Most of the trade carried by the canal was between Rochester and points east. For the first decade or so after its opening, the western section of the canal between Rochester and Buffalo served principally as a highway bringing westward-bound emigrants to Buffalo, where they boarded schooners and steamboats destined for Ohio, Indiana, and Michigan. Buffalo did not receive its first shipment of grain from the West until 1839. Hence despite the opening of the Erie Canal, the Holland Purchase continued to suffer from an unfavorable balance of trade with the markets of the East.[34]

How many settlers were affected by the land debt crisis in the Purchase? Both the Lockport and the Buffalo meetings estimated that two-thirds of the settlers faced the loss of their improvements should the company move against all delinquent buyers. The company estimated that there were "at least eight thousand families" or upward of forty thousand persons living in the Purchase on land for which the contracts had expired. This number

33. David Evans to John J. Vanderkemp, May 11, June 12, 1827, Reel 173, HLCP; Reports of David Evans in Robert W. Bingham, ed., *Reports of Joseph Ellicott*, 2 vols. (Buffalo, 1937–41), 2:1830, 476; Samuel King to David Evans, June 2, 1827, and Petition from settlers of Rushford to David Evans, June 14, 1827, Reel 153, HLCP.

34. Brunger, *Grand Canal*, 18; Shaw, *Erie Water West*, 264–67; David Gerber, *The Making of an American Pluralism: Buffalo, New York, 1825–60* (Urbana, Ill., 1989), 5.

constitutes about 35 percent of the population in 1825. So it appears that the convention's figure of two-thirds of the settlers is too high. Yet the company had not corrected the defect in its system of renewing contracts. Otto, like his predecessor, renewed contracts by computing a new purchase price, usually adding the amount of unpaid interest to the unpaid principal. Otto announced in early 1827 that under his tenure, contracts covering more than 625,000 acres had been renewed for $2,886,609.87. The amount of increase over the original purchase money was $1,140,623.71. The practical effect of Otto's system was to renew contracts at prices that exceeded the market value of the land in question. Hence while 35 percent of the settles lived under delinquent contracts, an equal number probably held under renewed articles in which the purchase price was greater than the land with improvements was worth. The company accepted this fact when it offered at the end of 1827 to renegotiate any land contract in which the cumulative debt exceeded the current market value of the land.[35]

The Agrarian Convention was wrong in its allegation that "great numbers of suits of ejectment and trespass" had been brought against the settlers. In fact, the company threatened legal action more often than it actually filed charges in court. But the threats of eviction were taken very seriously because they aroused the settlers' deepest agrarian fears. By appealing to these fears, the convention succeeded in building a coalition that united both poor and influential settlers against the moneyed landlords of the region. The fear of losing one's land, of becoming a "vassal" to some imperious "lordship," of being reduced to abject dependency, was the worst nightmare a small producer could imagine.

"The Clamor Got Up by Porter"

When Peter B. Porter's leadership of the Lockport and Buffalo meetings became known to John J. Vanderkemp in February 1827, the company's general agent attributed Porter's role to private business interests. "I know however," Vanderkemp said, "that General Porter and his brother the Judge, are holders of several lots of land, obtained by assignment, not having realized them in proper time and suffering the interest to accumulate, they are now desirous to throw some of them up and insist on an

---

35. Reports of David Evans, 1827, 440–41; Paul Evans, *The Holland Land Company* (Buffalo, N.Y., 1924), 353–54; Reports of Jacob Otto in Bingham, ed., *Reports of Joseph Ellicott*, 2:1826, 424–25.

allowance of discount." Porter's business interests had brought him into conflict with Joseph Ellicott and the company on several previous occasions. Porter, Barton and Company's control of the portage trade around Niagara Falls was contested by the Holland Company. Ellicott tried and failed to build a trade route from Buffalo to Pittsburgh that might have funneled commercial activity through the hinterlands of Chautauqua County. Ellicott's plans were in conflict with Porter, Barton and Company's Niagara portage monopoly, which continued to direct trade over Lake Erie to Presque Isle (Erie, Pennsylvania). In 1811 Ellicott used his political influence to deny Porter a renewal of the trade monopoly his firm enjoyed.[36]

During the same period, Ellicott rejected Porter's offer to buy a township near the village of Buffalo Creek. When Porter purchased a strip of land from the state, situated just to the north of Buffalo Creek, Busti told Ellicott to oppose any plans for development there. Porter built warehouses and wharves at Black Rock, hoping to make it the major trade outlet to the Ohio Valley as well as the Great Lakes region. Porter and Ellicott also disagreed about the best route for the Erie Canal. Porter favored a canal route that linked the Hudson River and the eastern shore of Lake Ontario. This route promised to funnel lucrative trade through the Niagara portage facilities his company controlled. Ellicott favored an inland canal that traversed company lands, opening markets and enhancing land values along the route. In 1826 Porter's business interests again brought him into conflict with the Holland Company. Porter sought concessions on a piece of commercially valuable land that he held under an article of agreement, but Otto refused to grant any concessions.[37]

Another source of conflict between Porter and the Holland Land Company originated in 1819, when Tracy published the Agricola letters. Porter's brother Augustus and his business partner Benjamin Barton openly supported Tracy's political assault on Ellicott and the company even though Tracy was a Clintonian and the Porters and Barton sided with the

36. John J. Vanderkemp to Thomas Ogden, Jan. 19, 1827, Reel 65, HLCP; Peter B. Porter to Jacob Otto, May 1, 1824, Reel 151, HLCP; Joseph Ellicott to Paul Busti, July 16, 1806, JEC; Evans, *Holland Land Company,* 341.
37. Grande, "Political Career of Peter Buell Porter," 230; Grande, *Peter B. Porter,* 2–3; Shaw, *Erie Water West,* 40; Chazanof, *Joseph Ellicott,* 71–74, 165–66; Joseph Ellicott to Paul Busti, July 16, 1808, JEC; Joseph Ellicott to Simeon DeWitt, July 30, 1808, JEC; Severance, ed., *Holland Land Co. and Canal Construction;* Peter B. Porter to Jacob Otto, Dec. 19, 1826, Reel 8, Peter B. Porter Papers, microfilm ed., Buffalo and Erie County Historical Society, Buffalo, N.Y.; cited hereafter as Porter Papers; Jacob Otto to Peter B. Porter, Jan. 5, 1827, Porter Papers.

Bucktails. Cooperation between these two aspiring commercial elites was quickly aborted, however, by the competition over the western terminus of the Erie Canal.[38]

IN the days and weeks that followed the adjourning of the Agrarian Convention, Porter emerged as the chief spokesman and lobbyist for the settlers' cause. On the day the convention adjourned, he prepared a petition to the state legislature. Condemning company policies that "had the effect to retard the growth and improvement of the country," Porter petitioned for a modification of the tax laws. He sought a revision of the tax system to make it "bear equally on all persons." The petition was accompanied by a copy of the proceedings of the Agrarian Convention. A week later, Porter sent a letter to all state senators and assemblymen representing the counties and townships of the Holland Purchase. He told them the Agrarian Convention planned to send Simeon Cumings and Robert Fleming to Albany to lobby for changes in "the present unequal system of taxation." "We calculate with confidence on your hearty and zealous cooperation in effecting a measure so perfectly just in itself and so vitally important to the interests of this section of the country," he wrote.[39]

On February 20 Porter wrote to John J. Vanderkemp, the company's general agent in Philadelphia, and to Jacob Otto, the resident agent at Batavia. Porter explained the convention's desire to secure some modification of the existing tax system, and he asked them to consider "some arrangement or compromise, that would alleviate the condition of the settlers, and, at the same time, promote the true interests of the Company." Porter referred the company's agents to an enclosed copy of the recent convention's proceedings to explain what relief the settlers hoped might be "extended . . . by the voluntary concessions of the Company." Porter further suggested that any move to eject the settlers "would lead to results as ruinous to the interests of the Company, as . . . to the settlers themselves." Finally, he informed the company's chief agents that Cumings and Fleming were on the way to Albany to represent the settlers' interests.[40]

Vanderkemp responded promptly, telling Porter and the other members of the Committee of Petitions and Correspondence that he had serious

38. *Niagara Journal* (Buffalo, N.Y.), Nov. 2, 1819; Evans, *Holland Land Company*, 341.
39. Petition to the state legislature, Feb. 8, 1827, and Peter B. Porter to state senators from the Eighth Senatorial District and to assemblymen from Niagara, Orleans, Genesee, Erie, Chautauqua, Cattaraugus, and Allegany counties, Feb. 17, 1827, Porter Papers.
40. Peter B. Porter to John J. Vanderkemp and Jacob Otto, Feb. 20, 1827, Porter Papers.

doubts about the legislative remedy they sought. "I must frankly declare, that an application . . . to the Legislature for the introduction of a new and oppressive principle of taxation does not appear to me to be calculated either to benefit the inhabitants or to promote the object which you seem to have in view." He added that company interests also would be represented in Albany. He had already asked Thomas Ogden, the company's attorney, to go to Albany if the "reformers" brought a petition before the legislature.[41]

In early March a select committee of the state assembly received the settlers' petition, but consideration of it proceeded slowly. Cumings and Fleming told Porter that the committee seemed willing "to try the road question" but was reluctant to push for a revision of "the general tax laws of the state." The settlers' petition drafted by Porter included two proposals for modifying the state's tax laws. The first urged the legislature to change the highway tax law by assessing all property in the Purchase. The other proposal recommended a basic overhaul of the tax system to equalize the burden "on all." The latter called for a new tax system "so framed as to reach property or the interest therein, to whatever shape it may exist." This meant the land debt due the company might be taxed—the single tax the great landlords of western New York feared the most. Every outbreak of agrarian protest beginning in 1819 stirred the landlords' fear that "the legislature might proceed to tax contracts, bonds, . . . mortgages, and securities taken for the sale of lands." Their fear was not groundless; the legislature eventually enacted such a measure in 1833.[42]

When the select committee finally reported a bill, it proposed an equalization of the highway tax making it applicable to all property, including that of nonresidents. The bill reported by Assemblyman Daniel Bucklin limited its provisions to the counties of the Purchase. Bucklin stood ready with an alternative bill making the new road tax applicable to the entire state, but supporters agreed that the more limited proposal was more viable. No action was taken on the question of a general revision of the state's tax system as Porter had proposed.[43]

Lobbying actively for the highway bill, Cumings and Fleming urged

41. John J. Vanderkemp to Peter B. Porter, Benjamin Barton, Albert Tracy, and Josiah Trowbridge, March 5, 1827, Porter Papers.
42. Simeon Cumings and Robert Fleming to Albert Tracy and Josiah Trowbridge, March 8, 1827, and Petition to the state legislature, Feb. 8, 1827, Porter Papers; New York, *Assembly Journal*, 50th sess. (1827), pt. 2, 843; R. W. Stoddard to Peter B. Porter, March 22, 1827, Porter Papers.
43. New York, *Assembly Journal*, 50th sess. (1827), pt. 2, 843–44.

Porter to come to Albany. When Cumings learned that Porter had delayed his planned arrival in Albany, he expressed deep disappointment and concern. He told Porter that personal business back home required his immediate return. Cumings also explained his reluctance to negotiate with John J. Vanderkemp without Porter present.[44]

Porter's decision not to come to Albany until sometime in April came in response to new revelations about the foreign landlords of western New York. These revelations offered an opportunity to increase public pressure against the Holland Company and the other foreign landholders of the region. In late March, Porter discovered that Robert Troup, agent for the English-owned Pulteney lands to the east of the Purchase, planned to oppose the settlers' political objectives. Troup believed Porter was behind this latest upsurge of agrarian discontent. Fearing that if it went unchecked the turmoil might spread like a brushfire, Troup sought to "curtail" Porter's "influence" before it aroused the settlers of the Pulteney lands. A disgruntled former employee wrote to Porter concerning Troup's intentions. The informant told Porter about Troup's questionable and repeated intrusions into state and local politics conducted on behalf of the English proprietors. This information opened the door for Porter to launch a vigorous public relations counterattack against any effort by the "foreign lobby" to defeat the settlers' objectives in Albany.[45]

Porter was given copies of the so-called Nunda letters documenting Robert Troup's partisan English loyalties "in the embargo times and during the war." The *Black Rock Gazette,* Porter's hometown newspaper, printed the full text of the Nunda letters. Over many years, the paper observed, Troup publicly admonished his subagents to refrain from any political activities, when privately he was advising them to do the opposite. The *Gazette* asked: "If foreigners, by our laws, may hold immense tracts of land, and be protected in the free exercise of the privilege, and too, with an exemption from the public burdens, does it become them to intermeddle in our national politics, and through their local agents, endeavor to favor the hostile pretensions of a foreign government, to influence our elections by extending the very money which they collect from our own citizens, or by overawing the electors by means of the power which their contracts for the sale of lands placed in the hands of those agents."[46]

---

44. Simeon Cumings to Peter B. Porter, March 15, 1827, Porter Papers.
45. R. W. Stoddard to Peter B. Porter, March 22, 27, 1827, Porter Papers.
46. Ibid.; *Black Rock Gazette,* March 31, 1827.

The Nunda letters also described how the foreign landowners of western New York had defeated the settler's previous efforts to revise the state's tax system. In 1820, for instance, Robert Troup and Philip Church, a large landholder from Allegany County, had combined their resources to host an "open house" for the members of the legislature at which the latter were "treated . . . in royal style and most sumptuously." The legislature later voted against a tax bill that had originated with the settlers of the Holland Purchase. Determined not to let the "foreign lobby" defeat the settlers again, Porter and the *Black Rock Gazette* called upon the foreign landowners "to quit their ducal and lordly establishments" and to "come and set themselves down as plain, unostentatious citizens." Porter and the *Gazette* admonished the landlords to give up their "exclusive privileges" and to accept the equal rights accorded every citizen in a republican society.[47]

Before public excitement about the Nunda letters subsided, Porter hurried to Albany to exert his personal influence in support of the highway tax bill. Porter fought efforts by opponents of the measure to weaken it. Proposed amendments threatened "to destroy the efficiency" of the bill. The "most destructive amendment," Porter believed, was one seeking to limit the tax of a "non resident company" to thirty days' labor in any one year. If the amendment was adopted, the counties of the Purchase "could not assess the Holland Company more than about $1500." This "would be a show of relief," Porter contended, "without the substance, and would be an absolute mockery of the people of the west." Finally, however, a highway bill taxing the lands of nonresidents for the construction of roads and bridges that was acceptable to Porter passed in the assembly by a vote of 73 to 33. But in the senate the bill languished and "was laid over . . . with other unfinished business."[48]

Meanwhile, Porter and others made some progress in their direct negotiations with the agents of the company. The Agrarian Convention's lobbyists in Albany, Simeon Cumings and Robert Fleming, met with John J. Vanderkemp and Thomas Ogden on March 22. The meeting went surprisingly well. Cumings described it as "a very amiable conversation." During the course of the meeting, Vanderkemp requested "a statement in writing of the principal grounds of complaint." Cumings and Fleming

47. R. W. Stoddard to Peter B. Porter, March 22, 1827, Porter Papers; *Black Rock Gazette,* March 24, 1827.

48. Peter B. Porter to John C. Spencer, April 15, 1827, Porter Papers; *Fredonia Censor* (Fredonia, N.Y.), May 2, Aug. 8, Oct. 24, 1827. See also John J. Vanderkemp to David Evans, April 7, 1827, Reel 65, HLCP.

consulted with Porter and drafted a statement of the settlers' main grievances against the company. After Porter reviewed it, the statement was
submitted to Vanderkemp.[49]

The "Grounds of Complaint" statement identified eight specific grievances and proposed an appropriate remedy for each. The first grievance
again drew attention to the unfairness of the highway tax system. The
second complaint criticized the company for not establishing a "permanent system" to accept "productions of the country" as payment for land.
The company was encouraged to "establish repositories" for the settlers'
wheat, pork, and cattle and to "fix the prices for a term of years." Guaran-
teeing prices was crucial. "This measure will induce the settlers," the
statement of grievances explained, " to make extra exertions to raise these
articles; because in that case they can be sure of a market and can therefore
afford to go to the expense of preparing their lands for the purpose;
whereas, the occasional, low prices of produce, and entire uncertainty of
markets, have discouraged them from raising more than sufficient for
their own sustenance, as attempting to raise much surplus, runs them in
debt."[50]

The third grievance concerned making all "new articles of agreement
. . . assignable." When Jacob Otto prohibited the buying and selling of
possession claims without his consent, many settlers resented the company's interference with their proprietary control. The fourth grievance
brought attention to the need for renegotiation of contracts when the
accumulated debt exceeded the market value of the land. The fifth
"Ground of Complaint" concerned the "great numbers of suits of ejectment and trespass" that company lawyers prosecuted against the settlers.
Cumings and Fleming asked the company to stop these suits, "or at least"
to stop "bringing them in the most expensive court, that of the United
States." The "Grounds of Complaint" also urged the company to reduce
its land prices and sell "for cash only." If the company did this, the
statement predicted, the Purchase would again attract "the best kind of
settlers." This last complaint underscores the fact that a united front of
opposition, joining small producers and more influential settlers against
the foreign landlords, did not completely submerge the latent class antag-
onism separating the poor hill country settlers from the lawyers, politicians, and entrepreneurs of the canal towns. The reference to "the best

49. Simeon Cumings and Robert Fleming to Peter B. Porter, March 24, 1827, Porter
Papers.
50. The draft copy of the "Grounds of Complaint" was attached to the letter cited above.
The "Grounds" were also printed in the *Black Rock Gazette,* May 12, 1827.

kind of settlers" and the call "for cash only" sales of land make it clear that Cumings, Fleming, and Porter shared some of the company's disdain for the woodchoppers.[51]

When agrarian opposition flared up in January and February of 1827, John J. Vanderkemp decided not to compromise with the "Agrarian Society." Confident that this latest episode had not created the "least excitement" among the settlers, Vanderkemp chose not "to treat" with the delegation sent by the Agrarian Convention to Albany. The success of that delegation in pushing the settlers' cause, however, eventually prompted Vanderkemp to change his mind. After meeting with Cumings and Fleming and considering the settlers' grievances, he decided to bring David Evans into the Batavia agency as a "coadjutor." Jacob Otto had fallen ill, and Vanderkemp became increasingly concerned about Otto's fitness to handle the job during this sensitive time. Consequently, he asked Evans to assist Otto as a "colleague clothed with equal authority." In addition to becoming a "coadjutor," Vanderkemp offered Evans the position of resident agent if Otto should die. Vanderkemp's decision to bring Evans into the Batavia agency was clearly a conciliatory gesture. Evans was a good choice for several reasons. He was a western New Yorker, and he knew the company and the settlers as well as anyone. He also possessed great political skill, having served as both a state senator and a member of the council of appointment. The general agent was aware of the political service he had rendered to the company. Vanderkemp believed Evans was the most qualified man for the job, but he insisted that Evans "retire from political life" once he assumed his official duties at Batavia.[52]

The news of Evans's appointment became public in May after Otto's death. The reviews were mixed. Evans was "well known" throughout the Purchase "as an honest and intelligent man," but his long-standing association with the company aroused concern. The *Buffalo Emporium* reminded its readers that Evans had acted as "the representative of the Holland Land Company," during his political tenure in Albany. Evans's opposition to Governor Clinton and his close ties to the Regency also raised questions about whether he was a friend of the West. In the aftermath of the highway tax bill's "defeat" in the state senate, Evans was linked to the "foreign lobby" that was blamed for killing the measure.[53]

51. Ibid.

52. John J. Vanderkemp to Thomas Ogden, March 5, 1827, and John J. Vanderkemp to David Evans, March 27, 1827, Reel 65, HLCP. David Evans was Joseph Ellicott's nephew, and before entering politics he worked for many years as a clerk in the Batavia land office.

53. *Fredonia Censor* (Fredonia, N.Y.), May 2, 1827; *Buffalo Emporium and General Advertiser*, June 11, 1827.

Evans's appointment as resident agent did not put the Agrarian Convention out of business; instead it emboldened the commercial dynamic that underlay the convention movement. The defeat of the highway tax bill produced a general call to elect representatives whose stand on the need to change the highway tax law was clear and unequivocal. The "great influence" of the foreign landlords and their agents could be counteracted only if "the people at Large" exercised their sovereign power at the polls. Only then could the highway tax law be amended. Meanwhile, the more fundamental question of a general tax revision again came under consideration. The editor of the *Buffalo Emporium* called for renewed consideration of the "propriety of taxing the bonds and mortgages" of the Holland Company and the Pulteney Estate. The principal appeal of this tax proposal was the revenue it would generate for internal improvement projects in the western part of the state, particularly the proposed state road.[54]

Governor Clinton had proposed that the state build a turnpike through the southern tier in March 1825. This road, its supporters argued, would do for the "sequestered counties" that lay to the "south of the great canal" what the canal was doing for the middle part of the state. The "idea of taxing the foreign landholders to raise a fund" for the state road garnered support from around the Purchase.[55]

In July 1827, the *Buffalo Emporium* printed an address to Erastus Root concerning the assembly's recent vote against the state road. Root was Speaker of the assembly and a supporter of the state road project. Authored by "Publius," this address recognized that the key objection to the road was financing, specifically the contention that the people of the state would not accept a general tax to pay for it. Critics carped that "nothing [could] be more unjust than to apply the property which belongs to the whole; for the benefit of a part." "Publius" argued that the road could be financed without a general tax. He proposed that the money could be raised through "a bonus upon the renewal of Bank charters and a reasonable tax upon the obligations for payment of money held by the agents of foreign landholders in the western country."[56]

"Publius" was proposing a tax on the money collected from the settlers as payment for land. Company agents were quick to point out that they remitted only small sums to the foreign proprietors, but "Publius" found

54. *Buffalo Emporium and General Advertiser,* June 11, 1827.

55. *Fredonia Censor* (Fredonia, N.Y.), May 2, 1827. The quotes are taken from the "Address of the Members of the Legislature friendly to the State Road to their Constituents."

56. *Buffalo Emporium and General Advertiser,* July 6, 19, 1827.

their assertions self-serving. The agents had a vested interest in drawing out the indebtedness of the settlers for as long as possible; their jobs depended on it.[57]

"Publius" justified the proposed tax against the "foreign landholders in this western country" on several grounds. Their selfish unwillingness to invest some of their profits for building roads and establishing other market outlets left the settlers "deeply in debt." The landholders' failure to help build an economic infrastructure undercut what few concessions they had made to settlers in the past. The poor condition of most roads in the Purchase, for instance, effectively limited the company's offer to accept wheat as payment for interest to a "small part of the settlers" living "near the appointed place of delivery." Overall, the foreign landlords' indifference and apathy entitled the settlers, "Publius" believed, to "the fostering care of the government of the state." The state road would liberate the settlers of the southern hill country, "opening to their industry a way to extricate themselves from that species of bondage" paralyzing their ambition and impoverishing their lives. "Publius" also argued that the state road would benefit the foreign landlords by helping them sell land in the more remote and inaccessible regions of their agencies.[58]

In September 1827, a new voice entered the public discussion of the Holland Company, the state road, and the tax question. "Citizen" reiterated the now familiar demand to make the highway law more equitable, but his proposal to tax the Holland Company differed on one critical point. "'Publius' recommends a tax upon the securities held by foreigners in proportion to their productiveness. I conceive that a tax upon the capital debt due to those foreigners, would be more proper than to levy it upon the income which may be received from the debt." "Citizen" objected that a tax "levied on the income" received by the agents put too much power in their hands. Since it was in their interest to collect only what was needed to operate their agencies, the revenue derived from taxing the landlords' income would prove too "fluctuating and uncertain" to provide a fund for the state road, which required a steady and predictable source of revenue. A tax "upon the capital debt due to those foreigners" was the answer. Taxing the debt due the Holland Company, as Porter had proposed in the settlers' February 9 petition, promised one other advantage. It might pressure the company to wind up its affairs in western New York, liberating the area from foreign domination.[59]

57. Ibid.
58. Ibid.
59. *Buffalo Emporium and General Advertiser*, Sept. 13, 1827.

The Local Elections of 1827

As the fall elections approached, the settlers in the Purchase remained both wary and hopeful about their relations with the Holland Company. In July the company announced its decision to receive wheat from the settlers at one dollar per bushel "for all interest on land contracts." If the wheat was not delivered at the canal, a deduction in price was made to cover the company's cost of shipping it to the canal. Other arrangements for receiving the settlers' beef and pork would be announced soon. The reaction to the company's July statement was not favorable. Porter's paper, the *Black Rock Gazette,* told the settlers this latest concession did not provide adequate relief. "This specious offer to allow a high price for wheat in payment of interest only, looks exceedingly like an article to wax the settler to part with his last farthing, and to continue to waste his energies in the improvement of lands which he must sooner or later abandon to the Company for want of means (and those means must be cash) to pay the principal," the *Gazette* concluded. Meaningful relief required a change in the highway tax law. The *Gazette* was optimistic about the prospect of securing such a change in the next legislative session. Still, it cautioned, that success depended upon the election of "candidates for the Legislature, favorable to the interests of the settlers."[60]

In early October, Peter B. Porter, Benjamin Barton, Albert Tracy, and Josiah Trowbridge, representing the Agrarian Convention's Committee of Petitions and Correspondence, published "a brief account of the progress of their agency" telling the settlers to stand firm. The "account" reviewed how the highway bill passed in the state assembly but "was lost" in the senate. Yet the committee predicted that the highway tax would be amended. The tide of history and progress was on the side of the settlers. "It is a relic of the feudal or aristocratic usages which prevailed in New York while in a colonial state, and has been preserved by the ascendancy which the great landholders of our cities have been able to maintain in the legislature. Its speedy downfall, however, may now be confidently anticipated, as well from the increasing influence of the country interest, as from the glaring injustice of the law itself, so strongly exhibited in its operation at this time, throughout the western counties of the state."[61]

60. *Fredonia Censor* (Fredonia, N.Y.), July 11, Aug. 8, 1827; see also *Buffalo Emporium and General Advertiser,* Aug. 23, 1827.

61. A draft copy of this statement, dated Oct. 10, 1827, may be found in the Porter Papers. See also *Fredonia Censor* (Fredonia, N.Y.), Oct. 24, 1827; *Buffalo Emporium and General Advertiser,* Oct. 15, 1827.

The committee's "account" praised the appointment of David Evans. He was a "westerner" who understood conditions in the Purchase from the perspective of both the company and the settlers. He also believed, according to the committee, that any attempt to enforce collection of the land debt "would be unjust as well as impractical." The appointment of Evans portended basic changes in company policy. First, Porter and his three colleagues believed the company would offer to renegotiate all contracts on which the amount of indebtedness exceeded the current market value of the land. Second, they predicted that a "leading object in the new system [would] be to give, as far as practicable, the benefits of improvements, on the lands of the Company, to the persons who actually made them" by extending the "most reasonable indulgences" to the settlers. Finally, the committee anticipated the company's plan to expand its payment in kind program and to do more to establish local markets for the settlers' surplus products. Porter was confident that these changes would infuse the settlers "with new life and activity and give a new aspect" to the general appearance of the Purchase.[62]

The Agrarian Convention's challenge to the Holland Land Company dominated local politics in the fall elections. Its activities produced a public call for candidates who would "secure and promote the great interests of western New York." For many settlers, this meant supporting candidates "without reference to party names or party attachments." The agrarian insurgency sparked a populist nominating convention that met at the Franklin House in Buffalo. Disregarding "all party distinctions," it nominated Peter B. Porter and Horace Clark, the latter from the town of Sardinia in southern Erie County, for the state assembly. In an address "to the Independent electors of Erie County" the convention outlined what was at stake in the next legislature: "Whether this County, in common with the rest of the Holland Purchase shall be REDEEMED from its present Embarrassed and truly Gloomy Condition and be permitted to march forward in the Road of Improvement to that state of Prosperity and Wealth, for which nature has so abundantly qualified it; or whether it shall continue to languish under Intolerable and Ruinous Pecuniary Burthens and remain in a state of Perpetual Tenancy to a Foreign Company."[63]

The Franklin House convention hailed Porter as "the champion of the People's Rights." His efforts over the last ten months on behalf of the settlers were impressive. The Franklin House meeting lauded Porter's

62. Ibid.
63. *Buffalo Emporium and General Advertiser,* Oct. 18, 22, 29, 1827.

support for local internal improvement projects. He favored the repair and improvement of roads traversing the Purchase, particularly those crossing the Indian Reservation south of Buffalo. He also supported the construction of a lateral canal linking Buffalo to the Allegheny River. This "independent" convention predicted that the Kremlin faction would oppose the nomination of Porter as well as the improvements he endorsed. The Kremlin's opposition, the independents charged, would stem from state senator Samuel Wilkeson's private commercial interest in "lake navigation." Wilkeson's investment in the transshipment of goods from Lake Erie to the canal, they believed, precluded any interest or support for other improvements.[64]

Meanwhile, the Kremlin faction met at the courthouse in Buffalo to nominate Thaddeus Joy and Horace Clark. But after Joy and Ebenezer Norton both declined the nomination for a seat in the state assembly, the Kremlin group met again on November 5, this time at the home of a local innkeeper. Peter B. Porter and David Burt were nominated. The late endorsement of Porter by the Kremlin convention signified that a coalition of aspiring commercial elites within the Purchase had arisen against the Holland Land Company. During the political insurgency of 1819–21, the Kremlin faction, the local supporters of Governor Clinton, appealed successfully to agrarian and egalitarian sentiments and won at the polls. But their appeal was directed primarily at toppling Joseph Ellicott and his influence. The agrarian and egalitarian sentiments aside, this was a political conflict between an aspiring commercial elite and the entrenched local establishment dominated by Ellicott and his family and friends. By November 1827, the Agrarian Convention embraced a coalition of agrarian and entrepreneurial interests that cut across lines of class and market orientation. The Agrarian Convention represented both the small settler who chiefly feared the loss of his equity and the local entrepreneur who blamed company policies for standing in the way of economic growth and diversification. Both could condemn the European bankers and moneyed landlords who lived without labor. Both could condemn the Regency's defense of the Holland Company and its system of political favors, privileges, and immunities that enriched the East at the expense of the West.[65]

Porter and Burt were elected to the state assembly. Only the Antimason vote in the towns of Erie, Clarence, and Amherst diminished the popular appeal of Porter and his support for the settlers' cause. The *Buffalo Em-*

64. *Buffalo Emporium and General Advertiser,* Oct. 29, 1827; *Black Rock Gazette,* Nov. 3, 1827.

65. *Buffalo Emporium and General Advertiser,* Nov. 5, 1827.

porium observed that Porter's election gave the "western country" an able advocate who would push the cause of "levying a tax upon the real and personal estates of non-resident landholders."[66]

The settlers' prospects looked bright in November 1827 for another reason too. The long-awaited but eagerly anticipated company reforms were made public in November 1. David Evans announced the company's willingness to renegotiate any land contract in which the amount of accumulated debt exceeded the current market value of the land. A modified contract required payment of one-eighth of the new purchase price and the balance in six annual installments. Evans also announced the company's decision to receive wheat and cattle as payment for principal and interest.[67]

The public reaction to the new company terms was very positive. The *Emporium* proclaimed that "a new era has commenced with the settlers on the Holland Company's lands." In late November the paper cited two instances of farmers living in Chautauqua County who had their land debts substantially reduced as a result of negotiating new contracts with the company. One settler had the price of his land reduced by $400, and another discovered he owed the company a mere $35. Porter noted approvingly: "The effects of the system are already wonderful in this part of the country, it has inspired new life and ambitions into the settlers, and almost everyone is taking advantage of the favourable terms that are offered." Privately Porter believed all of the settlers' "reasonable expectations" had been "fully realized." Similarly, the Agrarian Convention's Committee of Petitions and Correspondence observed that many of the settlers' objectives had "been happily and successfully attained."[68]

The success of the Agrarian Convention in winning concessions from the Holland Company prompted some of the movement's leaders to advise that they should "proceed with more moderation." The liberal terms announced by Evans in November put the movement on the defensive. Questions arose concerning whether the convention should meet in January as scheduled. When a delegate from Chautauqua County wrote to Porter to learn whether the convention planned to meet again, Porter gave a cautious answer. The convention would meet, he said, but it would not be as well attended "as it would have been, had we been less successful in

66. Ibid., Nov. 12, 1827.
67. Ibid., Nov. 5, 1827.
68. Ibid., Nov. 29, 1827; Peter B. Porter to Waterman Ellsworth, Dec. 24, 1827, and To the settlers on the Holland Purchase from the Committee of Petitions and Correspondence, Dec. 18, 1827, Porter Papers.

the attainment of the objects we had in view last winter." When a special session of the legislature in November modified the highway tax law to include the lands of the company, there was talk of dissolving or discontinuing the convention. Porter disagreed. He wanted the settlers to retain the "system of conventions," and he urged them not to lose sight of the "great principle" of taxation. Porter believed the ultimate solution to the settlers' problems required the enactment of a tax on the debt due the company.[69]

By the end of 1827 the Agrarian Convention could point to several accomplishments. Over the next few years, experience showed that the company's offer to renegotiate land contracts was more important than the new highway tax law. During the period of 1827–30, David Evans worked assiduously to process the business of modifying land contracts, whereas he noted in July 1829 that, surprisingly, "very few towns" in the Purchase had taken advantage of the new highway tax law.[70]

The Agrarian Convention promoted the interests of both small producers and more commercially oriented settlers. From the perspective of the former, the company's offer to renegotiate contracts promised protection for the settlers' "betterments" and affirmation of the dignity and status of productive labor. The modified contracts fixed land prices "at what the land independent of improvements [was] really worth." The practical effect was to encourage payments for land and to revitalize the regional market for improved farms. Hence poorer settlers might again sell their "betterments" and receive compensation for their labor. The commercially oriented settlers looked forward to greater economic diversification within the Purchase and a more fluid land market. These settlers believed that as a land changed hands it was improved. Buying and selling land, like any other exchange of commerce, was a vital and dynamic instrument of progress and economic development.[71]

69. Peter B. Porter to Waterman Ellsworth, Dec. 24, 1827, and Waterman Ellsworth to Peter B. Porter, Dec. 19, 1827, Porter Papers.
70. Reports of David Evans, 1827, 438; 1828, 455–56, 449–50; 1829, 461; 1830, 471–72.
71. Reports of David Evans, 1827, 444.

6

Rebellion

B y 1828, the Holland Purchase featured a distinctive pattern of land development that divided the region into several subregions. A line running between the tenth and eleventh tier of townships, continuing around the perimeter of the Buffalo Creek Indian Reservation, and extending to the southwest along the Erie Lake plain divided the Purchase into more developed and less developed subregions. The more developed area, located in the northern third of the Purchase, included a narrow strip of townships bordering Lake Erie. The less developed area occupied the hill country of the middle and southern two-thirds of the Purchase. The northern third of the region, in general, had higher property values, more improved acres, and a denser population (Tables 7–9). It included the longest settled townships, featured the largest urban sites, and offered the best transportation facilities. This region had always enjoyed easy access to Lake Ontario and the market center at Montreal, but beginning in 1825 it was transformed by the Erie Canal.

The Holland Company believed that this northern area was ready for an economic takeoff. The interior hill country, however, remained an area of frontier poverty and marginal economic growth. The new company policies announced in November 1827 did not measurably improve the immediate prospects of the hill country settlers. The economic independence and "comfortable subsistence" that these small producers pursued on their hardscrabble frontier farms could not withstand the effects of two far-reaching company decisions that threatened to turn their lives upside down. First, in 1833 the state legislature enacted a tax on the debts held by foreign landowners. The English and Dutch proprietors of the Pulteney

Table 7. Economic development, Genesee County

	Value per acre		Improved acres (%)		Population density per square mile	
	1825	1835	1825	1835	1825	1835
Area lying north of the tenth tier of townships						
Alabama		$ 5.55		25.2		31.5
Elba	$ 4.85	19.41	18.7	52.2	29.42	53.12
Pembroke	4.95	10.54	20.5	27.5	38.44	50.73
Darien		13.86		56.2		54.60
Batavia	12.90	23.95	29.7	50.5	44.29	83.59
Alexander	8.54	16.47	40.4	59.7	53.84	71.06
Bethany	8.44	20.62	43.6	67.2	59.39	70.33
Hill Country townships south of eleventh tier						
Bennington	$ 3.58	$ 7.15	18.9	38.0	28.81	48.66
Attica	6.58	13.21	36.9	52.8	54.47	71.69
Middlebury	7.39	15.82	43.4	63.5	59.33	71.94
Sheldon	4.12	6.28	18.3	36.0	28.03	46.51
Orangeville	4.33	7.89	21.6	40.4	34.19	51.17
Warsaw	7.30	15.53	31.3	49.5	59.41	76.74
Java		5.30		22.8		41.08
Wethersfield	3.35	5.54	14.4	30.3	23.18	46.37
Gainesville	4.87	10.39	25.4	46.3	40.36	59.86
China	3.86	4.56	9.3	18.8	19.96	26.65

Sources: New York State Census for 1825, in David Burr, *Atlas of the State of New York* (New York, 1829); Thomas F. Gordon, *Gazetteer of the State of New York* (Philadelphia, 1836).

Estate and the Holland Land Company responded through their agents by calling in all outstanding land contracts and rewriting them. The new contracts stipulated that a settler must pay that portion of the tax levied against his debt to the foreign landowners. Then in 1835 the Holland Land Company announced its decision to sell the Purchase to a group of American investors. The new proprietors, eager to profit, quickly announced plans to tighten the terms and conditions under which credit could be renewed. The new terms, stigmatized the "Genesee Tariff" by the settlers, produced an uproar in the "back towns." Fearing the impending loss of their homes and improvements, the small producers of the hill country helped to revitalize the Agrarian Convention movement in Buffalo, but the urgency of their situation drove them to open rebellion in 1836 against the aristocratic landowners of the Purchase.

Table 8. Economic development, Erie County

	Value per acre		Improved acres (%)		Population density per square mile	
	1825	1835	1825	1835	1825	1835
Northern townships						
Alden	$2.77	$ 6.89	13.1	38.1	25.38	67.45
Amherst	3.68	10.32	7.6	20.7	14.95	50.97
Clarence[a]	3.54	9.01	15.8	35.5	24.27	46.18
Erie	2.69		8.7		23.16	
Newstead		7.00		28.4		50.17
Lancaster (formed from Clarence, 1833)		8.64		30.0		53.90
Buffalo	11.40	114.83	9.4	58.5	45.84	577.64
Hill country townships south of Reservation						
Aurora	$2.68	$ 8.53	21.5	49.0	32.51	70.48
Boston[a]	3.22	4.91	14.0	37.0	28.85	47.15
Holland[a]	2.39	5.27	8.4	21.9	14.56	32.59
Colden (formed from Holland, 1827)		3.18		7.3		20.29
Collins	2.23	5.68	9.4	29.4	14.88	45.06
Concord[a]	2.30	4.35	12.1	23.6	21.73	38.17
Eden	2.99	5.78	12.4	23.4	22.99	50.69
Evans	1.97	4.31	6.4	24.0	11.73	44.20
Hamburg	3.66	8.73	15.8	36.8	29.36	51.65
Sardinia[a]	2.12	4.60	11.5	21.9	18.45	31.88
Wales	1.68	4.45	11.9	23.4	18.03	31.36

Sources: New York State Census for 1825, in David Burr, *Atlas of the State of New York* (New York, 1829); Thomas F. Gordon, *Gazetteer of the State of New York* (Philadelphia, 1836).
[a]Townships where public meetings approved of the destruction of the land office at Mayville.

MANY settlers responded voluntarily to the company's new terms of sale and credit announced in November 1827. A large part of the business transacted at Batavia and the other land offices during the period of 1827–30 involved modified contracts. In 1830, for instance, original sales involved 50,498 acres of land, but modified sales involved more than 225,000 acres. Over the period of 1827–30 the Holland Land Company renegotiated contracts for 832,000 acres of land, or 37 percent of all land sold from 1801 through December 31, 1826. The company told the state legislature in 1831 that more than 11,000 contracts had been modified with a net reduction of debt exceeding $700,000. By early 1833 more

Table 9. Economic development, Chautauqua County

	Value per acre		Improved acres (%)		Population density per square mile	
	1825	1835	1825	1835	1825	1835
Lakefront townships						
Hanover	$5.19	$ 8.54	18.9	41.4	67.74	76.06
Sheridan		7.12		41.0		55.29
Pomfret	5.20	10.76	14.9	35.0	42.68	79.78
Portland	3.77	7.81	20.7	44.9	39.05	67.14
Westfield		8.42		41.1		71.02
Ripley	3.25	5.46	16.3	25.4	24.59	44.66
Interior townships						
Arkwright[a]	$	$ 3.42		29.6		38.68
Busti[a]	2.08	3.59	11.5	31.9	22.88	42.43
Carroll		3.55		12.6		28.54
Charlotte[a]		3.26		24.4		33.01
Chautauqua	2.65	4.69	10.1	31.9	20.51	47.37
Cherry Creek[a]		2.19		13.0		26.00
Clymer	1.53	1.91	1.7	13.1	4.23	24.04
Ellicott[a]	3.85	6.32	9.3	20.5	24.04	67.60
Ellery[a]	2.50	4.30	18.0	39.1	22.07	49.15
Ellington	2.08	3.46	4.0	29.4	11.46	50.11
French Creek		1.67		6.5		15.32
Gerry[a]	2.45	2.80	6.3	18.7	16.10	29.93
Harmony[a]	2.06	3.11	4.5	18.5	10.93	36.42
Mina	1.56	2.13	2.0	11.1	7.76	23.52
Poland		2.39		13.0		26.89
Stockton[a]	2.93	4.46	12.4	24.9	20.53	45.71
Villenova	1.96	3.33	5.9	24.3	15.86	41.17
Sherman		2.20		18.4		23.91

Sources: New York State Census for 1825, in David Burr, *Atlas of the State of New York* (New York, 1829); Thomas F. Gordon, *Gazetteer of the State of New York* (Philadelphia, 1836).
[a]Townships that were prominently involved in the rebellion of 1836.

than 13,000 contracts had been renewed and modified, with "the whole amount of reductions" in excess of 1 million.[1]

The company decided to serve writs of ejectment on settlers who re-

1. Reports of David Evans in Robert W. Bingham, ed., *Reports of Joseph Ellicott*, 2 vols. (Buffalo, N.Y., 1937–41), 2:1830, 471–72; Reports of Jacob Otto, ibid., 2:1826, 424; Memorial of John J. Vanderkemp and Robert Troup to the Legislature of the State of New York, March 21, 1831, New York *Assembly Documents*, No. 282 (1831), 5; Memorial of John J. Vanderkemp and Joseph Fellows to the Senate and Assembly of the State of New York, March 9, 1833, New York *Assembly Documents*, No. 235 (1833), 5.

fused to have their contracts modified. It originally set a deadline of April 1, 1829. Common law rules required that the landlords give settlers six months' notice of their intention to serve such a writ. Evans planned to serve individual notices in the spring of 1828 warning settlers that their land would be resold unless they called the land office and took a new contract within the time stipulated. His plan was to resell such land and "let the new purchaser bring the ejectment." In fact, Evans anticipated that the new purchaser would compensate the previous owner for his "betterments" without resorting to coercive measures. "By this means the company will avoid bringing suits themselves," Evans explained, "which is desirable if possible."[2]

In 1829 Evans reported that five thousand expired contracts remained unmodified. "Five to six hundred" were contracts on "pieces" of land whose "purchaser either died or changed his mind." In other cases the land had been taken "by irresponsible men for the sake of the timber and abandoned." This left forty-five hundred contracts for land still inhabited by delinquent settlers. Some contracts had been expired for as long as fifteen years, and the company had little idea who occupied these lands. Evans believed half these contracts would be modified "within the time limited by the notices to quit," but the other half were held "by poor creatures from whom nothing like payment [should] be expected."[3]

Evans employed five persons to serve individual notices upon delinquent settlers throughout the summer and early fall of 1829. On February 1, 1830, he issued a "proclamation" warning that the company intended to enforce payment. Evans encouraged settlers unable to take new contracts to sell out. The company did not wish to expropriate any settlers' "betterments," but it expected delinquents to take advantage of the opportunity for a debt reduction or face certain eviction. Privately, Evans recommended to the company's general agent that some delinquent settlers, including "widows and orphan children . . . old people in a state of decrepitude, and those who had been recently visited by misfortune such as severe sickness, loss of property by fire or some other signal calamity," should be left alone. Evans noted the widespread prevalence of "fevers and agues" in the northern townships during 1828–29.[4]

2. Reports of David Evans, 1827, 442–43; Elizabeth Blackmar, "The Distress of Property Law: Landlord-Tenant Relations in Antebellum New York," in William Pencak and Wythe W. Holt, Jr., eds., *The Law in America, 1607–1861* (New York, 1989), 221.

3. Reports of David Evans, 1828, 451–52.

4. Ibid., 452; Paul Evans, *The Holland Land Company* (Buffalo, N.Y., 1924), 363–64; Reports of David Evans, 1829, 463; ibid., 1828, 453–54.

By the spring of 1830, 2,213 settlers in Genesee, Allegany, and Orleans counties had received individual notices, and 948 of them responded by coming to the land office and taking new contracts. In Genesee County, where 1,574 settlers received notices, the great majority of the delinquents lived in the hilly townships south of Batavia. The five townships of Orangeville (T9-R2), Attica (T10-R2), Wethersfield (T8-R2), Gainesville (T8-R1), and Middlebury (T10-R1) had 45 percent of the delinquent settlers in Genesee County (Tables 10 and 11).[5]

Evans attributed the stubbornness of settlers who refused to take new contracts to several factors. Some were determined, he believed, "to try how far the liberality of the company may be carried." But many others were simply too poor to pay for the land on which they lived. "There are . . . many so wretchedly poor as to require all their exertions to keep their families from absolute want of the necessities of life; from such," Evans predicted, "we can never expect to receive payment, and the time is not distant when measures must be taken to sell the land they occupy."[6]

To ascertain the particular circumstances of the most stubborn delinquents, Evans compiled lists of the offenders and arranged for a company representative to visit the lands of each. The company's agent assessed the value of the delinquent's farm, recording the number of improved acres, the quantity of fruit trees, and the existence and condition of houses and barns. The remarks used the phrase "buildings of no value" or "little value" again and again. For the most part, only frame houses and barns were acceptable. Log structures were judged to have little or no value. The company's representative also made a judgment concerning the present occupant's likelihood of renewing the article under which he claimed possession. Finally, if a case for "lenity" existed, the circumstances were noted and a recommendation was made.[7]

In Chautauqua County, where the Holland Company's land office was destroyed in February 1836, 505 visits took place during 1829–30. The largest number of visits occurred in the township of Ellery (T3-R12), where forty-seven contracts were investigated. These records highlight the active market for articles of agreement that the company tried to curtail in 1824. In the town of Ellery, for instance, the present occupant turned out to be the original purchaser in only ten of the forty-seven contracts under investigation. In three other cases it appears that the present occupant was a relative of the original purchaser. In six of these contracts the land was

5. Reports of David Evans, 1829, 462–63.
6. Ibid., 463.
7. Ibid., 464.

Table 10. Number of settlers notified during 1829 by township

Township	Range	Genesee County Notified	Modified	Remaining
8a	1	110	57	53
9a	1	88	76	12
10a	1	108	66	42
11	1	14	14	0
12	1	25	17	8
13	1	22	20	2
8a	2	122	26	96
9a	2	191	41	150
10a	2	177	116	61
11	2	84	77	7
12	2	53	41	12
13	2	17	14	3
7	3	17	1	16
8	3	22	5	17
10a	3	104	13	91
11	3	71	11	60
12	3	59	6	53
13	3	2	0	2
7a	4	41	7	34
8a	4	57	5	52
10a	4	52	9	43
11	4	90	16	74
12	4	47	4	43
13	4	1	0	1
		1,574	642	932

Township	Range	Allegany County Notified	Modified	Remaining
7a	1	109	59	50
7a	2	79	18	61
		188	77	111

Source: Report of David Evans, in Robert W. Bingham, ed., *Reports of Joseph Ellicott,* 2 vols. (Buffalo, N.Y., 1937–41), 2:1829, 462.
aHill country townships.

unoccupied or abandoned. The situation in other townships was similar. In Ellington (T3-R10) the present occupant was the same person to whom the land was sold in only four of fourteen contracts. In Pomfret (T5-R12) the present occupant was the original contractor in nine of thirty-five cases.[8]

8. These figures were taken from the lists of expired contracts, 1829–30, Reel 123, Inventory no. 555, Holland Land Company Project, State University of New York College at Fredonia; cited hereafter as HLCP.

Table 11. Expired contracts in the counties of Erie and Niagria during 1829–1830

Township	Range	Expired contracts	Contracts modified	Expired contracts remaining
6[a]	5	6	0	6
7[a]	5	69	19	50
8[a]	5	75	14	61
9[a]	5	101	16	85
11	5	53	19	34
12	5	65	18	47
13	5	11	0	11
6[a]	6	19	1	18
7[a]	6	49	10	39
8[a]	6	37	3	34
9[a]	6	58	20	38
11	6	27	12	15
12	6	29	11	18
13	6	3	0	3
Buffalo Village		19	11	8
6[a]	7	25	4	21
7[a]	7	64	12	52
8[a]	7	87	37	50
9[a]	7	24	17	7
11	7	11	4	7
12	7	14	4	10
13	7	9	2	7
6[a]	8	39	20	19
7[a]	8	70	24	46
8[a]	8	71	24	47
9[a]	8	43	20	23
11	8	2	0	2
12	8	9	2	7
13	8	10	1	9
14	8	18	10	8
15	8	57	13	44
8[a]	9	54	18	36
13	9	2	1	1
14	9	15	6	9
15	9	56	28	28
14	7	46	32	14
14	7	58	14	44
		1,405	447	958

Source: Reel 123, Inventory no. 558, HLCP.
[a]Hill country townships.

In addition to modifying land contracts for which the accumulation of debt exceeded the market value of the property, the Holland Company expanded its payment in kind policy. In November 1827 David Evans announced the company's decision to accept wheat and cattle as payment for both principal and interest. The earlier policy implemented by Evans's predecessor accepted wheat, cattle, and pork for payment of interest on land contracts. Actually cattle were accepted as payment for interest and principal during Otto's tenure, but in 1827 the company openly put the expanded provisions into general practice throughout the Purchase. Under the new provisions, settlers were required to deposit their wheat at designated depots on the canal. They received a credit of one dollar per bushel for payment of interest. When wheat was deposited as payment of principal, settlers received a credit equal to the current market price. If settlers chose to deliver their wheat at a site not on the canal, the company accepted it but deducted transportation charges.[9]

Local papers in the Holland Purchase praised the liberality of the modified payment in kind policy, yet the receipt of wheat in 1828 remained minimal. Evans attributed this to the failure of the wheat crop, to falling prices in the New York market, and to the ill health of the settlers. "The prevalence of fevers and agues in Orleans and Niagara counties and the north part of Genesee and Erie" greatly reduced the amount of grain sown and harvested.[10]

In 1831 Evans declared the taking of wheat for both interest and principal a failure and recommended abandoning the policy. The problem was that wheat possessed great value throughout the Purchase. Country stores and mills accepted it in trade for the debts farmers incurred throughout the course of every year, leaving little for the company. By 1835, as commercial agriculture radiated outward from the canal, growing prosperity in the northern townships led Evans to stop the practice of receiving any commodity as payment for land.[11]

After 1827 the company continued to receive cattle as payment for principal and interest, albeit more openly than before. The company continued to lose money, but because it received the greatest number of cattle from settlers in the "hilly parts of the southern counties," where delinquencies abounded, the program was continued. It was better, David Evans argued, to receive some form of payment from these settlers than

9. The announcement appeared in the *Buffalo Emporium and General Advertiser*, Nov. 5, 1827; Reports of David Evans, 1827, 442; Evans, *Holland Land Company*, 320.

10. Reports of David Evans, 1828, 453–54.

11. Reports of David Evans, 1835, 513–14.

none at all. Receiving cattle also presented company agents or drovers with an opportunity to pressure delinquent settlers to renew their articles.[12]

In the end, the company reforms put into operation during 1827 satisfied neither the small producers of the hill country townships nor the more commercially oriented settlers of the canal townships. In 1831 David Evans reported to the general agent that 2,268 expired contracts covering 391,905 acres were still unmodified. He recommended rigorous action against long-standing delinquents who refused to renew their contracts "through negligence, inability or perverseness." Evans urged the general agent "to bring ejectment suits against them in the names of the Company." His earlier proposal to sell delinquent lands to the first purchaser who came along, letting the buyer dispossess the occupant, flew in the face of widely shared agrarian values. "In general no good inhabitant wishes," Evans now explained, "to purchase a tract of land . . . or move into a neighborhood where, through sympathy for the old settler the people or a part of them will be prejudiced against him for dispossessing another to obtain the fruits of his labor." Rigorous action by and in the name of the company was the only alternative. Doubtless this step would "excite something like an insurrectionary spirit against the Company and their agents," but "a due regard" for the company's interest, Evans believed, required that such "measures should be adopted." As the company headed toward a final showdown with an agrarian culture whose conception of land and property rights was in conflict with its own hierarchical control of land development, cunning politicians sensitive to the populist value of endorsing the settlers' cause against the greedy, selfish, and monopolistic foreign landlords turned up the heat.[13]

The Political Setting of Agrarian Radicalism

The development of the second party system in the Holland Purchase does not fit the national profile that historians have drawn of the Jacksonian Democratic and Whig parties. In the Purchase the Whig party accomplished what the Democrats achieved at the national level. It became the popular party of the underdog, espousing the concerns of small producers who feared being oppressed and exploited by moneyed interests that used

12. Reports of David Evans, 1827, 444; ibid., 1830, 484; Reports of Jacob Otto, 1826, 423.
13. Reports of David Evans, 1831, 487; ibid., 1831, 488–89.

political power to govern on behalf of the privileged few. The local Whigs in the Purchase grew out of an uneasy alliance between Antimasons and National Republicans that was dominated by the Antimasons from 1829 to 1833. During these years the "blessed spirit" at work in the "infected eighth district" returned impressive majorities for local and state Antimasonic candidates. A radical egalitarian movement with distinctive evangelical overtones, Antimasonry in the Holland Purchase embraced both western agrarianism and some of the evangelical fervor that glowed more brightly in the heart of the burned-over district just to the east. Antimasonry expressed the small settler's fear of coercion and domination and his outrage over the intensifying assaults against his labor and liberty. Antimasonry's call to strike down the monster of Freemasonry was deeply rooted in the traditional agrarian fear of privilege, inequality, and commercial elites that lived on the labor of other men. But it also expressed the region's growing impatience with any obstacle that impeded the rise of the West. Both these dimensions were present in an "Address to the Electors of New York" issued by Albert Tracy, president of the state Antimasonic Convention held at Utica in June 1832. The "Address" castigated the "monster that threatens destruction to everything we hold dear." It assailed the "monied aristocracy" that had ruled the state for over a decade. But it also extolled the party's candidate for governor, Francis Granger, as a statesman who sought "to extend the benefits of internal navigation to a portion of our fellow citizens entitled to participate in the general prosperity."[14]

The important gubernatorial election of 1828 set the pattern for the heterogeneous party that the Antimasons became after they subsumed the National Republicans in 1829. In the Holland Purchase the race for governor in 1828 was a three-way contest between Democrat Martin Van

14. My discussion of Antimasonry is based on Michael F. Holt, "The Antimasonic and Know Nothing Parties," in Arthur M. Schlesinger, Jr., ed., *History of U.S. Political Parties,* 4 vols. (New York, 1973), 1:575–93; Whitney R. Cross, *The Burned-Over District: The Social and Intellectual History of Enthusiastic Religion in Western New York, 1800–1850* (Ithaca, N.Y., 1950), 114–20; Lee Benson, *The Concept of Jacksonian Democracy: New York as a Test Case* (Princeton, N.J., 1961), 14–46; Kathleen Smith Kutolowski, "Antimasonry Reexamined: Social Bases of the Grass-Roots Party," *Journal of American History* 71 (Sept. 1984), 269–93; Paul Goodman, *Toward a Christian Republic: Antimasonry and the Great Transition in New England* (New York, 1988); Ronald P. Formisano, *The Transformation of Political Culture: Massachusetts Parties, 1790's-1840's* (New York, 1983), 197–221; Ronald P. Formisano and Kathleen Smith Kutolowski, "Antimasonry and Masonry: The Genesis of Protest, 1826–1827," *American Quarterly* 29 (Summer 1977), 139–65. Albert Tracy's "Address to the Electors of New York" is found in Holt, "The Antimasonic and Know Nothing Parties," 669–74; the quotes are taken from 669 and 673.

Buren, National Republican Smith Thompson, and Antimason Solomon Southwick. The Albany Regency had been perceived by the voters of the Holland Purchase as a friend of the foreign landlords and an enemy of the West ever since 1819–20. Hence in the election of 1828 anti-Regency, anti-Jackson partisans could choose among two candidates. In Erie County, where aspiring commercial elites led by Albert Tracy and Peter B. Porter had challenged both the Holland Land Company and the state's eastern political establishment repeatedly during the previous eight years, 75 percent of the vote went against Martin Van Buren. Smith Thompson carried the county with 57 percent of the vote. Of the anti-Van Buren vote Thompson got 76 percent and Southwick 24 percent (Table 12).[15]

The majority of Thompson's vote came from the more settled townships of Buffalo, Clarence, Amherst, Hamburg and Aurora. Yet Thompson also received strong support from the poorer townships of southern Erie County. In Concord, Boston, and Colden electors gave over 80 percent of their votes to the National Republican candidate for governor. The Antimasons won a majority in only two townships and a plurality of the vote in a third town. But the Antimason strongholds of Erie, Alden and Clarence were among the fastest growing towns in the county. They, together with Amherst and Buffalo, were the only portion of Erie County that David Evans considered far enough "advanced in improvement" to secure the land debt owed the Holland Company. Antimason strength in these towns fits the profile that Kathleen Smith Kutolowski found in neighboring Genesee County. Contrary to standard interpretations of Antimasonry that link the "blessed spirit" with poorer, subsistence farming regions, Kutolowski has shown that in Genesee County the Antimasons were strongest in the "most economically mature townships."[16]

In Chautauqua County Solomon Southwick won with 40 percent of the vote to Martin Van Buren's 34 percent and Smith Thompson's 26 percent. Southwick got 61 percent of the anti-Van Buren vote (Table 12). The greatest percentage of Antimasonic votes were cast in the poorer townships that supported the agrarian rebellion of 1836. The townships of

15. The election returns for Erie County are taken from the *Buffalo Emporium and General Advertiser*, Nov. 20, 1828.

16. Reports of David Evans, 1835, 513; Kutolowski, "Antimasonry Reexamined," 275. During his campaign for a seat in the state senate during 1829, Albert Tracy noted that the "north towns" were strongly Antimason while the hill country towns of the south, "the worst part of the county," were less enthusiastic. See Albert H. Tracy to Millard Fillmore, Oct. 28, 1829, Reel 1, Millard Fillmore Papers, Buffalo and Erie county Historical Society, Buffalo, N.Y. For election results, see *Buffalo Republican*, Nov. 14, 1829.

Table 12. Gubernatorial election of 1828 (in percent)

Township	Chautauqua County		
	Thompson	Van Buren	Southwick
Chautauqua	14.5	44.5	41.0
Pomfret	53.4	19.4	27.2
Ellicott	20.3	45.0	34.7
Gerry	13.8	31.7	54.5
Hanover	67.1	29.8	3.1
Portland	18.7	31.1	50.1
Ripley	13.9	59.5	26.6
Harmony	6.9	17.4	75.7
Clymer	4.6	14.8	80.6
Ellery	10.3	34.2	55.6
Stockston	11.4	46.2	42.4
Villenova	32.5	48.5	19.0
Busti	8.5	21.2	70.3
Mina	5.1	41.7	53.2
Carroll	14.4	44.3	41.3
Ellington	37.3	37.3	25.4
Sheridan	46.8	20.2	33.0
	25.6	34.2	40.2

Township	Erie County		
	Thompson	Van Buren	Southwick
Alden	33.3	16.7	50.0
Amherst	59.5	10.5	30.0
Aurora	71.5	20.0	8.5
Boston	80.8	14.4	4.8
Buffalo	65.3	32.4	2.3
Clarence	42.3	14.9	42.9
Concord	82.5	15.6	1.9
Collins	38.0	31.5	31.5
Colden	81.1	18.9	00.0
Eden	55.9	44.1	00.0
Erie	20.2	8.2	71.6
Evans	65.9	34.1	00.0
Hamburg	66.6	27.1	6.3
Holland	17.3	47.5	35.2
Sardinia	53.8	45.6	00.1
Wales	53.8	25.4	20.8
	56.9	25.5	17.6

Sources: The Centennial History of Chautauqua County, 2 vols. (Jamestown, N.Y., 1904), 1:159–60; *Buffalo Emporium and General Advertiser,* Nov. 20, 1828.

Clymer, Harmony, Busti, Ellery, and Gerry gave Antimasonic majorities ranging from 81 percent in Clymer to 54 percent in Gerry. The greatest percentage of National Republican votes came from the more commercially developed townships along Lake Erie.[17]

"The validity of said company's title"

In February 1830 some Buffalo lawyers led by Henry White and Thomas Sherwood presided over a meeting called "for the purpose of taking into consideration . . . doubts concerning the validity of said Company's title to the lands claimed by them in this state." To shore up a weak title, White believed the company was petitioning the state legislature for a special act affirming the title of the heirs and survivors of the original trustees. From the company's perspective, the bill concerned a technical matter of little consequence. Some of the settlers saw it differently. At a second meeting, also held at the Eagle Tavern in Buffalo, White assailed the company's title, charging that the foreign proprietors dared not bring any ejectment suits against the settlers because they knew their title was defective. In addition, he focused renewed attention on the still growing debt owed by the settlers. He estimated "the debts due the company at about ten millions of dollars." In what represented as radical an agrarian scheme as would ever issue from the Holland Purchase, White proposed expropriating the debt and using it for common schools and internal improvements throughout the Purchase. He failed to explain just how this could be done.[18]

The Buffalo meetings created a "prodigious excitement" among the settlers living in the southern part of Erie County. The town of Hamburg sent forty delegates to the second meeting; the nearby town of Aurora sent fifteen delegates. The "commotion" underscored the hill country settlers' growing concern about losing their farms and improvements. Some of them believed that if the company's title was shown to be invalid, the entire Purchase might revert to the state and they could buy their land "at one dollar and twenty-five cents per acre." Other settlers hoped "the state would, without requiring any payment whatever, convey to the actual occupants all the land they held under contracts with the Company." At the very least, the settlers of the south towns anticipated the "commo-

---

17. The election returns for Chautauqua County are taken from *The Centennial History of Chautauqua County*, 2 vols. (Jamestown, N.Y., 1904), 1:159–60.

18. Handbill, Feb. 4, 1830, Ira Blossom to David Evans, Feb. 4, 5, 1830, and David Evans to John J. Vanderkemp, Feb. 18, March 30, 1830, Reel 90, HLCP.

tion" would result in more "lenient terms" from the landlords. Still, some of them worried about the consequences of creating doubts about the company's title. Once "a shadow of doubt" existed, few emigrants "in search of a farm" would "stop to investigate" the lands for sale in the Holland Purchase, making it even more difficult for a settler to sell his improvement and recover the value his labor added to the company's land.[19]

The commotion over the validity of the company's title subsided almost as quickly as it began. Several factors contributed. First, White and the other Buffalo lawyers were accused of political expediency. Critics said they sought "to create a party in opposition to anti-masonry" exploiting the settlers' hatred of the foreign landowners just as the Antimasons had taken advantage of the people's outrage over the Morgan affair. Second, the title question failed to enlist the support and leadership of Peter B. Porter, who refused to attend the Buffalo meetings and announced that he "disapproved of the proceedings." Porter's disapproval was followed by an "Address," bearing the names of thirty-six leading Buffalonians, that appeared in the local newspapers. It cautioned the settlers of the Holland Purchase about the consequences of agitating the title question: "It is as easy to perceive that farther emigration will be greatly retarded, if not wholly interrupted; that new investments of capital within our borders will cease; that existing ones will be gradually withdrawn; and that all the mature advantages and varied blessings arising from the increase of healthful population, from the progress of productive industry, and from the development of our immense and yet unexplored sources of wealth must be lost for years."[20]

Finally, concern about the negative effect the commotion was having on business at the land offices prompted David Evans to recommend prosecution of White and his colleagues for slandering the company's title. "It is all important," he declared, "to convince this community that the H. L. Co. rights will not be permitted to be sported with, with impunity." A lawyer from the company prepared a brief of evidence against White and sent it to the general agent in Philadelphia, but prosecution never took place because of Evans's success on another front.[21]

David Evans went to Albany to push along the company's bill that had given rise to the title question in the first place. Prevailing upon "old

19. David Evans to John J. Vanderkemp, Feb. 18, March 30, 1830, ibid.

20. *Buffalo Journal*, Feb. 24, 1830; see also *An Address to the Landholders and Inhabitants of the Holland Purchase* (Buffalo, N.Y., 1830).

21. David Evans to John J. Vanderkemp, Feb. 8, March 30, 1830, Reel 90, HLCP.

friends" in the state legislature, he succeeded in expediting its consideration and prevented "much angry debate which would have encouraged the malcontents at Buffalo." He also succeeded in having a clause the company found particularly offensive removed from the final language of the bill. The objectionable phrase stipulated "that the act should not be construed by implication or otherwise to confirm to Wilhem Willink and others the title to any land claimed by them within this state." This clause would have raised further doubts concerning the company's title. The company's bill passed on March 9, 1830.[22]

"Taxing the debts due to nonresident land holders"

The controversy stirred by the title question subsided. The threat of prosecution caused the Buffalo lawyers to retreat from their earlier boldness. In the fall of 1830, however, the idea of taxing the debts owed to foreign landlords, first advanced by Peter B. Porter and the Agrarian Convention of 1827, received new attention. The impetus this time came from the settlers of the nearby Pulteney Estate who shared the same problems as their counterparts in the Holland Purchase. The unrest that beset the Pulteney Estate beginning in 1828 was greatly influenced by the proceedings of the Agrarian Convention held in Buffalo. In November 1830, David Evans told his general agent to anticipate a proposal for "taxing the debts due to nonresident land holders" from the settlers of the Pulteney Estate. Evans believe there was little support for such a tax among the settlers of the Holland Purchase, and he attributed the petitions circulating throughout Allegany and Steuben counties to land speculators who wished to rid western New York of foreign landowners so as to create opportunity for themselves.[23]

Nonetheless, Evans warned that the tax might be enacted because the state needed more revenue. The state's two most reliable sources of income, the salt and auction duties, were committed "to the redemption of the canal debt," so new taxes appeared inevitable. If the state comptroller asked for a tax on debts, Evans conceded, "it would be hard to resist." Yet he remained optimistic because strong opposition from foreign merchants doing business in New York City (Evans could not imagine the legislature

22. David Evans to John J. Vanderkemp, March 8, 1830, ibid.; *Laws of the State of New York,* chap. 74, 53rd sess. (Albany, N.Y., 1830), 75–76.
23. David Evans to John J. Vanderkemp, Nov. 8, Dec. 23, 1830, and Joseph Fellows to David Evans, Dec. 28, 1830, Reel 90, HLCP.

imposing a tax on foreigners "for debts due them for land and not for debts created by the sale of merchandise") might dissuade the comptroller.[24]

In February 1831, however, the state legislature's Committee of Ways and Means introduced a bill to tax debts due nonresidents of the state of New York. Evans rushed to Albany and laid plans to defeat it. But after discussing the proposed tax with the state comptroller and "several members of both houses" of the legislature, he became convinced the new tax could not be avoided. He decided to direct his lobbying efforts at restricting the tax to an assessment based on the net annual income that foreign landlords derived from their holdings. Evans hoped to protect the foreign proprietors from local assessors who might levy the new tax against all debts owed to the Holland Land Company, even those that local agents had written off as uncollectible. His efforts were aided by a memorial submitted to the assembly by the general agents of the Holland Land Company and the Pulteney Estate. The intense lobbying paid off, and the bill was never called up.[25]

The proposal to tax debts owed to nonresident landowners arose again in February 1833. As before, David Evans realized that foreign landlords could not "oppose the principal entirely." Hence he recommended that the company assert its influence toward "obtaining some provision to protect" the property of "all non-resident creditors" from the exorbitant assessments of local public officials. Evans also advised the company's general agent to "present a remonstrance" to the state legislature. As the new bill again originated from a petition sent by settlers in the Pulteney Estate, the Holland Land Company joined forces with Joseph Fellows, Robert Troup's replacement in the post of general agent for the Pulteney Estate, submitting a joint remonstrance on March 9, 1833.[26]

The memorial accompanying the petition explained how the Holland Company had opened its entire tract of land in western New York to small farmers. Settlement of the Purchase, the memorial noted, "was commenced in the year 1800, upon the system of long credits to actual settlers; a system which, whilst calculated to postpone for a long time the reimbursement of the capital employed in it, was supposed to be well adapted to the then circumstances of the country." The Holland Company had always treated its settlers fairly and as a consequence suffered serious

24. David Evans to John J. Vanderkemp, Dec. 23, 1830, ibid.
25. David Evans to John J. Vanderkemp, March 1, 9, 1831, ibid.
26. David Evans to John J. Vanderkemp, Feb. 20, 1833, and David Evans to Joseph Fellows, Feb. 1, 1833, ibid.

financial losses. "It is notorious that in all new settlements, a large proportion of the land contracts are surrendered; that in many cases the lands are
abandoned, and that in others, the conditions of the contracts are wholly
unfulfilled by the settlers; whilst in these cases, the debts prove to be
worthless and irrecoverable." Vanderkemp and Fellows asked the legislature to reject the proposed tax because of the "peculiar character" of the
debts due the foreign landowners of western New York. But if the legislature insisted on such a tax, they urged that the levy "ought to be applied to
the net receipts of the estates annually remitted to the proprietors, and not
to the nominal amount of the securities."[27]

David Evans and Joseph Fellows rushed to Albany to try to modify the
tax bill. They did not succeed. The bill passed the assembly on April 5 by a
vote of 69 to 32. The assembly passed the bill without extending any of its
provisions to all the "inhabitants of this state." When it became clear that
the new tax would apply exclusively to nonresident landowners, the company became alarmed that the tax question had begun "to assume a
belligerent appearance." On April 23 the senate passed the same version
of the bill previously approved by the assembly. "It was not possible,"
Evans lamented, "to amend the bill."[28]

The passage of the tax bill had ominous consequences for both the
Holland Land Company and the settlers. For the company the tax on
debts due foreign landowners meant an added financial burden it was
unwilling to carry. For the settlers the tax marked the beginning of a get
tough policy that represented a departure from the long-standing attitude
of indulgence. Throughout the 1820s the company blustered, privately
and publicly, but took little legal action against the settlers. In September
1833 Evans sought legal counsel to advise the company about the "proper
course" to take with its delinquent settlers. The immediate concern for
Evans and the company was how to reduce the amount of land debt liable
for taxation after January 1, 1834. After conferring with Joseph Fellows
and learning how he planned to modify "all his contracts, obligating the
settler to pay the tax on the debt he owed," Evans adopted a similar policy.
He sent notices to all settlers under contract with the company, instructing
them to bring in their old agreements for renewal and modification or face
ejection. Evans put a clause into the modified contracts requiring the
debtors to pay the new tax. "In consequence of the service of the notices
on the settlers," he explained, "we shall be authorized to consider such as

27. New York *Assembly Documents*, No. 235 (1833), 4–6.
28. David Evans to John J. Vanderkemp, March 2, April 4, 5, 1833, Reel 90, HLCP.

do not comply, as having forfeited their contracts and our return of the amount due on the first of January next may be immensely reduced from what it would otherwise be."[29]

At first, many settlers complied with the new policy. "The settlers are flocking to the offices," Evans reported, "and taking new contracts." Staley Clarke, the company's subagent for Cattaraugus County, observed: "I commenced giving the new kinds of Articles. . . . No one objects to taking them, and indeed it appears to be the opinion of the people, that unless the law is repealed, they will have to pay the tax as a matter of course." The initial complacency of the settlers faded quickly. In November, some elections in the Purchase "turned solely" on the tax issue. The local Jacksonians came out in opposition to the tax while the Antimasons took a position "in its favor." Only weeks after the elections, Staley Clarke reported that the notices had created "considerable excitement." In December 1833 a meeting of settlers in Jamestown called for a convention of delegates representing all the towns of the Purchase. Clarke reported that "a very great alarm prevails among the settlers throughout the County so much so, that many persons have sold their improvements, for less than a third or a fourth of their value and a great many others are offering to sell at almost any price they can get. From this state of things you will readily perceive that unprincipled demagogues have it completely in their power to create an excitement against the Company which it may be hard to allay."[30]

The situation throughout Chautauqua County was much the same. In the town of Stockton, settlers condemned the effort by the Holland Land Company to foist payment of the new tax upon them. The law taxing debts due foreign landholders was "just and equitable," and they called upon fellow settlers throughout the Purchase to resist any effort to repeal it. The Stockton meeting provided a foretaste of the growing militancy that soon characterized the backwoods settlers of the inland towns. Before adjourning, these settlers resolved: "We will spend our fortunes before we will leave those hard earned possessions which we have cleared and prepared for cultivation, the threats of the Company's emissaries and agents, to the contrary notwithstanding."[31]

29. David Evans to John J. Vanderkemp, Sept. 20, 27, 1833, ibid.
30. David Evans to John J. Vanderkemp, Nov. 12, 1833, ibid.; Staley Clarke to David Evans, Oct. 22, Nov. 19, Dec. 4, 1833, Reel 175, HLCP.
31. David Evans to Joseph Fellows, Dec. 30, 1833, Reel 90, HLCP; *Fredonia Censor* (Fredonia, N.Y.), Jan. 8, 1834.

Nevertheless, David Evans believed there was widespread support throughout the Purchase for repealing the tax law. He believed the settlers "by a spontaneous movement" would "petition for a repeal of the law at the next session of the legislature." In late December 1833, Evans told Joseph Fellows that any petition calling for repeal of the tax law should originate with the settlers "to prevent the appearance of concert among the agents of nonresident landholders." Some of the settlers did not disappoint Evans. In early January 1834, settlers from the town of Attica gathered at the house of T. G. Goodwill and called for the repeal of the law "taxing debts due to nonresident creditors." They argued that this tax was "detrimental to the welfare not only of the individual indebted to the Company, but to the merchant, the mechanic, the farmer, and in short, to the whole population residing on the territory known as the Holland Land Company's purchase.[32]

The Agrarian Convention of 1834

The popular excitement caused by the company's decision to make the settlers pay the new tax revitalized the Agrarian Convention. As in 1819, 1827, and 1830, the movement centered in Buffalo. It was led by Thomas Sherwood, one of the Buffalo lawyers who had challenged the company's title in February 1830. Dyer Tillinghast, another of the company's critics during the flare-up of 1830, also figured prominently in this movement. On February 19, 1834, 139 delegates representing towns in Erie, Chautauqua, Cattaraugus, Genesee, and Niagara counties convened at the courthouse in Buffalo. The delegates represented the geographical diversity of the Holland Purchase. They came from the isolated back towns of the southern region as well as from the more commercially advanced areas in the north. These latter areas included Buffalo and the ring of towns surrounding it, Lockport in Niagara County, as well as the lakefront towns of Chautauqua County.

Merchants, mill operators, and local town officials were heavily represented in this convention as they had been in 1827. But some of the poorest towns were represented by small settlers with genuine agrarian grievances. Only five towns from Genesee County were represented, but they constituted the poorest and most indebted townships in the county. These five townships were home to many of the settlers who stubbornly

---

32. David Evans to John J. Vanderkemp, Nov. 12, 1833, Jan. 18, 1834, and David Evans to Joseph Fellows, Dec. 30, 1833, Reel 90, HLCP; *Fredonia Censor,* Jan. 15, 1834.

refused to renew expired contracts. Daniel Kemp, a delegate from the town of Bennington and a member of the committee that reported resolutions, was later selected as one of five settlers against whom the company brought suits of ejectment in federal district court. Similarly, William Cooper from the township of Perrysburg in Cattaraugus County attended this convention, and he too became one of the five settlers the company moved against. It seems that both Kemp and Cooper were outspoken in their belief that the company's title was weak. Staley Clarke, the subagent for Cattaraugus County, recommended an ejectment suit against Cooper less than a month after the Buffalo convention, noting that this settler "openly proclaims the Company's title to be bad."[33]

When the convention began, the delegates chose an Executive Committee and asked it to prepare "an abstract of the several acts of the Legislature, grants, charters and deeds, under which the Company claim to hold lands in this state." The committee's responsibility included lodging a protest against "the passage of any law confirming" the company's title. The Executive Committee was also asked "to prepare and present a memorial to the Legislature upon the relations subsisting between the settlers and the Holland Company." The committee's *Report* attacked the company's title, alleging that it was not "well founded at law." Tracing the complicated and sometimes veiled transfers of title to western New York dating from 1784, it declared the company's title neither "valid" nor "deserving of farther protection." The claims of the company should be "submitted to the solemn determination of the Legislature and the people."[34]

The Executive Committee's *Report* also addressed the question of the relations "subsisting between the settlers and the Company." This part of the *Report* reiterated some familiar criticisms of the company, yet the popular alarm over the company's decision to make the settlers pay the tax of 1833 gave the old charges new meaning. The Report reviewed the company's speculative motivations. As long as the Dutch investment in western New York continued to earn interest at the rate of 7 percent when the same capital invested in Europe could earn no more than 3 or 4

33. The five townships were Bennington, China, Java, Orangeville, and Darien. See *Buffalo Patriot*, Feb. 25, 1834; Reports of David Evans, 1834, 510; Staley Clarke to David Evans, March 8, 1834, Reel 175, HLCP.
34. For the proceedings of the Agrarian Convention, see the *Buffalo Patriot*, Feb. 25, 1834, and the *Fredonia Censor*, March 15, 1834; *An Appeal to the People of the State of New York; Being a Report of the Executive Committee of a Convention of Delegates from the Several Counties within the Holland Purchase, Held at Buffalo the 19–20th of February 1834* (Buffalo, 1834), 23; cited hereafter as *Executive Committee Report*.

percent interest, the proprietors had no incentive to close out their investment. The *Report* stigmatized the rapacious agents of the company, who
let the cumulative debt of the settlers grow to monstrous proportions, as
the "real party in this controversy with the people." The agents used their
"discretionary powers" to reserve and speculate in the choice lands of the
Purchase. As a result, they "acquired an amount of influence and amassed
an extent of wealth" that rendered them a "terror to the settlers."[35]

What gave the old charges new poignancy, however, was the company's
decision to circumvent the tax law of 1833. The *Report* declared:

> To show to the entire satisfaction of every candid mind, the deep laid scheme
> by which they could, with impunity extort still farther from the people, it is
> only necessary to call your attention to the measures adopted by the Com-
> pany immediately after the passage of the law. Notices were prepared and
> individuals employed to serve them upon every occupant throughout the
> Purchase holding articles on which any thing was due; informing him that he
> must within sixty days come to the office of the agent and take a new
> contract; if not, they should require him to pay the installments, that were
> due, or consider the contract void and drive him from his farm.

The principal condition exacted in the new contracts required the settler's
consent to pay the tax on his indebtedness. By doing this, the *Report*
charged, the company signified its utter disregard for the rights of the
settlers. To escape the tax on debts due foreign landowners, the company
was prepared to deprive many small farmers of the fruits of their labor
without offering any compensation for the property their labor created.[36]

The collective land debt owed by the settlers remained a powerful
symbol of the control the foreign landlords held over the region's growth
and development. It served as a constant reminder that "the honest settlers" of western New York had "virtually become the hewers of wood
and the drawers of water" for foreign speculators and "their purse-proud
agents." The Executive Committee's *Report* estimated the indebtedness of
the settlers at more than $10 million. The annual interest that regularly
fell due exceeded $700,000. Unless the tax was repealed, the *Report*
predicted, the agents of the company "have resolved to enforce the collection of this debt and withdraw their money from the country." An enforced collection would compel settlers who possessed the means to
"gather up all the money of the country . . . to save their farms." This

35. *Executive Committee Report,* 25.
36. Ibid., 28, 26.

would bankrupt the Purchase, leaving no money for "other business" or "the common demands of society." Collection of the debt meant "distress" for the entire community and "ruin" for the marginal farmers of the inland towns.

> In conclusion the committee would say that gratitude demands, if not the cancelling of the debt, at least such an abatement as shall bring it within the ability of the people to pay. The Company have long participated largely in the public patronage and favor. They have gathered a golden harvest from the long continued smiles of the legislature; but, like corporations that have no souls, they seem to cry give-give-give-and will never be satisfied, till they have brought the settlers in ruin and misery at their feet.[37]

The Agrarian Convention met again in September 1834, again organized and led by prominent local opponents of the Democratic party. Thomas Sherwood and Dyer Tillinghast, the Buffalo lawyers, were both prominent Whigs. A large delegation from Buffalo that included Samuel Wilkeson, mayor of the newly incorporated city of Buffalo, and Roswell W. Haskins, editor of the *Buffalo Whig*, dominated the convention. But some of the poorest towns in the southern hill country region of the Purchase were also represented. Daniel Kemp from the town of Bennington in Genesee County was again present.[38]

The convention called for a speedy resolution of the title question while endorsing the tax law of 1833. It also pledged to stand "with all persons who may be prosecuted by the Holland Company." The convention's Executive Committee believed these suits would finally settle "the question of title" to the lands of the Holland Purchase.[39]

The fall political campaign turned heavily on the issue of the company's oppression of the settlers. The local Whigs stigmatized Governor William Marcy and the Democrats as being in league with foreign bankers and monopolists. When Antimasonry began to give way to the emerging Whig

37. This figure is probably too high, although company records make it difficult to know exactly how much was owed in 1834. When David Evans took over the Batavia office, he estimated the debt was $7.5 million. In the years that followed, the company modified thousands of contracts reducing the nominal debt by $1 million. Following the enactment of the tax law of 1833, the company worked assiduously to reduce the settlers' debt. See David Evans to John J. Vanderkemp, June 12, 1827, Reel 173, HLCP; New York *Assembly Documents*, No. 235 (1833), 5; *Executive Committee Report*, 27, 30–32.

38. *Buffalo Whig*, Oct. 8, 1834.

39. Ibid.

party in 1834, the most eager Whigs came from the more economically developed towns, while the most reluctant Whigs came from the isolated back towns. Albert Tracy told William H. Seward in June 1834: "We shall find Antimasonry and Whiggery not exactly the same material or capable of amalgamation without some loss." Tracy quoted from a letter he had recently received from James Lowry, a leading Antimason from Chautauqua County. "A general want of confidence prevails among our antimasons and especially towards the leading men in the eastern section of the state. It cannot be remedied by the disorganized process of becoming Whigs." A few weeks later, Tracy spent several days in Chautauqua County to see for himself. "It happened to be court week and the people were gathered from all quarters, and full of anxiety and differences of opinion as to their future political direction. The old nationals most of whom are masons," Tracy explained, "were anxious to make a summary disposal of antimasonry and raise the banner of Whiggery while the antimasons were determined to preserve their organization and their power." In Chautauqua County the "old national" strongholds were located in the lakefront townships of Hanover, Sheridan, and Pomfret. The same tension between nationals and Antimasons also existed in Erie County, according to Tracy.[40]

In an effort to reassure Antimasons, who reluctantly raised the new Whig banner, Erie County Whigs aggressively took up the cause of the settlers, a cause that by 1834 had become particularly desperate in the poorer towns of the hill country. Taking their cue from Antimasons who openly embraced the settlers' plight in 1833, Erie County Whigs active in the Agrarian Convention slammed away at the Regency. The most telling blows were directed at Martin Van Buren's long-standing friendship with David Evans and against several leading members of the Regency who had speculated in Holland Purchase lands. In early October Roswell Haskins's *Buffalo Whig* reported that Martin Van Buren had stopped in Batavia to see David Evans. "This is Van Buren's annual visit," the *Whig* observed, "he regularly has such interviews with his leader in western New York, previously to important elections." The same edition carried a report from the *Batavia Advocate* that drew the familiar connection between Van Buren and the Holland Land Company even more explicitly. "We are

---

40. Albert H. Tracy to William H. Seward, June 9, July 5, 1834, Reel 2, William H. Seward Papers, University of Rochester Library, Rochester, N.Y.; James Lowry to Albert H. Tracy, June 3, 1834, Albert H. Tracy Papers, New York State Library, Albany, N.Y.

credibly informed that Mr. Van Buren . . . has been for the last few days and nights plotting in secret conclave at the Palace with his Local Agent and his feed attorneys." This same story charged that Van Buren had loaned Evans $20,000.[41]

Buffalo and Erie County Whigs also pointed to a large speculative purchase of land in 1827 by three leading members of the Regency. Benjamin Knower, Charles Dudley, and Thomas Olcott bought 80,000 acres within the Holland Purchase for one dollar per acre. Exploiting the struggle over dominion of land that underlay the more general conflict between landlords and settlers that had arisen with the crisis of the 1820s, the *Buffalo Patriot* asked settlers: "What confidence can you place in political partisans that are sold to the interests of Van Buren, Marcy, Olcott, Dudley, Knower and Co.—men who are speculating with the Holland Company, in the purchasing of large tracts of land at $1 per acre, to sell again to you who honestly toil for subsistence at $10 per acre."[42]

Meanwhile, Whigs denounced the Holland Company for being a "monster" and a "soulless corporation," which like "the insatiable horse leech" fed upon "the labor of the settler." In the southern towns of Erie County, where Antimasons chafed at their new political identity, local Whigs waged virtually a single-issue campaign. Whigs proclaimed themselves the friends of the settlers. In the town of Hamburg local Whig candidates for the offices of state assembly, sheriff, clerk, and coroner were praised for "their uniform devotion to the interests of the Holland Land settlers, and firm . . . opposition to the encroachments of a foreign monopoly." In the November election Whig candidates for local and statewide offices won impressive majorities in the counties and townships of the Holland Purchase. Governor Marcy was reelected by a margin of

41. An Antimason political broadside from Chautauqua County issued in 1833 called upon the "freemen of Chautauqua" to "stand fast" and "acquit yourselves like men!" It thundered: "Scarce have you triumphed over one insidious foe, ere you are met by another, the corps de reserve of the first and not less corrupt, powerful and desperate—we mean the HOLLAND LAND COMPANY, combined with the Monied Monopolies and Bank Influence of the country." Elial T. Foote Papers, vol. 2, item 174, Chautauqua County Historical Society, Westfield, N.Y. *Buffalo Whig*, Oct. 1, 1834.

42. *Buffalo Patriot*, Nov. 4, 1834; the eighty-thousand-acre purchase included land in Erie, Niagara, and Orleans counties located in townships 12–15 and ranges 1–8. See Memorandum of Lots of Land conveyed in 1828 to Charles E. Dudley, Thomas W. Olcott Papers, Rare Book and Manuscript Library, Columbia University. For the negotiations leading up to this purchase, see David Evans to John J. Vanderkemp, May 28, June 16, 27, Oct. 16, Nov. 8, 1827, Reel 173, HLCP. See Charles Sellers, *The Market Revolution: Jacksonian America, 1815–1846* (New York, 1991), 111–12; Richard E. Ellis, *The Union at Risk: Jacksonian Democracy, States' Rights, and the Nullification Crisis* (New York, 1987), 141–44; John Niven, *Martin Van Buren: The Romantic Age of American Politics* (New York, 1983), 91.

12,936 votes, winning 52 percent across the state. In the eighth electoral district, containing the Holland Purchase, however, William Seward, the Whig candidate for governor, won by a margin of 10,318, getting 59 percent of the vote.[43]

Following the election, the Agrarian Convention's Executive Committee issued an "Address to the Inhabitants of the Holland Purchase" written by William Moseley, one of the successful Whig candidates for the state assembly from Erie County. The "Address" recounted the familiar story of oppression "by a knot of European Bankers." "Company policy has condemned," Moseley wrote, "the toil worn pioneers in this western wilderness to the condition of a dependent tenantry—they must work hard and die poor." But the "Address" also invoked "your sympathies and your aid" for five settlers against whom the company had brought suit in the United States District Court at Albany. After meeting with leaders of the Agrarian Convention, the Holland Company had agreed to prosecute only five of roughly one hundred cases of ejectment prepared by company lawyers. The convention hoped the five cases would settle the question of the company's title. The company hoped to resolve this matter too, but it also wished to make an example of the five settlers. It chose the five cases carefully, bringing suit against settlers from poor back towns who had publicly doubted the landlords' title.[44]

"I never doubted the power of the Company to destroy me entirely"

The five settlers against whom the company brought suit were Sylvester Locke, Daniel Kemp, Seth Cole, William Cooper, and Ira Kibbe. All five lived in poor hill country towns, three in Genesee County and two in Cattaraugus. The Genesee townships of Orangeville, Bennington, and China, where Locke, Kemp, and Kibbe lived, were heavily indebted to the company. In 1828 Orangeville and Bennington each had 99 expired contracts while China had 88. In Orangeville 46 percent of the land was held under an expired contract. In nearby Bennington 37 percent of the land was held under a delinquent contract. These three townships also responded poorly to the notices served by Evans in 1829. In Orangeville only 27 percent of the settlers who were notified came in and took new

43. *Buffalo Whig*, Oct. 1, 22, 1834. For election results, see *Buffalo Whig*, Nov. 11, Dec. 10, 1834; *Albany Argus*, Nov. 25, 1834.
44. *Buffalo Whig*, Dec. 3, 1834, Jan. 28, 1835.

contracts. In Bennington and China the figures were 13 and 17 percent respectively.[45]

During 1834 Evans received a report from a company representative just returned from the southern part of Genesee County where the above townships were situated.

> The inhabitants on most of those lands appear to be of that unfortunate class, who have removed from the older and better parts of this Company's land and from the small tracts east of this, where they could not pay for the land, and were compelled to leave it, and they have got in these south townships in such numbers as to feel confident (in their numbers) that the company cannot remove them suddenly, and they say individuals dare not buy separate farms of the Company and settle among them which I believe to be true. It appears as if the poorer parts of this south country had become the great poor-house, not only of the older and better parts of this Company's land, but for all the older and better settled parts of the tracts east of this. They are in the habit of dividing the lots in small pieces which enables the poor man to get possession of such a piece, with a poor house, for a small sum and they are generally too poor to pay the company anything.

Evans told the company's general agent that Orangeville was "being settled by the worst inhabitants in the county. Most of them are miserably poor, and they are dividing the lots into small pieces of twenty and twenty-five acres and disposing of the right of possession for anything they can get."[46]

From the company's perspective, the southern Genesee townships were desperately poor, filled with transients, squatters, and "birds of passage." But what the company really objected to was the stubborn resiliency of agrarian culture among these settlers. The "inhabitants are now," Evans concluded, "merely able to support themselves . . . they could not pay for the land." The fundamental shortcoming of these small marginal producers, according to Evans, was their practice of husbanding labor rather than land. The company saw this as leading directly to rotating land instead of crops, "badly improved" lots overrun with brush and small trees, and common use rights under which settlers recognized an absolute right of property only when land was enclosed by a lawful fence and in

45. The number of expired contracts and amount of land under delinquent contracts is taken from the Register of the buyers of the lots of tracts M, O, P, Q, H, W, T, and R with statement of the surface area of the land, purchase price, and amount paid, 1802–27, Reels 178–79, Inventory no. 802, HLCP. The figures concerning the number of settlers notified are taken from the Reports of David Evans, 1829, 462.

46. Reports of David Evans, 1834, 508–10.

use. That land was divided into small parcels in the Genesee south towns made common use rights especially important to the settlers living there.[47]

Local fencing ordinances that kept large areas of these townships open to common use rights continued well into the twentieth century. This region's local historian Harry Douglass could still write in 1947: "The problems attendant upon roaming livestock have persisted to this day." Another author of this same history wrote that "as a boy in his teens he accompanied his father in driving through Allegany County (just south of the region described by Douglass) with a horse and carriage for the purpose of purchasing young calves to drive one hundred miles north to our farm in Niagara County, said calves to be fattened for the market."[48]

The company's report concerning the poorer townships of southern Genesee County was right when it predicted that the settlers of this region would oppose any buyer who purchased land from the company and ejected the rightful occupant without compensation for his improvements. During 1835–36 settlers from these towns and others "called themselves nullifiers" and talked about the "necessity of nullification." So said the settlers who put Sylvester Locke back on his land after the company evicted him. The appeal to the idea of nullification is very revealing. Agrarian values exalted natural over positive law when a fundamental question of right and wrong was at issue. These settlers were saying that the fundamental right of a man to have dominion over the fruits of his labor justified their "nullifying" the company and anyone purchasing under its authority. After settlers from the town of Arkwright helped to "nullify" the company's land office at Mayville, they proclaimed: "That according to the strictest principles of moral philosophy the productions of a man's labor are his own property; and whoever shall purchase the land occupied by any settler, without his consent, and paying a reasonable consideration therefor, we should consider an enemy to justice, and such a one would very probably be treated with the contempt such an intruder might deserve. He had better repair to the wilderness and make his own improvement. A word to the wise!" The settlers' use of this idea points to the concept of a "moral economy," but the specific term to nullify has a particularly Jacksonian-era flavor.[49]

47. Ibid., 506.
48. John T. Horton, Edward T. Williams, and Harry S. Douglass, *History of Northwestern New York: Erie, Niagara, Wyoming, Genesee and Orleans Counties*, 2 vols. (New York, 1947), 1:518–20, 2:511.
49. David Evans to John J. Vanderkemp, April 23, 1836, Reel 91, HLCP; Staley Clarke to David Evans, March 7, 1835, Reel 175, HLCP; Evans, *Holland Land Company*, 384;

The company's report about southern Genesee County exaggerated the transient character of its residents. The three settlers from this area against whom the company brought suits of ejectment did not fit the profile of "birds of passage." Sylvester Locke took an article of agreement on 139 acres on June 2, 1807. This contract was renewed on June 3, 1817. Company records show that when the second article expired in 1825, Locke's farm included 25 improved acres, a frame house, and 125 fruit trees. When he was evicted in June 1835 from lot 63 in township 9, range 2, he had been on this land for twenty-eight years. Daniel Kemp came to the town of Bennington in 1815; he took 100 acres at $3.75 per acre and paid a dollar down. Kemp's property featured 22 improved acres, a log house, and 25 fruit trees. When Kemp was ejected in 1835, he had been on this land for twenty years. Likewise, Ira Kibbe arrived in the town of China during October 1817. He had been on the land for eighteen years when he was ejected.[50]

The other two settlers against whom the company brought suit were Seth Cole of the town of Burton and William Cooper from Perrysburg. Both towns lay in the steep hill country of Cattaraugus County. Seth Cole came to Cattaraugus from the town of Phelps in Ontario County with his father, the Reverend Benjamin Cole, and his brother Elijah. They followed two of Benjamin Cole's other sons who had gone to the wilds of Cattaraugus in 1822 "with only one dollar in money." The local economy of the town of Burton was dominated by the lumber trade. Seth Cole made a living like most other settlers in the region raising livestock and harvesting timber. Cole dragged his logs to local sawmills and received a share of the lumber that was cut. Living in a frontier society that put a high value on physical strength and courage, Cole became a champion collar and elbow wrestler. Doubtless as a measure of grudging respect, some of his conquered opponents helped elect him town supervisor in 1829 and 1831. He

---

Fredonia Censor, March 9, 1836. Lawrence Kohl sees the exalting of natural law as a Jacksonian value, but I believe the agrarian beliefs and values upon which the Jacksonian movement stood were wider and deeper than Kohl acknowledges. See Lawrence Kohl, *The Politics of Individualism: Parties and the American Character in the Jacksonian Era* (New York, 1989), 161–62, 170–71. For the idea of a moral economy, see E. P. Thompson, "The Moral Economy of the English Crowd in the Eighteenth Century," *Past and Present* 50 (Feb. 1971), 76–136; Eric Foner, *Tom Paine and Revolutionary America* (New York, 1976); Jonathan Prude, *The Coming of Industrial Order: Town and Factory Life in Rural Massachusetts, 1810–1860* (New York, 1983); Ruth Bogin, "Petitioning and the New Moral Economy of Post-Revolutionary America," *William and Mary Quarterly* 45 (1988), 391–425.

50. Register of the buyers, 1802–27, Reel 123, Inventory no. 557, 22, 41.

was elected to serve as a justice of the peace for the town of Allegany in 1834.[51]

Seth Cole's problem with the Holland Company, shared by William Cooper and Daniel Kemp, concerned his outspoken criticism of its title. Staley Clarke later explained the suit against Cole: "He not only doubted the title himself, but took every opportunity to instill his doubts into others." Daniel Kemp and William Cooper appear to have been singled out by the company for their activism in the Agrarian Convention movement.[52]

The five ejectment cases were tried in a federal district court at Albany presided over by Judge Alfred Conklin. The decisions handed down in January and February 1835 "resulted in sustaining the Company's title." The company maintained throughout these trials that its purpose was not to punish certain settlers but rather to prove its title. The company insisted that each of the five settlers pay the legal costs of the suit against him. William Cooper "paid the costs" and was allowed to keep his land. Some of the other settlers did not fare as well. Sylvester Locke was evicted by the marshall in June 1835; his house was torn down by company officials shortly afterward. Seth Cole, unable to pay the costs of his suit, was legally ejected from his land and then jailed.[53]

From his jail cell in the town of Lyons, Wayne County, Seth Cole wrote a long letter to Staley Clarke that documents one small settler's experience of direct conflict with the Holland Land Company. Cole was in jail because he could not pay the $440 in legal costs incurred by the company in bringing suit against him. The company took possession of his land and improvements, intending to sell the improvements to help recover its court costs. Cole figured his improvements, consisting "mainly [of] meadow and pasture," were worth at least $500. Cole had a buyer for his improvements; a settler named Learn agreed to pay $350. This was less "than their real value," but Cole was prepared to return Learn's note letting him pay the company for the improvements. Cole was ready to sacrifice his equity if the company agreed to discharge him from the unpaid court costs.[54]

51. William Adams, *Historical Gazetteer and Biographical Memorial of Cattaraugus County* (Syracuse, N.Y., 1893), 724–25, 728; Seth Cole to Staley Clarke, Dec. 22, 1835, Reel 175, HLCP.

52. Staley Clarke to David Evans, April 10, 1836, Reel 175, HLCP.

53. Staley Clarke to David Evans, Aug. 10, 1835, April 10, 1836, Reel 175, HLCP; Evans, *Holland Land Company*, 384–85.

54. Seth Cole to Staley Clarke, Dec. 22, 1835, Reel 175, HLCP.

"I have now offered you all I have left," he wrote, "but if you choose to extort anything from me by continued oppression, I tell you now, frankly, that no good can come from it, and much evil may." Cole believed the company's action in bringing suit against him violated "justice." The justice to which he referred inhered in a rural exchange ethic that regulated creditor-debtor relations. As we have seen, this ethic held that debtors should pay what they could as circumstances permitted. Negotiation and accommodation should govern the relationship between creditors and debtors, affirming the mutual trust, obligation, and reciprocity upon which rural culture was built.[55]

Not three or four months before the commencement of the suit, Cole spoke with company agent Staley Clarke during a visit to Ellicottville. Standing in the common between Clarke's office and Barrow's Tavern, Cole told Clarke he "could not command money enough to take a contract." As experience was about to attest, from Cole's perspective, the company's demand for a cash payment underscored the fact that money was an instrument of privilege and oppression in a cash-poor frontier economy. Indeed, the Agrarian Convention held at Buffalo in February 1834 had complained about the effect new company policies were having in changing "the credit system into a cash system." Seth Cole knew firsthand what this meant.[56]

Cole told Clarke he "had some good stock" that he planned to "turn out" during the "course of the ensuing season." He agreed to "take a contract" for all or part of the land when circumstances allowed. According to Cole, Clarke consented to this arrangement. Cole returned to his land, feeling "bound and determined to do all [he] possibly could to pay for the land that season, or to take a contract at least." Just months after his conversation with Clarke, the "process of ejectment came up" on him "like a clap of thunder." His "prospects [were] blighted," and the land "seemed no more like home." The company's resort to legal action shackled his initiative: "My calculations were all set afloat, my business deranged," he lamented. Plans to build a house, "which was very much needed," and work "making new fences" were cut short.[57]

Cole reminded Clarke of what he said when the trial was about to begin. "You assured me that . . . the suit was an act of necessity to prove

---

55. Ibid.; Christopher Clark, *The Roots of Rural Capitalism: Western Massachusetts, 1780–1860* (Ithaca, N.Y., 1990), 47.
56. Seth Cole to Staley Clarke, Dec. 22, 1835, Reel 175, HLCP; *Buffalo Patriot*, Feb. 25, 1834.
57. Seth Cole to Staley Clarke, Dec. 22, 1835, Reel 175, HLCP.

the title—that you did not intend to injure my interest." Yet the suit went forward; Cole was ejected and charged with paying court costs that were beyond his means. The company's offer to let Cole have his land back by paying the court costs and taking a deed was disingenuous, "unreasonable, as well as unjust," because Clarke knew it to be beyond Cole's "power." The company had violated the spirit and principle of negotiation and accommodation governing landlord and settler relations in the Holland Purchase for over thirty years. Worse yet, by putting him in jail, the company had reduced him to a point "below poverty itself." His freedom gone, he no longer commanded the resources necessary to provide for his family and sustain his patriarchal authority. Cole's story is unique in its particular details, but the composite picture of which it formed a part points to the more general story of an agrarian culture of small producers in conflict with large capitalist landlords for control over land and productive resources. As American liberty and equality rested upon the dignity and opportunities enjoyed by ordinary laboring men, Cole and his fellow settlers believed company action like this undercut the nation's republican social order.[58]

The Holland Land Company's Decision to Sell

The Agrarian Convention of 1834 underscored the fact that opposition to the foreign landlords had brought together a coalition of interests and groups. David Evans believed at least three different groups gave "rise to the agrarian convention." The first and most numerous consisted of local politicians who were determined to use the language of agrarian opposition to succeed at the polls. The second group included the Buffalo lawyers who raised doubts about the company's title, "expecting thereby to compel the company to institute a great number of suits, which they hoped to be employed to defend." Speculators made up the third group, "a class of men generally possessed of more ability," according to Evans, "than moral principle . . . who had their agents secretly co-operating with the other two, with the hope of inducing the Company to believe their property to be insecure and that their interest would be promoted by a sale of it on almost any terms."[59]

By the early 1830s the northern region of the Holland Purchase, particularly the area around Buffalo, Lockport, and the other canal towns,

58. Ibid.
59. Reports of David Evans, 1834, 502.

began to prosper. Buffalo's future as an important trading center was ensured by its strategic location as the point of transshipment for all commerce passing between the upper Great Lakes and the Erie Canal. Throughout this northern region of the Holland Purchase commercial agriculture was taking hold as wheat became the staple crop raised for market. In 1834 47,000 barrels of flour were milled at Lockport from grain raised in Niagara County. In his 1835 report Evans judged "the counties of Niagara and Orleans and those portions of Genesee and Erie, lying north of the tenth tier of Townships . . . so far advanced in improvement" that only money should be received as payment for land.[60]

The continuing development of the northern section of the Holland Purchase attracted the interest of investors and speculators, including the New York Life Insurance and Trust Company. Established as an investment firm to provide capital for long-term economic development, the New York Life Insurance and Trust Company exchanged $400,000 of stock certificates for an equivalent amount of Holland Company contracts secured by mortgages in 1833. This business deal constituted the first step in the Dutch proprietors' ultimate decision, made two years later, to sell all their land, debts, bonds, and mortgages. The decision to sell the Purchase was influenced by the Holland Company's recognition that American speculators, including the investors, trustees, and officers of the New York Life Insurance and Trust Company, enjoyed several advantages that gave them an edge in the land development business. The New York firm made capital loans throughout the western agricultural regions of the state, issuing bonds and mortgages "payable in from five to ten years with the interest payable semi-annually." Any failure to comply with the letter of these terms resulted in "an immediate foreclosure of the mortgage." Assessing the advantages enjoyed by the Trust Company, David Evans observed: "We can never expect the same punctuality, for the reason that we have no choice in the selection of our debtors, we have to take them as they are, good and bad together, and make the best we can of them, whereas the Life and Trust Company lend no money but upon security to at least twice the amount, independent of buildings and with a perfect understanding that a rigid compliance in the payment of interest will be exacted."[61]

60. Thomas F. Gordon, *Gazetteer of the State of New York* (Philadelphia, 1836), 559; Reports of David Evans, 1835, 513–14.
61. For the New York Life Insurance and Trust Company, see John Denis Haeger, *The Investment Frontier: New York Businessmen and the Economic Development of the Old Northwest* (Albany, N.Y., 1981), chap. 2. See also William Bard to Potter and Babcock, Nov.

Evans appreciated that the New York firm invested only in agricultural lands that were fully integrated into the market economy. The Trust Company's portfolio followed the Erie Canal into the new regions it opened to commercial farming. In the Holland Purchase of western New York, these businessmen issued bonds and gave mortgages primarily to the settlers of the canal townships in Erie and Niagara counties. The Holland Land Company, however, could not enjoy the advantage of managing carefully selected farmlands. It had to oversee the southern part of the Purchase as well as the rapidly developing northern region. In the hill country of the southern Purchase, where small farmers continued to eke out a living by exploiting the resources of the woodlands, the land remained generally uninviting and unimproved. "Not more than one-ninth part" of Cattaraugus County was under improvement. Similarly, less than 25 percent of Chautauqua County's 650,000 acres were improved in 1835. The new breed of capitalist land developers that had arisen with the Market Revolution showed no interest in the latter regions because they were a bad investment risk.[62]

The combination of factors that convinced the Holland Company to sell its lands and securities in 1835 was explained by Thomas Olcott, a leading member of the Albany Regency, in a confidential letter to David Evans. Speculative interest along with growing "public feeling" against the company would cause the Dutch landlords to "dispose of all their interest in this state." Olcott asked Evans to join him in "the purchase of the whole or a part of" the company's lands and contracts, but Evans

23, 1830, G Letter books, GA-1 series, New York Life Insurance and Trust Company Papers, Baker Library, Harvard Business School, Boston, Mass.; cited hereafter as New York Life Insurance and Trust Company Papers. For details of the business deal struck between the New York firm and the Holland Company, see William Bard to J. J. Vanderkemp, Oct. 10, 16, 1833, G Letter books, GA-3 series, New York Life Insurance and Trust Company Papers. William Bard to David Evans, Oct. 17, 1833, ibid.; William Bard to David Evans, Oct. 31, Dec. 6, 12, 1833, G Letter books, GA-4 series, New York Life Insurance and Trust Company Papers. Reports of David Evans, 1834, 503; David Evans to John J. Vanderkemp, Feb. 20, 1833, Reel 90, HLCP.

62. William Bard described the Trust Company's investment strategy: "The property the Company loan on must be either a good farm in a settled and well cultivated country—or a good house of stone in one of the larger inland towns." Bard noted that "the Company prefer good farms, in good order, and in well cultivated districts." With respect to undeveloped property, Bard said: "Wild lands, producing no rent and of course no means to pay interest, we avoid altogether." See William Bard to William Loomis, June 21, 1830, William Bard to Charles Butler, July 15, 1830, and William Bard to Ebenezer Mack, Aug. 21, 1830, G Letter books, GA-1 series, New York Life Insurance and Trust Company Papers. Haeger, *Investment Frontier*, 28–29; Reports of David Evans, 1834, 513–14; Gordon, *Gazetteer* (1836), 366, 382.

informed him that other investors had already reached a tentative agreement with John J. Vanderkemp. The company had agreed to sell its "entire interest in the counties of Genesee, Erie, Niagara and Orleans" to Jacob LeRoy and Herman Redfield, agents of the Farmers Loan and Trust Company. In November 1835 Evans recommended that the Holland Company accept an initial payment of $1 million with the balance due in three months. The total purchase price was just over $2,282,000.[63]

The Holland Company sold its lands in Chautauqua County to George Lay and Trumbull Cary of Batavia. They acquired the still unsold lands for two and three dollars per acre and the contracts at a discount averaging between 10 and 15 percent. Cary and Lay went to Philadelphia to borrow some of the purchase money, yet it seems clear they were counting on exacting heavier payments from the settlers to help finance the deal. In early December 1835 the company sold its remaining lands in the isolated townships of Cattaraugus, Allegany, and Genesee counties to Nicholas Devereux, Gould Hoyt, Russell Nevins, Rufus Lord, and William Kent. These investors were betting on the success of the projected Erie Railroad. More than 417,970 acres of land were sold for one dollar per acre. Both Devereux and Hoyt had been shareholders in the New York Life Insurance and Trust Company.[64]

As news of the sale spread throughout the Purchase, nervous settlers waited to see what would happen to them. Ironically, many settlers scrambled to company land offices during the closing weeks of 1835 to secure a title and deed from the foreign landowners. William Peacock, the sub-agent at Mayville in Chautauqua County, observed: "It makes me laugh to see the change that has taken place in one short year."[65]

Herman Redfield announced the new terms of sale and credit for the settlers of Genesee, Erie, Niagara, and Orleans counties on November 30, 1835. He explained the conditions under which the new proprietors agreed to renew old contracts upon their expiration. The first condition required immediate payment of one-eighth of the purchase money with the balance due in ten annual installments. The new terms also included a system of surcharges based on the outstanding debt. For instance, if the

63. Thomas Olcott to David Evans, Oct. 8, 1835, David Evans to Thomas Olcott, Oct. 13, 1835, and David Evans to John J. Vanderkemp, Nov. 21, 1835, Reel 91, HLCP; Evans, *Holland Land Company,* 392–93.

64. Trumbull Cary to David Evans, Oct. 19, 1835, and David Evans to John J. Vanderkemp, Oct. 22, 1835, Reel 91, HLCP; Evans, *Holland Land Company,* 393; Haeger, *Investment Frontier,* 23.

65. William Peacock to David Evans, Oct. 22, 1835, Reel 91, HLCP.

balance due on the old contact was less than three dollars per acre, the surcharge was one dollar per acre. The graduated schedule of surcharges, outlined by Redfield and LeRoy, increased the price of some lands by as much as three dollars per acre. Finally, Redfield urged every settler holding land under an expired contract to come forward and take a new contract or face certain eviction.[66]

Trumbull Cary and his partner George Lay drafted new terms of sale and credit for the settlers of Chautauqua County on December 23, 1835. Their terms were harsher than those proposed by Redfield and LeRoy. Any contract that had expired during 1835 had to be renewed immediately by paying 25 percent of the purchase price or one dollar per acre. The balance was due in five annual payments. Cary also announced the imposition of surcharges, the amount determined by the outstanding debt per acre. The surcharges ranged from $1.00 per acre when the cumulative debt did not exceed $3.00 per acre to $2.50 per acre on contracts for which the debt was $8.00 or more per acre. Any land held "by widows and orphan children" was exempted.[67]

Cary and Lay offered to issue deeds whenever the value of the land, including improvements, was "twice the amount of the purchase money." Finally, they called upon settlers holding land under expired contracts to make a new agreement within six months. Failure to comply, the new proprietors warned, would result in speedy eviction from the property.[68]

Rebellion in the Back Towns

The new terms of the sale and credit created great anxiety among the settlers, especially in Chautauqua County, where a group met at Mayville on January 8, 1836, to consider a response. Elial T. Foote and several other leading men from the county informed the convention about their visit to Batavia to open a dialogue with the new owners. Foote reported that Trumbull Cary seemed unwilling to enumerate the specific terms of what the settlers were already calling the "Genesee Tariff." Foote and the others finally learned the specific terms from a clerk in the Batavia office. Upon returning home, Foote sent a letter to Cary, a draft of which he presented to the convention. His letter remonstrated against "the terms called the Genesee Tariff" and warned the new owners that the "people of

66. David Evans to John J. Vanderkemp, Jan. 8, 1836, ibid.
67. Ibid.
68. Ibid.

this county would not submit to such terms: That they were oppressive and unjust, and if persisted in would reduce the people to a state of vassalage."[69]

In light of Foote's information, the Mayville convention adopted a series of resolutions denouncing the injustice of the new proprietors. They warned the new owners not to undertake "any sudden and unexpected change in the policy towards the settlers which shall increase the difficulties of payment, becloud their hopes of future prosperity, and deprive them of the avails of their labor." The settlers also declared that "the actual improvements on the lands in this county, ought to be considered and actually are the property of the settlers." Another resolution denounced any effort by the new proprietors to charge more than the "value of the soil" in its wild condition. Before adjourning, the convention appointed a committee of three men "to correspond with the recent purchasers."[70]

In the weeks following the Mayville convention, local newspapers joined the "whole community" in condemning the new owners and their Genesee Tariff. The *Fredonia Censor* asked its readers: "Are such Shylocks, who appear to be intent on the last pound of flesh, entitled to the benefit of laws intended for the good of society? No. They should be thrust out, not only of the pale of the law, but—we had nearly have said— of every honorable community." Similarly, the *Mayville Sentinel* castigated the new proprietors for expropriating the labor and industry of the settlers. The *Sentinel* reminded the new owners that "the industry of the settler" had given the land the value it now possessed. The paper declared: "The settlers are now placed at the mercy of a few monied speculators . . . we cannot suffer them to step one pace beyond their limits—beyond justice . . . . Every man ought to, and we have no doubt will, disregard their measures, and promptly arise in defense of his just privileges and rights."[71]

On the evening of February 6, 1836, the long-standing frustration of the backcountry settlers, exacerbated by news of the Genesee Tariff, erupted into violence. About half past six o'clock in the evening a "mob" of between 500 and 700 men assembled two miles outside Mayville at Barnhart's Inn. They were principally from the back towns of the eastern and southern part of the county. "They organized under command of one

69. *Fredonia Censor,* Jan. 13, 1836.
70. Ibid.
71. *Fredonia Censor,* Jan. 30, 1836. The article from the *Mayville Sentinel* appeared in the issue of the *Fredonia Censor* cited above.

of their number . . . and took up their line of march for the village, in military order." Local folklore has it that an old pioneer, Nathan Cheney, listened as the settlers made speeches, trying to determine what to do. Growing impatient, Cheney stepped forward and proclaimed: "Those who are going to Mayville with me fall into line." Upon reaching Mayville, the men marched to the land office, surrounded it, and began "their work until it was demolished." When they had accomplished "their object," the *Mayville Sentinel* noted, the men "again formed in line of march and left the village, each man with a book or bunch of papers under his arm. After arriving at Hartville a bonfire was made of the books and papers."[72]

The subagent of the Mayville land office, William Peacock, fled for his life, and the next morning he sent a hurried note to David Evans. "My office was destroyed last night by a mob of about 300 men from the east part of the county; they came armed with guns, rifles and clubs . . . . They threatened death to the whole of us. It was given out by them that all the offices would share the same fate." The following day, Peacock reported that his life was again threatened by the settlers who appeared to grow "more bold."[73]

The destruction of the land office did embolden the settlers. In the southern towns of Erie County, "a majority of the people" approved of "the measures pursued in Chautauqua County." In the towns of Boston, Concord, and Sardinia the settlers approved "openly and loudly . . . of the Mayville outrage." In Holland and Wales the excitement suspended all ordinary business. The settlers crowded into local taverns where they threatened both the Holland Company and the new proprietors with "every kind of violence." Since many settlers believed the sale was only a "pretext" employed by the Holland Company "to exact more money from the people," their anger encompassed the old as well as the new owners.[74]

In the meantime, settlers from the back towns of Chautauqua County met and passed resolutions denouncing the landlords and praising the destruction of the land office. In the town of Charlotte, the settlers said the sale was "a mere hoax . . . for the express purpose of evading the law of the land which subjects them to a tax on debts." They commended "the public spirit of our fellow citizens, who assembled at Mayville last week in

72. From the *Mayville Sentinel* as reported in the *Fredonia Censor,* Feb. 17, 1836; *Centennial History of Chautauqua County,* 138–39.
73. William Peacock to David Evans, Feb. 7, 8, 1836, Reel 91, HLCP.
74. Thomas Tufts to Ira Blossom, Feb. 20, 1836, and Ira Blossom to David Evans, Feb. 20, 1836, ibid.

imitation of our forefathers who threw the British tea into Boston Harbor, demolished that public nuisance which has stood for years unmolested, but now that she has through her proud inmates defied the whole people, has been humbled, as was a powerful nation by her colonies." In the town of Gerry "at least two thirds of the voters" cheered "the destruction of the land office at Mayville, as an act of retributive justice." "Any further submission on the part of the people," these settlers declared, "would evince a servile spirit more becoming a Russian serf than an American citizen." In the town of Ellery the settlers hailed "those enemies of oppression who destroyed the public nuisance in this county." They boasted harboring "no fears of becoming vassals and serfs, to a monied aristocracy, so long as the people show the same fearless patriotism that they have shown of late."[75]

These meetings also pointed to the specific grievances that pushed the settlers into open rebellion. Settlers from the town of Charlotte warned "all persons against purchasing the lands from under any settler in this town . . . until he shall have gained the entire consent of the occupant." They warned that "if any person neglects the admonition in the above resolution, and buys the lands from under any settler without compensating such occupant to his full satisfaction for his improvements, then and in that case we will approve and assist in bringing the culprit to merited and condign punishment: and we shall be surprised if the scenes of Mayville are not reacted in a more tremendous form." In the town of Ellery, the settlers admonished "every person against purchasing the lands occupied by a settler, without first making him satisfactory compensation." Settlers from the town of Stockton declared that "the improvements made on the lands are rightfully the property of the settlers."[76]

Some of the Chautauqua settlers tried to be more conciliatory. James Mullett, Leverett Barker, and Chauncy Tucker, representing the settlers who attended the Mayville convention, wrote a letter to Trumbull Cary on February 18. They acknowledged Cary's right to fix the terms by which he chose to sell his property, yet they pointed out that this sudden change of policy threatened to reverse thirty years of "lenity and indulgence towards the settlers." The sudden reversal threatened to "embarrass" the back-country settler, particularly by increasing "the burden of his debt" and by compelling "a sacrifice of his property." The settlers of Chautauqua County, Mullett and his colleagues explained, viewed the new owners as

75. *Fredonia Censor,* Feb. 17, 24, March 2, 1836.
76. Ibid., Feb. 17, March 2, 9, 1836.

the agents and representatives of the Holland Company. Hence the long-standing policy of the Holland Company formed the standard of justice and fairness against which the settlers judged the new terms.[77]

Trumbull Cary's response to the Chautauqua settlers signified the new proprietors' defiance, but it also underscored the speculative interest that induced Cary and his partner to take advantage of the business opportunity afforded by the Holland Company's agrarian problems. Cary told the settlers' representatives: "The Holland Land Company have adopted, it is true, towards the settlers upon the Holland Purchase, a policy more liberal and lenient than any other Land Company in the State. But I have much doubt whether this policy has in the main been beneficial to the settlers." Cary believed the indulgence of the Holland Company spoiled the settlers and thwarted its efforts to manage the economic development of the region. Jacob LeRoy and Herman Redfield, agents for the purchase of Holland Company lands in the northern region of the Purchase, concurred. When David Evans warned them that their new terms "could not be enforced in Erie County," they "treated the matter very lightly." The "new proprietors," Evans noted, "pretty plainly intimated that the Company's agents had heretofore been deficient in energy." The overreaching ambitions of the "new proprietors," he believed, left them unwilling to "yield up any part of the princely fortunes they considered just within their reach." There was little doubt in Evans's mind that the "united opposition" of the settlers would force the new owners to make concessions.[78]

On March 30, 1836, the Holland Purchase Convention reconvened at Buffalo to consider "the present contest between the Holland Company and those claiming under them" and the settlers. One hundred delegates from Erie County, eighteen from Genesee County, seven from Chautauqua County, and one from Niagara County assembled. The Buffalo lawyers who had played a leadership role in the agrarian movement since 1830 were again prominent. Dyer Tillinghast was appointed president of the convention, and Thomas Sherwood served on the committee that drafted resolutions. Sherwood laid out the case against both the old and

77. James Mullett, Leverett Barker, and Chauncy Tucker to Trumbull Cary, Feb. 18, 1836, Reel 91, HLCP.
78. Trumbull Cary to James Mullett, Leverett Barker, and Chauncy Tucker, Feb. 24, 1836, and David Evans to John J. Vanderkemp, Feb. 20, March 4, 1836, ibid. The company's subagent at Buffalo also blamed the settlers' uprising on the greed of the new proprietors. See Ira A. Blossom to H. J. Huidekoper, Feb. 8, 1836, Ira A. Blossom Papers, Buffalo and Erie County Historical Society.

the new proprietors. The violent attack on the Mayville land office had "grown out of the last attempts of the company and their retainers to possess themselves of farms cleared, cultivated and rendered valuable by the labor of the settlers without compensation for such improvements." A second cause of the violence stemmed from the owners' "endeavors to evade the payment of taxes imposed on their lands by the government of this state, and to fix such burthens on the settlers themselves."[79]

The new terms of credit and sale proposed by Jacob LeRoy and Herman Redfield were unacceptable to the Buffalo delegates. The surcharges were "unjust and oppressive." Yet the delegates insisted that the settlers were willing to pay a "fair price" for their lands, which meant a purchase price equivalent to the value of the land in "a state of nature." After explaining the settlers' position, the delegates warned the new owners: "To compel the settler to surrender his land without an equivalent for his improvements, or to pay an enhanced price for the privilege of remaining would be a tyrannical and arbitrary act, to which the people of western New York will never submit." Finally, the delegates called upon all members of the state legislature from the Holland Purchase "to oppose any attempt" to repeal the tax against debts owed to nonresident landowners.[80]

In the days and weeks that followed the Holland Purchase convention at Buffalo, small farmers from the back towns organized to protect themselves from dispossession. David Evans described how at Varysburg in southern Genesee County, five hundred settlers decided "to put" Sylvester Locke back "in possession of the premises from which he was ejected by the Marshall." On April 1, 1836, "an armed force of about sixty men" accompanied Locke and his son to their contested land. When they arrived, they found a young man, Lewis Patterson, living in a new house built since the eviction. After Locke's eviction, the Holland Company had sold the property to Horace Patterson, who built a house for his nephew Lewis. Young Patterson was ordered "by the mob" to leave "the premises," but he refused. "Some of the mob then took a fence rail and after cutting it to a sharp edge threatened to put him on it and run him off the lot, but as this was opposed by others, they desisted from actual violence but turned his cattle into the road and deposited what few effects he had in the house there also, and put Locke's family in possession."[81]

79. *Fredonia Censor,* April 6, 1836.
80. Ibid.
81. David Evans to John J. Vanderkemp, April 9, 1836, Reel 91, HLCP.

Horace Patterson promptly began a legal proceeding to dispossess Locke, but the ill health of the sheriff along with "extremely bad weather" delayed any immediate action. Meanwhile, "the people . . . guarded Locke with from ten to fifty men," threatening "to defend him with powder and ball." Finally, however, the sheriff did arrest "the elder Locke" and took him to a tavern in Varysburg several miles from the disputed land. Locke's supporters made several more efforts to protect his rights. As darkness fell, the sheriff "heard a heavy firing of muskets and rifles in the neighborhood and about fifty men came to the tavern, calling themselves nullifiers, and showed a disposition to rescue the prisoner." But when two deputies joined the sheriff, the men withdrew into the nearby woods, where they shouted and fired guns throughout the night. The next morning the sheriff went out to Locke's residence to "dispossess the family." Gunfire erupted again. As the sheriff approached the house, "twenty five men armed with muskets and bayonets fixed" suddenly appeared. The sheriff's firmness prevailed again, and the men dispersed into the woods to watch as he dispossessed Mrs. Locke and put Horace Patterson back into possession.[82]

The efforts by settlers in the south towns of Genesee County to put Locke back in possession of property he had improved took place in the midst of continuing popular demonstrations against the Holland Company. A deputy sheriff told David Evans that "secret meetings had been held in most of the school districts in the south towns to organize a force to attack" the land office at Batavia. Evans received another report warning that "the malcontents were waiting to see the result of the experiment they had tried in forcibly reinstating Locke." Alarmed, Evans secured fifty muskets and a thousand ball cartridges from the arsenal "and kept the office guarded at night by several young men." On the evening of May 14, bells began to ring throughout the village of Batavia, "as if to give an alarm for fire." As village residents swarmed into the streets, Evans learned that seven hundred men had gathered at Alexander to the east and were headed toward Batavia. The next morning three hundred men crossed the bridge at the east end of the village and pushed toward the land office. Only sixty "were armed with muskets and rifles"; the rest carried crowbars, sledgehammers, "bludgeons or nothing at all." When they reached the land office, Evans "positively declined" to talk with them.[83]

82. David Evans to John J. Vanderkemp, April 21, 23, 1836, ibid.
83. David Evans to John J. Vanderkemp, April 9, June 20, 1836, ibid.

Moments later the sheriff arrived with 120 men "armed with bright muskets and bayonets fixed," and the disaffected settlers soon "felt the awkwardness of their position." After the sheriff declared he was ready to give the order to "fire a full volley among them," the settlers moved down the street, and following "a boisterous consultation" the "greatest part thought it best to go home." In the days that followed, Batavia remained "in a high state of excitement." Evans arranged to have two pieces of cannon brought in from artillery companies at LeRoy and Bethany, and later he had two blockhouses constructed to protect the land office and its records.[84]

The Batavia office was not directly threatened again, but the settlers of the isolated back towns remained agitated. A letter sent to Evans from "many settlers" in the southern Genesee County town of Attica expressed their anger and fear. "David you have distressed multitudes of poor people by selling their lands from under them to ruthless speculators. The cries of those poor have entered into the ears of the lord of sabbath and the vengeance of an incensed God hangs over you (if not in pestilence) in the indignation of the people of this country. The storm is gathering blackness." The letter warned Evans that he could not "avert the threatening storm" unless the company and the new owners agreed to respect the settlers' rights.[85]

In Chautauqua County another settlers' convention met at Mayville on June 15. The settlers reiterated their complaints. They should not pay any "additional price" for the land. The new proprietors should charge only what the land was worth in a state of nature. If a settler could not pay for all the land he held under contract, "he ought to be permitted to pay for and receive a title of such part as he" could manage. The settlers should not pay the tax "imposed upon the debts due to the Holland Company." Finally, the Chautauqua settlers held William Peacock, the Holland Company's subagent at Mayville for many years, responsible for "a great proportion of the difficulties and disturbances that have arisen in this country."[86]

By the time of this last convention, however, the widespread alarm and discontent convulsing the back towns had already forced the new proprietors to make concessions. Jacob LeRoy and Herman Redfield announced their modified terms of credit and sale in March 1836. First, they pledged

84. David Evans to John J. Vanderkemp, June 20, 1836, ibid.
85. "Many settlers" to David Evans, June 13, 1836, ibid.
86. *Fredonia Censor,* June 22, 1836. See also James Milnor to David Evans, June 17, 1836, and James Mullett to J. A. Smith, June 17, 1836, Reel 91, HLCP.

not to charge compound interest, and second, they forswore any plans to expropriate the settlers' lands for "the non-payment of installments." LeRoy and Redfield also proposed reducing the amount of surcharge per acre by one-half on contracts extending five years. They relaxed the terms of credit and sale even further for "the towns in the south parts of the counties of Genesee and Erie." In these areas they offered "to renew contracts without any advance." As David Evans predicted, the announcement of these modified terms helped to alleviate the concerns and fears of the settlers. With the immediate threat of dispossession over, relative calm returned to southern Erie and Genesee counties.[87]

In Chautauqua County, Trumbull Cary and George Lay also made concessions to the settlers. In late July local newspapers announced the formation of the Chautauqua Land Company. William H. Seward joined Cary and Lay as a partner and undertook the job of local agent replacing William Peacock. The *Fredonia Censor* described Seward as "a distinguished citizen, whose character is a sufficient guarantee to the settlers, that their rights and interests will be scrupulously respected." Seward opened a new land office at Westfield and announced modified terms of sale and credit. He promised to renew all expired contracts if application was made before January 1, 1837. In cases of hardship, he required only nominal payments. He also offered to modify contracts when the "debt due" exceeded the value of the land. Within a short time, Seward was able to quiet the fears of the settlers from the back towns of Chautauqua County.[88]

With peace restored throughout the back towns, the agents of the Holland Company closed down their agencies. The Farmers Loan and Trust Company completed the necessary payments and title passed to the new proprietors at the end of 1837. In Chautauqua County William H. Seward quickly became the dominant partner, arranging a loan from the American Life Insurance and Trust Company which enabled him to make final payment to the Dutch proprietors on July 14, 1838. David Evans, who had served as resident agent since 1827, tendered his resignation on July 18, 1837. But Evans's departure was neither smooth nor amicable. Officials for the Holland Land Company soon discovered that Evans's personal finances had become completely enmeshed with the company's accounts. Evans owed the company over $300,000. He attempted to repay,

87. *Fredonia Censor,* March 23, 1836; Jacob LeRoy and Herman Redfield to David Evans, March 13, 1836, and David Evans to John J. Vanderkemp, March 10, 1836, Reel 91, HLCP.
88. *Fredonia Censor,* July 20, Aug. 10, 1836.

offering some bonds that were secured by property and railroad stock, but final settlement between the company and Evans's trustees did not occur until September 1841. In accordance with this settlement, the company received more land, which was sold in 1846. The Holland Land Company's long-standing interest in western New York was over.[89]

THE rebellion in the back towns during 1836 illuminates the complex nature of the agrarian movement in the Holland Purchase. The small settlers of the isolated interior towns fought to protect their homes and improvements and to defend their hard-earned property from grasping landlords who threatened to expropriate years of labor and toil. The destruction of the land office at Mayville was certainly the most dramatic expression of the backcountry settlers' discontent, yet the efforts by Sylvester Locke's neighbors to reinstate and protect him highlighted the specific agrarian grievances that had sparked the open rebellion. The ejection of Locke without any compensation for his equity violated several canons of agrarian culture. Small independent producers could agree that land might be an article of trade and commerce and could even serve as collateral security for a loan, but land was still the chief source of sustenance and life itself. To deny a man control over the fruits of many years of labor relegated both him and his family to dependence upon others. No fate could be worse.

The dominion that the company stripped away from Sylvester Locke, the same control it wished to deny so many of the settlers after 1821, was primarily a matter of choosing what mix of labor and land yielded the highest return and offered the best guarantee of security for a settler's family. The settlers' relations of production were based on the scarcity of labor and the abundance of land and nature. The dynamics of this person-to-land ratio pushed settlers into economic activities that husbanded labor and spent land, encouraging extensive agricultural practices that were supplemented by the harvesting of woodland resources for grazing, potash, and lumber.

The legal action taken against Locke also violated the rural exchange ethic that governed relations between creditors and debtors. This ethic was built on the mutual reciprocity and interdependence that were hallmarks of rural life. Recognizing the highly capricious nature of a farm household's fortunes, it held that creditors should accept payment from their debtors as circumstances permitted. During the rebellion of 1836 the

89. Evans, *Holland Land Company,* 424–27.

settlers reminded the landlords of what this trust entailed. "Under this system of indulgence and lenity, and an implied promise of its continuance, the present settlers took their contracts. No matter what the written conditions of those contracts were—not one in a hundred ever read them—the policy of the landholders was known, established and relied on; and implicitly, and in many instances, expressly, became a part of the contract." By substituting a market conception of creditor and debtor relations for the more traditional arrangement, the landlords had chosen to ignore the cultural and social considerations that structured economic activity within the settlers' agrarian world.[90]

If the rebellion of 1836 highlighted the truly radical nature of the small settlers' challenge to the Holland Company and its hierarchical market aspirations, what did it reveal about the political challenge to the company that was inspired and led by local entrepreneurs and boosters? Ambitious office seekers and aspiring elites took up the settlers' cause beginning in 1819. Albert Tracy, Peter B. Porter, and others helped to build their political careers and to promote their private business interests along the way. Yet whatever personal ambitions may have underlain their political challenge to the company, these local boosters and entrepreneurs touched on the small producer's deepest fear and his chief political grievance when they took up the cause of defending the laboring majority against the privilege and power of the moneyed few. Tracy and everyone who followed him pointed to the "hidden design" governing company policy. Lenient terms of sale and credit attracted many to the Holland Purchase, but the indulgent treatment was merely a scheme to get these lands settled and improved. When the rising value of the settlers' betterments equaled the land debt they owed, the foreign capitalists planned to expropriate the settlers' hard-earned property and to resell it for a large profit. As long as the foreign capitalists and a corrupt eastern political establishment were the enemies, everyone in the Purchase, small settler and aspiring entrepreneur alike, could identify as members of the producing classes. The political success of a host of local factions and parties in the Holland Purchase from the Clintonian Republicans to the Antimasons and the Whigs turned on their ability to stand publicly against the "aristocrats" who beguiled and exploited the majority in their pursuit of wealth and power accumulated without labor.

90. James Mullett, Leverett Barker, and Chauncy Tucker to Trumbull Cary, Feb. 18, 1836, Reel 91, HLCP.

7

"To take contracts at the point of the bayonet"

The new American landlords quickly discovered the very real class tensions that would pit their pursuit of hierarchical control against the small settlers' defense of individual managerial freedom. The battle was still a fight to control the meaning and use of land and a struggle to determine whether some men's dominion over the means of subsistence and production should depend on the consent of others. When William H. Seward joined Trumbull Cary and George Lay as a managing copartner of the Holland Company's former lands in Chautauqua County, he was an outspoken defender of the "democratic" West in opposition to the "aristocratic" East. Yet his new position as local agent for the Chautauqua Land Company tested the limits of his egalitarian sentiments. As a political leader of the Antimasons he had forcefully appealed to agrarian and democratic ideals, but as a new landlord, he denounced those same sentiments. "My observation of Mayville [where the land office had been destroyed] resulted in the conviction," Seward explained, "that it would be a most uncomfortable place for the sale of lands, that its secluded position subjected it to the control of turbulent spirits who lived in the hills around it, and that, if I meant to be independent of the dictation of those who assume to direct the land agency by popular votes, I must avoid placing myself within their power."[1]

Despite Seward's glowing account of how he "happily pacified the settlers," the record shows that he did so only by making substantial

---

1. Frederick W. Seward, ed., *William H. Seward: An Autobiography,* 2 vols. (New York, 1891), 1:306.

concessions. He renegotiated any contract for which the debt due exceeded the market value of the land, requiring as a condition only a nominal down payment. In October 1836 he acknowledged the persistent tension that continued to divide land agent and settler in Chautauqua County. Making a curious distinction "between debtors who come in fair weather and those who come in the mud," Seward explained that settlers who visited the land office during the pleasant weather of early September had money to pay their debts "promptly," and they went away satisfied. But those who trudged to the office "in the mud" came later in the season because they hailed from the more remote hill country of the interior townships. They possessed little money and grumbled loudly about the advantages that went to the privileged few who were lucky enough to have cash. When dealing with these latter settlers, Seward often feared the worst. "I don't know but my office will be pulled down over my head," he fretted. On one occasion he "was annoyed by a squatter" who had come down out of the hills "to purchase the land he was upon." Seward demanded nine dollars an acre, but the settler insisted that three dollars was fair. "He was drunk," Seward noted, "and, after abusing me roundly in the office, he went into the street, and made a boisterous harangue to the multitude gathered round him, calling me all manner of names."[2]

When Seward ran for governor again in 1838, his status as a landlord and land agent opened the door for local Democrats to exploit the class tension between landlords and settlers that Seward and the Antimasons had once tapped. In October 1838 the *Cattaraugus Republican* printed an open letter to Seward. "It is said that you have boasted of having effected an arrangement by which you and your associates are to be enabled to wring the sum of six hundred thousand dollars out of the sweat of the farmers' brows of this country. That is to be done through a system of 'sweating' bonds and mortgages taken from the hardy settlers to secure their homesteads from the remorseless grasp of speculators and land pirates." Seward was no longer accepted by the settlers as a member of the producing classes. His entrepreneurial ambitions were in conflict with the settlers' small producer outlook.[3]

Relations between the new American landlords and the settlers of Niagara, Orleans, Genesee, and Erie counties were also tense. The Farmers Loan and Trust Company started out with a tough policy toward delinquent settlers, requiring that they take new contracts, make punctual

---

2. Ibid., 314, 312, 309.
3. *Cattaraugus Republican* (Ellicottville, N.Y.), Oct. 17, 1838.

payments, or get off the land. As a result of the rebellion of 1836 and the persistent tension that continued until long afterward, the Farmers Loan and Trust Company devised two policies—one for the more economically mature areas under its control and another for the isolated townships of southern Erie and Genesee counties. These latter towns were still populated by settlers, Herman Redfield explained in 1843, with the capacity to "subsist whether they have an immediate market for the produce of the soil or not."[4]

For "the counties of Orleans, Niagara, and the county of Genesee and that portion of Erie County north of the Indian Reservation," the company's policy called for immediate foreclosure when the interest was "in arrears one year." But in "the county of Wyoming and in that part of Erie south of the Indian Reservation greater indulgence" was extended. In the summer of 1844 the Farmers Loan and Trust Company agreed to accept cattle, sheep, and hogs as payment in kind for back interest. Local agents Herman Redfield and Benjamin Pringle were authorized to conduct a one-year experiment. The company's offer was extended only to those delinquents who were in arrears for at least one year. The landlords received cattle at a 50 percent loss, yet they judged the program a success because livestock were the only means of payment available in the back towns. Cattle agents reported being welcomed "even in Holland and Wales," where company agents sometimes feared to visit. During the decade after the rebellion of 1836, the Farmers Loan and Trust Company generally proceeded against delinquent settlers from the back towns of Wyoming and southern Erie County with great caution. Company president R. C. Cornell warned one of his Batavia agents in April 1845 that it was dangerous "to commence many foreclosures" at the same time. "A prudent course of collections should be steadily pursued," Cornell admonished, "selecting as far as possible the worst cases and debtors not living near each other."[5]

The most serious conflict between the new American landlords and the small independent producers of the isolated hill country townships occurred in Cattaraugus County. A continuing struggle over the use and

4. R. C. Cornell to Herman J. Redfield and Benjamin Pringle, Oct. 22, 1842, Letterbooks, roll 3, microfilm ed., Farmers Loan and Trust Company Papers, Department of Manuscripts and University Archives, Cornell University Libraries, Ithaca, N.Y.; cited hereafter as Farmers Loan and Trust Company Papers; Herman J. Redfield to James McNaughton, May 12, 1843, Letterbooks, vol. 3, folder 19, Farmers Loan and Trust Company Papers.

5. R. C. Cornell to Herman J. Redfield and Benjamin Pringle, Oct. 22, 1842, July 20, Aug. 7, Dec. 30, 1844, and R. C. Cornell to John Lowber, April 1, 25, 1845, Letterbooks, roll 3, Farmers Loan and Trust Company Papers.

meaning of land there triggered the "Dutch Hill War" of 1844–45. The Dutch Hill region of eastern Cattaraugus County had been settled by ethnic Germans from the Wyoming Valley in northeastern Pennsylvania. Two of these settlers, Jacob and George Learn, migrated to Cattaraugus County in 1823. Both were veterans of the War of 1812, and they arrived in the Holland Purchase with little more than the oxen and wagons that brought them. They purchased 329 acres at a cost of two dollars per acre. They made a down payment of ten dollars, signed an article of agreement, and pledged to pay the rest over the next ten years. The contract exempted them from any interest assessment for the first three years but then required seven annual payments with interest. Over the next fourteen years the Learns failed to make any additional payments[6]

Jacob and George Learn were marginal hill country farmers. As was true of other settlers of the back towns, rearing livestock constituted the basis of their livelihood. Cattle and horses provided dairy products and draft animals, sheep yielded wool, and hogs furnished the staple animal protein of their diets. Every fall a few of their animals were "turned out" to earn some cash. Both of the Learn brothers used a significant portion of their farms to provide pasture, hay, and oats for their livestock. Buckwheat was the principal cereal crop tilled by the Learns, providing most of the bread consumed by them and their families. Considered poor man's food, buckwheat could be grown where high altitudes, short seasons, and poor soils made cultivation of wheat impossible.[7]

When title to their farms and to Cattaraugus County passed to the Devereux Company in July 1837, Jacob and George Learn agreed to take two separate contracts on the lot they originally purchased from the Holland Company. Both brothers paid the new proprietors $50 and consented to pay the balance of $508.50 plus interest over the next six years. Neither brother honored the new contracts, and in July 1843 title to their farms went to Gould Hoyt and Russell Nevins. Both the new landlords were partners in the Devereux Company. When Hoyt called upon Jacob Learn for payment, Learn agreed to drive some cattle, valued at $105, to Ellicottville as partial payment for his land. The cattle were never delivered. Consequently, at the end of the summer of 1843, Jacob and

6. Sally Pettengill, "The Dutch Hillers," *Sandpumpings* (Summer 1983); *Cattaraugus Republican,* July 15, 1844.
7. My sketch of Jacob and George Learn is drawn from state manuscript census records for the town of Hinsdale (1835) and for the town of Ischua (1855), as well as from federal manuscript census records for the town of Hinsdale (1850). These records are kept at the Cattaraugus County Historical and Memorial Museum, Little Valley, N.Y.

George Learn had occupied their lands for twenty years, violated three separate contracts, and failed to pay three successive owners. The passage of time added $800 of unpaid interest to the original purchase price of $658. The $110 that they had paid constituted only about one-eighth of the interest that was now due.[8]

The new owners waited until March 1844 and then went to court to begin suits of ejectment. The Learns did not contest the suits, and judgments by default were awarded to Hoyt and Nevins. On June 12 the local sheriff, George White, went to Dutch Hill to evict the Learn brothers. When the sheriff and the six or seven men he had taken along to help remove furniture from the houses arrived, they "were surrounded by a mob, numbering from a hundred to a hundred and fifty men, many of them armed and disguised as Indians." After the sheriff persisted in the execution of his duty, the "Indians" attacked and forced him "to leave the premises."[9]

The adoption of White Indian tactics by the Learn brothers and their neighbors was a throwback to an earlier tradition of extralegal rural violence, yet it was a style of resistance that stopped short of open insurrections involving large crowds of yeomen. The settlers combined this more traditional expression of rural resistance and unrest with an appeal to their rights as citizens of a democratic and participatory society.[10]

Several weeks later, settlers alarmed about the attempt to dispossess the Learn brothers gathered in the town of Machias to discuss their grievances against the landlords. They questioned whether the Devereux Company and the individual proprietors who constituted it held a valid title to the land. They also charged that land prices were "unjust and oppressive." Many Cattaraugus settlers had purchased land during the boom years following the War of 1812 when prices were high. In the wake of the Panic of 1819 and the prolonged stagnation that gripped the southern counties of the Holland Purchase, land prices had tumbled. Nevertheless, the present landowners, like their predecessors, continued to add interest to the

---

8. *Cattaraugus Republican,* July 15, 1844.

9. *Cattaraugus Republican,* Feb. 3, 1845; for White Indians on the Maine frontier, see Alan Taylor, *Liberty Men and Great Proprietors: The Revolutionary Settlement on the Maine Frontier, 1760–1820* (Chapel Hill, N.C., 1990), 2–3, 22, 58, 117–18, 128, 181–205, 235, 238, 240, 242–43, 264–79.

10. For the transition from extralegal rural violence to electoral politics, from White Indians to republican citizens, see Taylor, "Regulators and White Indians: The Agrarian Resistance in Post-Revolutionary New England," in Robert A. Gross, ed., *In Debt to Shays: The Bicentennial of an Agrarian Rebellion* (Charlottesville, Va., 1993), 145–60.

original price. The effect, the settlers argued, was to make it "utterly impossible" for them to pay what the landlords demanded.[11]

At the heart of the settlers' grievances was a conflict over land use and property rights. Aside from the failure to make punctual land payments, the most serious offense committed by the settlers, according to Devereux Company spokesmen, was the "injury" they inflicted upon the land. The company referred to the Learns and their Dutch Hill neighbors as "timber thieves" who measured "respectability . . . by the contempt with which" they treated "their written obligations." Clearing land for lumber and potash and then letting it revert to brushland and woodlots remained an important economic activity. In keeping with long-standing rural tradition, the Cattaraugus settlers used unfenced timberlands as a common resource open to anyone's use and enjoyment.[12]

The Devereux Company's proprietors appreciated, as had the Holland Company's agents before them, that timber constituted the primary value of their lands. They tried to protect the timber on their unsold lands by preferring criminal charges and bringing indictments for stealing timber. The Devereux Company also tried to prevent the settlers from cutting more timber than was needed for improvements. The landlords used writs of replevin to recover lumber that they judged to have been cut solely for sale and profit. The settlers complained that the company "replevied lumber" even when it was cut on lands that were held under a good contract.[13]

The settlers who met at Machias adopted a set of strong resolutions explaining their grievances: "That these pretended land holders in preferring charges of a criminal nature against a large number of persons under pretense of protecting their property from trespassers plainly shows they have no feeling in common with us, but are determined to make us pay the expense of protecting that property which has been made valuable by our own labor." The settlers rejected "the idea of setting the laws of our country at defiance or of violating them in any case whatever," yet they warned the landlords not to push them too far. If the provocations continued, they would be morally justified in violating the "letter of the law," if it was done to defend their natural rights and protect their families "from the iron grasp of aggression."[14]

11. *Cattaraugus Republican,* July 22, 1844.
12. Ibid., July 15, Aug. 5, 1844.
13. Ibid.
14. Ibid., July 22, 1844.

In the weeks following the confrontation between Sheriff White and the "Indians" of Dutch Hill, "eleven of the participants in the outrage" were indicted. Meanwhile, rumors about an impending rebellion abounded. A local newspaper reported:

> Associations were formed, for the avowed purpose of resisting the execution of the laws, in certain cases, embracing particularly those cases in which persons wished to be indulged in taking pine timber from lands not their own—pledges of mutual protection were adopted—threats of violence to any who should give information concerning timber stealers, or who should contract or pay anything for land to the proprietors, have been frequently and openly repeated—and in case the officers should succeed in making any arrests of the guilty, the jail and land offices were to be demolished.

To quell the "excitement," the sheriff, "under the advice of the public authorities," decided to delay the "execution of the laws" until after the election.[15]

Finally, on January 20, 1845, Sheriff White and Judge Benjamin Chamberlain went to Dutch Hill to persuade the indicted persons to surrender. When the settlers refused, the sheriff appointed several men to return to Dutch Hill and make arrests. The deputized men arrested one settler but then fled back to Ellicottville after another encounter with armed and angry "Indians." Rumors flew again. Sheriff White prepared to defend Ellicottville against an expected attack by settlers sworn to destroy the land office and the jail if any arrests were made. Another rumor alleged that the Senecas at the Allegheny Reservation had joined the ranks of the Dutch Hill "Indians" as allies.[16]

Fearing an imminent attack, Sheriff White called out the militia, and on Sunday evening, January 26, eleven hundred men set out in sleighs for the "infected district" of Dutch Hill. When the militia arrived early Monday morning, they found no "Indians" and no resistance. The troops surrounded the homes of Jacob and George Learn, who surrendered peacefully. The land agents allowed the Learns to stay on their land in return for taking new contracts that added the costs of the ejectment suits to what they already owed. The militia retired, and the rest of the indicted "Indians" surrendered the next day. In the days that followed, Sheriff White came under severe criticism for overreacting. Calling out the militia cost the county $700, and many taxpayers grumbled about the expense.[17]

15. Ibid., Feb. 3, 1845.
16. Ibid., Feb. 3, Feb. 17, 1845.
17. Ibid.

The settlers of Dutch Hill viewed the calling up of the militia as a manifestation of the vast power, reinforced by the law, that the monopolistic landlords sought to exercise over the producing majority. The militia went to Dutch Hill not to put down rebellion or to arrest indicted persons, but to force the settlers to sign new contracts. The people's militia had become a tool of oppression in the hands of the moneyed landlords. A "Settler on Dutch Hill" observed: "Raise an alarm that such and such persons cannot be arrested, get out an army of men, then, use that body to compel settlers to take contracts at the point of the bayonet. Is this the laws of our country? I trust not." This settler understood that the landlords' assertion of hierarchical control was an assault upon his small producer values and aspirations. If that control was allowed to stand, the opportunity for ordinary men to govern themselves and participate in democratic markets where buyers and sellers negotiated as equals was at an end. To the settlers, what was at stake that wintry morning in 1845 when the militia surrounded the homes of Jacob and George Learn, was no less than their right to live as free men and to enjoy the material comforts that their capacity and desire to subdue nature could provide.[18]

But the political power of the capitalist landlords was not allowed to stand. The Dutch Hill settler quoted above explained the significance of how the "war" had ended. Neither the sheriff nor the officers in command of the militia ordered any violent measures against the "Dutch hill Boys." If they had, the settler predicted, at least "three quarters of the general's men would have joined" the rebels. Nor did this military force dare to dispossess either one of the Learn families. In the aftermath of the confrontation, the sheriff was widely criticized for permitting the landlords to use the power and resources of the county to oppress the settlers in the name of law and order. This act of tyranny was an egregious violation of the great revolutionary principle that government should not grant special privileges or favors to any individual or group, however rich and powerful they might be.[19]

To make this point perfectly clear, several months later one hundred men from the Dutch Hill region once again resisted the sheriff "in the

18. Ibid., March 31, 1845. For a discussion of democratic markets, see Michael Merrill and Sean Wilentz, "'The Key of Libberty,' William Manning and Plebeian Democracy, 1747–1814," in Alfred F. Young, ed., *Beyond the American Revolution: Explorations in the History of American Radicalism* (DeKalb, Ill., 1993), 273–74 n. 5. See also Michael Merrill, "The Anticapitalist Origins of the United States," *Review* 13 (Fall 1990), 465–97.

19. *Cattaraugus Republican*, March 31, 1845; Franklin Ellis, *History of Cattaraugus County, New York* (Philadelphia, 1879), 46–51, esp. 50–51.

discharge of his official duties." From the settlers' point of view, he was
again guilty of using his official powers to do the landlords' bidding.
Apparently chastened by the public outcry that followed his recent calling
for the assistance of the militia, he chose another course this time. The
matter ended with negotiation and accommodation on both sides. None
of the "Dutch hill boys," including George and Jacob Learn, ever lost
their land and improvements. Aided by the high ratio of land to labor that
constituted the primary structural underpinning of frontier settlement and
land development in the Holland Purchase, they persevered in the defense
of their small producer aspirations. George Learn finally received a deed
for his land in 1850; his brother Jacob secured legal ownership of his farm
four years later. During the twenty-seven years it took George Learn to
pay for his land and the thirty-one years that passed before Jacob Learn
achieved fee simple ownership of his, both men created property out of
wilderness and raised large families. Both patriarchs added seven children
to their households during the years of struggle with the land and the
absentee owners. In the final analysis, their agrarian vision had prevailed
at least as much as landlords' capitalist one.[20]

THE small settlers and producers of the Holland Purchase were active
participants in the economic changes that underlay the Market Revolution in western New York and in the rest of Jacksonian America. New
land and market development was at the heart of the economic growth
that transformed the pre-white settlement forests of the region into frontier farms and cultivated woodlots. Small and influential settlers alike
contended with the Holland Company for dominion over the region's
land and other productive resources. The settlers' strong preference for
individual managerial control animated their struggle against the capitalist landlords, who pursued a different vision of development that was
based on more centralized control. The settlers used and changed the land

20. Ellis, *History of Cattaraugus County,* 50–51. Charles Sellers has argued that the
Market Revolution transformed American society during the period from 1815 to 1846,
overwhelming and sweeping aside all resistance to the new capitalist order with breathtaking
speed and power. Recently several historians who participated in a symposium on Sellers's
book have raised questions about the hegemony of this revolution. See "A Symposium on
Charles Sellers, *The Market Revolution: Jacksonian America, 1815–1846* featuring Richard
E. Ellis, Mary H. Blewett, Joel H. Silbey, Major L. Wilson, Harry L. Watson, Amy Bridges,
and Charles Sellers," *Journal of the Early Republic* 12 (Winter 1992), 445–76. For a
different view of yeoman society that deemphasizes the agency of ordinary rural people,
see Allan Kulikoff, *The Agrarian Origins of American Capitalism* (Charlottesville, Va.,
1992), 8.

in ways that reflected their intense commitment to a system of production and exchange by and for small producers.

When shifts in company policy and the deepening crisis of the 1820s challenged the settlers' democratic and egalitarian aspirations, their response was complex and ambiguous, combining traditional rural elements with more liberal and democratic sentiments. In defending their improvements, their families, and their status as free men, they drew upon their own cultural resources and experiences. No one had to tell them what their labor was worth; nor did anyone have to tell them that they must always stand ready to defend their property and liberty against moneyed men who stood equally ready to deny free men their due.[21]

As changes in company policy exacerbated the general crisis of the 1820s, the settlers appealed to the company's fairness and respect for their rights, they participated in the new democratic political culture of popular conventions and formal petitions to the state legislature for redress of their grievances, and, in the end, they resorted to extralegal acts of violence and rebellion against the moneyed few who were determined to exploit and oppress the producing many. Their response to crisis cannot be understood simply in terms of opposition or accommodation to the big transition that was under way in the Holland Purchase. Rather, it combined elements of resistance and confrontation with a spirit of negotiation. They never denied that the Dutch landlords or the American owners who followed them had a right to sell wild land, but they did insist that the proprietors respect their individual freedom to create and enjoy property without undue interference.[22]

The small settlers of the Holland Purchase were not opposed to land and market development, but they wanted it on their own terms. They mined the varied resources of the forest for both subsistence and market value, but they did so on behalf and for the benefit of small producers. Their conception of land and property rights likewise pointed to the admixture of negotiation, accommodation, and resistance that marked this culture of small independent producers as it struggled to pursue its own vision of the good society in the age of the Market Revolution. And so this book ends where it began—with Orsamus Turner's sketches of pioneer progress in the Holland Purchase. In his fourth sketch Turner tells the reader that this imaginary settler has triumphed in his personal battle

---

21. My discussion here is based on Alfred F. Young, "Afterward: How Radical Was the American Revolution?" in Young, ed., *Beyond the American Revolution,* 317–64, esp. 318–25.

22. Ibid.

to sustain the agrarian vision of what kind of society America should be. "The pioneer is an independent Farmer of the Holland Purchase. His old 'article' has long ago been exchanged for a deed in fee. He has added to his primitive possessions; and ten to one that he has secured lands for his sons in some of the western states, to make pioneers and founders of settlements of them. He has flocks and herds; large surplus of produce in his granaries, which he may sell or keep as he chooses. He is the founder, and worker out, of his own fortunes."[23]

23. Orsamus Turner, *Pioneer History of the Holland Purchase of Western New York* (1850; rpr. Geneseo, N.Y., 1974), 566.

Index